# VOLUME EDITOR

PATRICK GOOLD is Associate Professor of Philosophy at Virginia Wesleyan College. His current research focuses on defining rationality. He is co-editor with Steven Emmanuel of the Blackwell anthology *Modern Philosophy from Descartes to Nietzsche*. Patrick is passionate about sailing, and, in addition to maintaining a small daysailer and a cruising boat of his own, frequently crews on the boats of others. The bays and sounds of Virginia and North Carolina are his home waters but he has sailed the length of the East Coast of the United States from Hilton Head to Long Island Sound, made a Bermuda crossing, done club racing in Brittany, and cruised in the Lesser Antilles.

# SERIES EDITOR

FRITZ ALLHOFF is an Associate Professor in the Philosophy department at Western Michigan University, as well as a senior research fellow at the Australian National University's Centre for Applied Philosophy and Public Ethics. In addition to editing the *Philosophy for Everyone* series, he is also the volume editor or co-editor for several titles, including *Wine and Philosophy* (Wiley-Blackwell, 2007), *Whiskey and Philosophy* (with Marcus P. Adams, Wiley-Blackwell, 2009), and *Food and Philosophy* (with Dave Monroe, Wiley-Blackwell, 2007). His academic research interests engage various facets of applied ethics, ethical theory, and the history and philosophy of science.

# PHILOSOPHY FOR EVERYONE

Series editor: Fritz Allhoff

Not so much a subject matter, philosophy is a way of thinking. Thinking not just about the Big Questions, but about little ones too. This series invites everyone to ponder things they care about, big or small, significant, serious… or just curious.

*Running & Philosophy: A Marathon for the Mind*
Edited by Michael W. Austin

*Wine & Philosophy: A Symposium on Thinking and Drinking*
Edited by Fritz Allhoff

*Food & Philosophy: Eat, Think and Be Merry*
Edited by Fritz Allhoff and Dave Monroe

*Beer & Philosophy: The Unexamined Beer Isn't Worth Drinking*
Edited by Steven D. Hales

*Whiskey & Philosophy: A Small Batch of Spirited Ideas*
Edited by Fritz Allhoff and Marcus P. Adams

*College Sex – Philosophy for Everyone: Philosophers With Benefits*
Edited by Michael Bruce and Robert M. Stewart

*Cycling – Philosophy for Everyone: A Philosophical Tour de Force*
Edited by Jesús Ilundáin-Agurruza and Michael W. Austin

*Climbing – Philosophy for Everyone: Because It's There*
Edited by Stephen E. Schmid

*Hunting – Philosophy for Everyone: In Search of the Wild Life*
Edited by Nathan Kowalsky

*Christmas – Philosophy for Everyone: Better Than a Lump of Coal*
Edited by Scott C. Lowe

*Cannabis – Philosophy for Everyone: What Were We Just Talking About?*
Edited by Dale Jacquette

*Porn – Philosophy for Everyone: How to Think With Kink*
Edited by Dave Monroe

*Serial Killers – Philosophy for Everyone : Being and Killing*
Edited by S. Waller

*Dating – Philosophy for Everyone: Flirting With Big Ideas*
Edited by Kristie Miller and Marlene Clark

*Gardening – Philosophy for Everyone: Cultivating Wisdom*
Edited by Dan O'Brien

*Motherhood – Philosophy for Everyone: The Birth of Wisdom*
Edited by Sheila Lintott

*Fatherhood – Philosophy for Everyone: The Dao of Daddy*
Edited by Lon S. Nease and Michael W. Austin

*Coffee – Philosophy for Everyone: Grounds for Debate*
Edited by Scott F. Parker and Michael W. Austin

*Fashion – Philosophy for Everyone: Thinking with Style*
Edited by Jessica Wolfendale and Jeanette Kennett

*Yoga – Philosophy for Everyone: Bending Mind and Body*
Edited by Liz Stillwaggon Swan

*Blues – Philosophy for Everyone: Thinking Deep About Feeling Low*
Edited by Abrol Fairweather and Jesse Steinberg

*Tattoos – Philosophy for Everyone: I Ink, Therefore I Am*
Edited by Robert Arp

*Sailing – Philosophy for Everyone: Catching the Drift of Why We Sail*
Edited by Patrick Goold

Edited by Patrick Goold

# SAILING
## PHILOSOPHY FOR EVERYONE

Catching the Drift of Why We Sail

Foreword by John Rousmaniere

A John Wiley & Sons, Inc., Publication

This edition first published 2012
© 2012 John Wiley & Sons, Inc

Wiley-Blackwell is an imprint of John Wiley & Sons, formed by the merger of Wiley's
global Scientific, Technical and Medical business with Blackwell Publishing.

*Registered Office*
John Wiley & Sons, Ltd., The Atrium, Southern Gate, Chichester, West Sussex,
PO19 8SQ, UK

*Editorial Offices*
350 Main Street, Malden, MA 02148-5020, USA
9600 Garsington Road, Oxford, OX4 2DQ, UK
The Atrium, Southern Gate, Chichester, West Sussex, PO19 8SQ, UK

For details of our global editorial offices, for customer services, and for information
about how to apply for permission to reuse the copyright material in this book please
see our website at www.wiley.com/wiley-blackwell.

The right of Patrick Goold to be identified as the author of the editorial material
in this work has been asserted in accordance with the UK Copyright, Designs
and Patents Act 1988.

Wiley also publishes its books in a variety of electronic formats. Some content that
appears in print may not be available in electronic books.

Designations used by companies to distinguish their products are often claimed
as trademarks. All brand names and product names used in this book are trade
names, service marks, trademarks or registered trademarks of their respective owners.
The publisher is not associated with any product or vendor mentioned in this book.
This publication is designed to provide accurate and authoritative information in regard
to the subject matter covered. It is sold on the understanding that the publisher is not
engaged in rendering professional services. If professional advice or other expert
assistance is required, the services of a competent professional should be sought.

*Library of Congress Cataloging-in-Publication Data*

Sailing : philosophy for everyone : catching the drift of why we sail / edited by
Patrick Goold; Foreword by John Rousmaniere.
    p.  cm.
  Includes bibliographical references.
  ISBN 978-0-470-67185-6 (pbk.)
1. Sailing–Philosophy.  I. Goold, Patrick Allen.
  GV811.S25515 2012
  797'.124–dc23

                                                    2012009766

A catalogue record for this book is available from the British Library.

Set in 10/12.5pt Plantin by SPi Publisher Services, Pondicherry, India
Printed in Singapore by Ho Printing Singapore Pte Ltd

1  2012

# CONTENTS

Foreword: *The Craft and the Mystery*                              viii
John Rousmaniere

The Philosophical Sailor: *An Introduction to*
Sailing – Philosophy for Everyone                      xiv
Patrick Goold

Acknowledgments                      xxiii

### PART I   PASSING THROUGH PAIN AND FEAR IN THE PLACE OF PERPETUAL UNDULATION    I

1 Ships of Wood and Men of Iron: *Voyaging the
Old-Fashioned Way and Seeking Meaning in Adversity*    3
Jack Stillwaggon

2 Winning Philosophy: *Developing Patience, Inner Strength,
and an Eye for the Good Lanes*    12
Gary Jobson

3 "Hard a' Lee": *Why the Work of Sailing Can Be Great Fun*    23
Crista Lebens

4 Solo Sailing as Spiritual Practice: *A Phenomenology
of Mastery and Failure at Sea*    36
Richard Hutch

PART 2   THE MEANING OF THE BOAT
         *THREE SCHOOLS OF THOUGHT*                          47

  5  Buddha's Boat: *The Practice of Zen in Sailing*           49
     James Whitehill

  6  Freedom of the Seas: *The Stoic Sailor*                   61
     Gregory Bassham and Tod Bassham

  7  Sailors of the Third Kind: *Sailing and Self-Becoming
     in the Shadow of Heraclitus*                              72
     Steven Horrobin


PART 3   BEAUTY AND OTHER AESTHETIC ASPECTS
         OF THE SAILING EXPERIENCE                            83

  8  What the Race to Mackinac Means                           85
     Nicholas Hayes

  9  Sailing, Flow, and Fulfillment                            96
     Steve Matthews

 10  On the Crest of the Wave: *The Sublime, Tempestuous,
     Graceful, and Existential Facets of Sailing*             109
     Jesús Ilundáin-Agurruza, Luísa Gagliardini Graça,
     and José Ángel Jáuregui-Olaiz

 11  Navigating What Is Valuable and Steering a Course
     in Pursuit of Happiness                                  122
     Jesse Steinberg and Michael Stuckart


PART 4   PHYSICS AND METAPHYSICS FOR
         THE PHILOSOPHICAL SAILOR                            133

 12  Do You Have to Be (an) Einstein to Understand Sailing?   135
     Sebastian Kuhn

 13  Paradoxes of Sailing: *The Physics of Sailing
     and the Import of Thought Experiments*                   148
     John D. Norton

14   The Necessity of Sailing: *Of Gods, Fate, and the Sea*       164
     Tamar M. Rudavsky and Nathaniel Rudavsky-Brody

15   The Channel: *An Old Drama by Which the Soul
     of a Healthy Man is Kept Alive*                             176
     Hilaire Belloc

Notes on Contributors                                            180

# FOREWORD

## The Craft and the Mystery

This welcome collection of essays about the examined life under sail touches many of my nerve endings. A topic I call "the meaning of the boat" has been high on my agenda for many years, and I have long been fascinated by the passionate connection that so many of us feel with boats and the sea. Who reading this does not agree or at least sympathize with E. B. White's declaration, "With me, I cannot not sail"?[1] For most sailors, this intense engagement is much more than a mere intellectual decision. It is a transforming connection between mind and heart, thought and belief, boat and sea.

This is what Joseph Conrad referred to when he wrote of "our fellowship in the craft and the mystery of the sea" in his seafaring memoir, *The Mirror of the Sea*, one of the crucial texts of meaning-of-the-boat studies.[2] Here is a fine match: *craft* (what might be called "the physics of sailing") and *mystery* ("the metaphysics of sailing"). Craft we all know – or at least we know we *should* know. It is the skills and equipment needed to get a boat from one place to another. Mystery, however, is a little more complex.

Recently, during a panel discussion of an upcoming race across the Atlantic, the moderator, Gary Jobson, asked me to describe my most vivid memory of transatlantic sailing. I could have mentioned the thrill of starting a race to Spain, or exuberant days of fast running before westerly gales in seas seemingly as high as the boat was long. Stretching the subject a little, I might have said something about a brutal beat out to Fastnet Rock in a force-ten storm, or carefully skirting Bermuda's reef after four days at sea, sailing the boat like a dinghy as we fought to win a Newport Bermuda Race. I might well have recalled many of those memories of great excitement, but, somewhat to my surprise, my mind went immediately to an altogether different moment.

Deep into a moonless night during my first long Atlantic voyage, a perfect calm enveloped the big ketch. The skipper came on deck, took a look around, and cut the engine. He didn't have to explain why; we understood. The boat carried her way for a few minutes as the bow wave trickled into silence, and our little world was inhabited by stillness. The only sound was the occasional flutter of empty sails or confused birds. The single sign of reckoning time was the slow march of constellations across the great dome of darkness overhead. We could have been anywhere, at any moment.

After a while – I can't say how long because minutes and hours were abstractions – someone switched on the spreader lights, and we tiptoed to the rail and peered down many fathoms into the clear, magical sea. Suspended between those two worlds in that moment, decades ago, I felt more connected to the eternal mysteries than any prayer or song or poem has ever allowed.

I am reminded of this magical moment by a photograph on my study wall. An anonymous sailor, his back to us, stands on the deck of a sailboat becalmed on a still dawn, peering ahead at the rising sun. Is he searching for land? For wind? Or for himself?

FIGURE F.1    Photo used by permission of Mystic Seaport.

Many sailors of all levels of ability have told me that they have had similar moments afloat, when time stood still and they discovered another world. The mystery of the sea is shared by all sailors, even (perhaps especially) the most technically gifted masters of the craft. The man who took this photograph was one of the most successful ocean racing sailors who ever lived, Carleton Mitchell. The high naval official Samuel Pepys was taking a row on the Mediterranean in 1683 when he was overwhelmed by one of these moments. He later wrote in a journal, "I know nothing that can give a better notion of infinity and eternity than the being upon the sea in a little vessel without anything in sight but yourself within the whole hemisphere."[3] Pepys was no flake but a tough-minded inspector of warships whose outbursts (as anyone who has read his diary knows) tended to be sexual, not spiritual; yet on this day the sea took on a whole new meaning for him.

More than two hundred years later, a self-promoting New York City magazine editor and ocean sailor named Thomas Fleming Day explained why he founded a race to Bermuda in this way: "Sailors wanted to get a smell of the sea and forget for the time being that there is such a thing as God's green earth in the universe."[4] In short, they were seeking another world. So was an exceptionally experienced English writer-sailor, Maurice Griffiths, who laid out his feelings upon heading out in a small cruising boat in these words:

> I found my pulse beating with suppressed excitement as I threw the mooring buoy overboard. It seemed as if that simple action had severed my connection with the life on shore; that I had thereby cut adrift the ties of convention, the unrealities and illusions of cities and crowds; that I was free now, free to go where I chose, to do and to live and to conquer as I liked, to play the game wherein a man's qualities count for more than his appearance.[5]

A few years ago the champion long-distance racer Ellen MacArthur wrote in her log as she neared the finish of a solo transatlantic race:

> I now feel so wonderfully in tune with the boat and the sea that I know I shall really miss this once the race is over. At night I watch the sun go down and in the morning the sky is there above me, a wonderful feeling of space and timelessness.[6]

And a pioneer British ocean racer of the 1920s, George Martin, noted that there are times when, "except for the knowledge of contact with the deck, one seemed to have passed right out of the world."[7]

One point to make about these visions is that nobody should ever feel embarrassed to have them. Not only are they common – sometimes so much so as to be commonplace – but they are paths to valuable truths. In fact, they carry considerable philosophical weight. The adjective often applied to them is "numinous," a term originated by Rudolph Otto (1869–1937), a German theologian and authority in the field of comparative religions. In his influential book *The Idea of the Holy*, Otto defined a numinous event as a non-rational, non-sensory experience or feeling whose primary and immediate object is outside the self.[8] That object might be called God or "the wholly other." The experience of confrontation, the "*mysterium tremendum*," inspires great awe, distance, humility, and even fear.

Two decades before Otto, the American philosopher and psychologist William James (1842–1910) described this engagement with the sacred slightly differently. Collecting reports of mystical states, he noted patterns. Some included a sense of déjà vu. In others, everything seemed to carry special meaning. A common theme was oneness with the absolute, which sometimes had a maritime setting; one of James' sources described a mystical state in which he was "immersed in the infinite ocean of God." James emphasized that, while these states may appear non-rational, they can influence and even team up with our thinking. Their existence, James wrote, "absolutely overthrows the pretension of non-mystical states to be the sole and ultimate dictators of what we may believe."[9]

A sailor living an examined life could do a lot worse than read up on William James. He is mentioned briefly in this volume in Chapter 10, but more really should be said about this great thinker and man who so well appreciated the call of the sea. James did a little sailing as a young man in Newport, and evidently learned something because he employed a clever nautical metaphor to make a point about one of his favorite causes, free will. How can human beings be automatons, he asked, if, when they are passengers in a sailboat, they freely volunteer to take the helm or help with the reefing when the wind comes up?[10] James' own sport of choice was mountain hiking. That and his own psychology and intellectual work gave him an intimate understanding of the needs and life of the thoughtful adventurer. He urged opening ourselves up to making choices, pushing aside dogmatic determinism, and trusting that feeling can be a reliable adjunct to thinking (all good options for sailors, I would say). Finding meaning and mental health in vigorous adventures, he propounded a notion familiar to any sailor who has ever been at one and the same time wet, worn out, and exhilarated (and what sailor hasn't?): "It is indeed a remarkable fact that sufferings and hardships do not, as a rule, abate the love of life; they seem, on the contrary, usually to give it a keener zest."[11]

The philosopher Charles Taylor has described James as "our great philosopher of the cusp," explaining, "He tells us more than anyone else about what it's like to stand in that open space and feel the winds pulling you now here, now there."[12] The analogy is apt; few people face more decisions than the typical sailor on an average day. Should we reef now? Tack now? Anchor here? Heave to? Do nothing? There is no room for indecisiveness or complacency either in William James or in the best-sailed boats.

I have long wondered whether James knew about the extraordinary Richard T. McMullen, a pioneer cruising sailor who was never happier than when things were toughest. He first headed out in 1850 and was still at it forty-two years later, when he died at the helm while singlehanding. In his collection of sea stories, *Down Channel*, first published in 1869, he laid down a personal philosophy of vigorous yacht cruising that he summarized in the phrase, "my hard sailing habits." He loved a hard beat to windward in a strong breeze, an activity that he called "terrible but very grand." McMullen memorably said of good sailing that it "is not unlike the pleasure human nature has invariably found in successfully gathering roses off thorns." There may be the occasional bloody finger, but there are great rewards.[13]

There is much in these pages to prove that the joy in nautical rose-picking and the old sense of mystery both remain alive among sailors. Nicholas Hayes, in Chapter 8, for instance, describes the second day in a typical Chicago to Mackinac race as "a day of transcendence and transformation. Sailors will tell you that every person who starts this race will finish as someone new." Yet mystery and romance cannot suffice on their own. It has been wisely said that, in a boat at sea, "piety is no substitute for seamanship."[14] Romantics who have fallen in love with "the dream" head out with too little knowledge, and they and their rescuers suffer for it. The most famous example of inappropriate romance is the poet Percy Bysshe Shelley. So incompetent a seaman that he bragged about it, he built himself a boat that was "fast as a witch" but utterly unseaworthy, and he drowned in it. We certainly don't want to encourage more Shelleys by suggesting that all it takes to sail around the world (much less around the harbor) is one numinous experience.[15]

Mystery and craft, feelings and intellect – they function at their best when they team up to work together. As Joseph Conrad, himself a consummate mariner, knew very well, a numinous experience is not at all

  JOHN ROUSMANIERE

incompatible with competence and technology. In fact, they often nurture each other, making sailing even more of an obsession than it already is.

## NOTES

1  E. B. White, "The sea and the wind that blows," in Peter Neill (Ed.), *American Sea Writing: A Literary Anthology* (New York: Library of America, 2000), p. 612.

2  Joseph Conrad, *Mirror of the Sea* (Doylestown, PA: Wildside Press, 2003), p. 177.

3  Claire Tomalin, *Samuel Pepys, The Unqualified Self* (New York: Knopf, 2003), p. 330.

4  John Rousmaniere, *Berth to Bermuda: 100 Years of the World's Classic Ocean Race* (Mystic, CT: Mystic Seaport and Cruising Club of America, 2006), p. 17.

5  Maurice Griffiths, *Magic of the Swatchways* (Dobbs Ferry, NY: Sheridan, 1997 [1932]), p. 50.

6  Ellen MacArthur, *Taking on the World* (New York: McGraw-Hill/International Marine, 2003), pp. 137–138.

7  E. G. Martin, *Deep Water Cruising* (New York: Yachting, 1928), p. 99.

8  Rudolf Otto, *The Idea of the Holy* (New York: Oxford University Press, 1958), pp. 10–11.

9  William James, *Varieties of Religious Experience* (New York: Viking Penguin, 1982 [1902]), p. 427.

10  Robert D. Richardson, *William James: In the Maelstrom of American Modernism, a Biography* (Boston, MA: Houghton Mifflin Harcourt, 2007), p. 199.

11  William James, "Is life worth living?" In *Will to Believe and Other Essays in Popular Philosophy* (New York: Dover, 1959), p. 47.

12  Charles Taylor, "Risking belief," *Commonweal*, March 8 2002, pp. 14–17.

13  Richard T. McMullen, *Down Channel* (London: Rupert Hart-Davis, 1949 [1869]), pp. 147, 272.

14  Donald Wharton, "Biblical archetypes." In John Rousmaniere (Ed.), *Oxford Encyclopedia of Maritime History*, vol. 1 (New York: Oxford University Press, 2007), p. 285.

15  John Rousmaniere, *After the Storm: True Stories of Disaster and Recovery at Sea* (New York: McGraw-Hill/International Marine, 2002), p. 12.

# THE PHILOSOPHICAL SAILOR

## An Introduction to *Sailing – Philosophy for Everyone*

Why philosophize about sailing? Because people sail! Serious people – that is, people serious about life – pour their time and treasure into sailing. They drag their families into it, or abandon friends and family to do it. They even risk their lives. Why do they do this? Can there be any sense to it? Every activity is a possible subject for philosophical reflection, the more so the more deliberately and passionately the activity is pursued and the more demanding it is. Committed action pre-supposes goals, values, and meanings. These give it its structure. Philosophical reflection wants to explicate these goals, in order to comprehend them, to see how they hang together with one another and with the larger set of commitments that the actor shares with others, and, finally, to interpret them as a signpost pointing us toward wisdom. Philosophical reflection focuses attention on what matters in the activity and on the fit and finish of its implicit ideals. Connections with the larger human drama are made. Lines of improvement in the activity might be suggested. Meaning and value grow. The activity becomes a practice, with a code of conduct (perhaps unspoken), an unfolding tradition with recognizable heroes and reformers, a sense of camaraderie with others similarly engaged, and more or less formal modes of organization to protect it. And so it could be with sailing. Philosophical sailors have more fun sailing. Sailing becomes bigger for them and more real.

It might be, too, that sailing could add life to one's philosophy. Do philosophers who sail find themselves liberated as philosophers? Do traditional categories take on a different appearance when viewed from "a place of perpetual undulation"?[1] Could seamanship under sail, a species of practical wisdom with ancient roots, serve as a model for wisdom in general? Philosophy can help us grasp the meanings, aims, and satisfactions of sailing. Perhaps reflecting on sailing can also help us grasp the meanings, aims, and satisfactions of philosophy itself. Philosophers might find a path to more *philos* in their philosophy. Philosophy might become something bigger for them and more real. The reader will find suggestions to this effect in the essays that follow.

What is sailing? Traditionally, Socrates set the form of the fundamental philosophical question: *Ti esti?* – What is it? What is courage? What is piety? What is knowledge? What is love? For Socrates, the path to wisdom leads through questions of this form. He rejects mere examples as an answer. He wants a statement of the essence of justice. His way of constructing such a statement set the pattern for philosophical reflection ever since: one listens to how those around one use the term, maps what inferences are sanctioned by this use, and then tests the set for consistency. Theoretically, this process continues until no further inconsistencies appear. Breathe easily! None of the essays below takes this approach. It is worthwhile, however, to take a moment to consider the *ti esti* question with regard to our subject.

What is sailing *really*? Is there a timeless essence that can be put into words? I doubt it. Try something like "moving a boat through water by means of the wind." Counterexamples will not be long in coming: iceboating, windsurfing, sailing stones in Death Valley, an imagined spaceship harnessing solar winds, and so on. More importantly, even if we set aside these possible counterexamples, the definition will not be able to capture what sailing means to us now. The function of sailing has changed. Sailing vessels were once movers of goods and passengers, tools for the exploitation of fisheries, the only way to cross seas, and powerful weapons of war. Other machines have taken over these functions. Something other than the necessities of commerce and war prompt contemporary men and women to sail. Ignoring this different function would lump together practices that ought to remain distinct. It would put us at a level of abstraction at which something essential is lost.

What then has sailing become? The genus "hobby" cannot contain it without remainder. A hobby is an activity done regularly in one's leisure time for pleasure. While some sailors may be hobbyists, many are not. Sailing has its professionals as well as those strange birds the circumnavigators and long-term cruisers – people for whom sailing is not a leisure-time activity but the focus of their lives. The physical effort required in these more strenuous forms of sailing, as well as the risks involved, sit uneasily with the ideas of pleasure and of toys or pursuits lacking seriousness, part of the connotation of "hobby."

Sport, which the *American Heritage Dictionary* defines as "an activity involving physical exertion and skill in which an individual or team competes against another or others for entertainment," does better perhaps. But, of course, sailing need not involve competition. This clause might be a mistake in the definition of sport since hunting and mountain climbing are universally considered to be sports but seldom involve competition. We might try looking inward for the competition in these cases, to some sort of self-overcoming, but this would be an unusual use of the word. The awful word "entertainment" also connotes an ultimate lack of seriousness that is inadequate to the circumnavigator or long-term cruiser as well as the hunter and the mountaineer. If these activities entertain, once again it must be in some very special sense of the word.

Many do call sailing a sport. The National Sailing Hall of Fame circulates a brochure that describes what the Hall is and what it does.[2] On the second page of that document a statement by Walter Cronkite contains these sentences: "Baseball, basketball, football, tennis, soccer, golf and lacrosse all have halls of fame. I believe the sport of sailing should have a similar facility that will focus attention on our sport and recognize its heroes as role models for our youth." On the whole, however, the National Sailing Hall of Fame, in this publication and on its website, uses the word "sport" very sparingly. In fact, the word "sport" occurs only two more times in the brochure. More often "the art of sailing" or "the science of sailing" are referred to. There is a gallery in the Hall of Fame dedicated to "The Spectacle of Sailing." Well, is it also a sport?

This simple question takes us back full circle: What is sailing? And what is a sport? The first, we have seen, is not as straightforward to answer as one might hope. Even if we stipulate away the funky counterexamples and stick to boats moved by the wind, the second question cannot be answered unequivocally. In this sense, if you are racing sailboats you are sailing, and if you are cruising sailboats you are sailing. James Cook was sailing when he explored the South Pacific in *Endeavour*, and so was the previous master of that ship when he took it from Grimsby to Hull, delivering coal. If sailing is anything done to move a boat using the wind, then clearly at least some sailing is not a sport. Getting clear about what sailing means to us today may cut away Cook and the collier. It leaves other unclear cases like that of the long-term cruising couple. They are clearly sailing; are they engaged in a sport?

This little exercise is salutary. Concepts that we might otherwise deploy in a thoughtless and reified way are thematized – set in motion, so to speak – and, instead of bricks out of which to build a final answer, they become hypotheses that we must test continually against our own intellectual experience. We are freer now to philosophize, philosophy being, as Adorno has said, "thought in a perpetual state of motion." To put it another way, philosophy is the attempt to think in a disciplined way about something when we don't know exactly what it is we are thinking about. We cannot begin until we have realized that we don't know. To ordinary consciousness this loss of certainty is a step backward. To the philosopher, and to the reflective sailor, it is progress; now one may begin.

There is another traditional philosophical question: What is the ultimate purpose of the thing in question? Aristotelians use the terms *telos*, or final cause, to name this motive. What is it that draws the soul to sailing? The four essays in Part I of this volume reflect on the fact that effort, uncertainty, and sometimes pain and danger are inescapable parts of sailing. If we are thinking in the direction of pleasure or entertainment, toward which the categories of hobby and sport would point us, then this is a particularly salient question for sailing: Where is the fun of it? If pleasure or entertainment is not the final goal, what is? How does one explain a pursuit that commits one to so much discomfort and even danger?

A common thread runs through the answers the first four essays give to these questions. Facing the uncertainty and the technical challenge of sailing can lead to self-knowledge and to increased virtue. One finds out what one is made of and, perhaps, takes heart, becoming more confident, more open to experience and more self-directed.

Jack Stillwaggon, in "Ships of Wood and Men of Iron," recounts a voyage he took as a young man on a replica of Captain Bligh's *Bounty*. Jack encountered considerable danger and discomfort and yet, despite the passage of years, this voyage has remained a high point in his life. Reflecting on this, Jack asks about the point of making such journeys: "Do we strive to experience the past as amateur historians or are we atoning for our frivolous modern lifestyle? Are we like the actor who takes up a political cause to prove he can do more than just play make-believe? Does the fact that we endured a risky trial and survived add importance to an otherwise silly existence?" His answer is that we face the perils of the sea in order to prove something to ourselves about our abilities and our personal worth. To face such a challenge successfully is life-changing. "Like the rock climber who maintains an inner self-confidence because of having scaled challenging heights, or the marathon runner who completes a race, I was more at peace with myself for reaching new horizons and I expected more from myself from that point onward."

In "Winning Philosophy," Gary Jobson takes up the themes of courage and self-confidence from the perspective of a long and distinguished career racing sailboats. He describes the exhilaration and the anxiety of competition and offers tips for overcoming the latter. "Winning takes inner strength and even courage. The big question for every competitive sailor is how to generate the will to overcome fear and to win." While Gary speaks directly from his long experience, using no philosophical vocabulary, his essay answers the question: What must I do to acquire the virtues I need to succeed at sailing? Strength of character and the power of self-transformation have been the aim of philosophical exercises since the beginning of philosophy. Gary's essay links up in especially illuminating ways with the essay of Greg and Tod Bassham on stoicism and sailing and with the Aristotelian approach that Jesse Steinberg and Michael Stuckart take in their essay.

Crista Lebens, in "'Hard a' Lee,'" agrees with Jack and Gary that the opportunity to face down danger and to win the respect of others is part of sailing's allure. She sees this, however, as one element of a larger pursuit, the pursuit of *eudaimonia*. This ancient Greek word she translates as "human flourishing." Perhaps it is Crista's different sailing experience that gives her this perspective: "I have sailed almost exclusively in small craft on inland lakes with family and friends. I have raced in informal afternoon regattas that are about as competitive as a game of touch football in the park. The life lessons I have learned from sailing are drawn from my experiences of these enjoyable afternoons." Themes of sociability, beauty, and enjoyment emerge here. They will be developed at length in Part III.

In "Solo Sailing as Spiritual Practice," Richard Hutch rounds out this opening section on the motives and rewards of sailing with an analysis based on his own experience as an open-ocean sailor and on his study of the writings of a number of single-handed ocean sailors. Richard introduces the notion of "moral presence" and argues that this is what these sailors seek. They sometimes describe their goal in terms of personal quest (as we see in Jack's essay), sometimes in terms of a cosmic quest, and sometimes as the pursuit of technical finesse. Richard shows how these varying self-descriptions describe different pathways to moral presence.

The confluence of the views in these four essays is striking. It is even more striking when one reflects on the very different experiences of sailing that ground them: a crewman on a square-rigger, high-level racing of dinghies and large-keel boats, clubbing on a C-Scow in Lake Michigan, and single-handed ocean sailing.

The essays of Part II develop this fundamental idea that sailing can be a pathway to moral fulfillment by looking at it through the lens of particular historical schools of philosophy.

Sailing his catboat is for James Whitehill a Zen practice. In "Buddha's Boat," he says that "Buddhist tradition holds the view that there are countless ways to the difficult goal of an awakened, flourishing self. Sailing, I believe, can be one of those ways or practices." James describes how archery and meditation have been taught by traditional Zen practitioners as a means to enlightenment and then develops, out of his own carefully observed experience of sailing catboats around Cape Cod, an account of how he approaches sailing in a similar spirit.

In "Freedom of the Seas," Greg and Tod Bassham find in the teachings of Cicero, Seneca, Epictetus, Marcus Aurelius, and the Stoic school a guide to the most successful sailing. "For sailors," they write, "Stoicism has much to offer as a means to create and sustain the sense of joy we seek in sailing." They explain the Stoic metaphysics of fate and agency, the complementary virtues of cheerful resignation and self-sufficiency, and the all-important technique of negative visualization, and demonstrate their value for the sailor.

Steven Horrobin, in "Sailors of the Third Kind," takes his inspiration from Spinoza, leading the reader on a metaphysical journey the goal of which is to break the hold on him or her of a substantialist view of things. A sailor of the third kind is one who recognizes that everything is process: not just the weather and the waves but persons, boats, everything. Citing Spinoza, Steven describes this person in process of becoming as "in essence a move of the universal super-process toward its own self-realization, with persons achieving greater or lesser moves toward representing, in themselves and their own being, an approximation of the whole." For Spinoza, "the good was manifest in the direction of movement, within a person, toward the accurate reflection of the whole of nature, in microcosm." Heavy stuff! But Steven connects it to his experience of a certain sort of sailing and of sailors he calls sailors "of the third kind." Those who have perused the literature of ocean sailing, or who have much acquaintance with those who do such sailing, will recognize this sort of sailor at once. And, anyone who spends time maintaining a boat will be moved by Steven's eloquent depiction of the boat as a process unfolding in interaction with other surrounding processes.

The essays in Part III explore in detail various aspects of the "flourishing" or "fulfillment" to be found in sailing. In "What the Race to Mackinac Means," Nicholas Hayes gives a compelling account of competing in the Chicago to Mackinac Island Race. His racers encounter natural beauty, camaraderie, "lessons about work, reward, luck, and injustice," and a new sense of "our relationship with time." "Everything is now," says Nick near the end of his essay.

If it is not the same sort of consciousness, Nick's "nowness" is closely related to the one that Steve Matthews unpacks in his essay on the phenomenon he calls "flow." In "Sailing, Flow, and Fulfillment," Steve draws on both Daoism and the work of contemporary psychologists to explain the special value he finds in sailing, and especially in the sort of sailing of particular interest to him, windsurfing. Here, I think, specific features of the "boat" are important. Steve emphasizes the tight connection between the windsurfer and his board, a feeling of oneness with the kit.

Though I feel something similar in sailing my small skiff in a fresh breeze, it is very different sailing my five-ton yawl. There the feeling is more one of sovereignty. Set the course, trim the sails, and, once the boat is comfortable, set the tiller pilot and step back. The joy in this sort of sailing arises from the felt difference between the boat and me. The boat is an orderly world and I am its contemplating spirit. This contemplation does have an "everything is now" aspect to it, but for me at least it also has a time-soaked quality. When I sail, I feel the continuity with a long tradition. These differences in the experiences of various sorts of sailing are worth noting. We must not pull our conceptual nets too taut, lest we arrest "the motion of thought/and its restless iteration."[3]

Jesús Ilundáin-Agurruza, Luísa Gagliardini Graça, and José Jáuregui-Olaiz, in "On the Crest of the Wave," rhapsodize on many of the themes touched on in this book. They make playful use of common expressions with roots in the sailing world in order to evoke, as well as describe, the special aesthetic aspects of sailing. Slocum, Gautier, MacArthur, and other heroic sailors are brought in to testify to the natural beauty encountered in sailing, awe in the face of the sublime, the cultivated beauty of boats and of the precise and pertinent motions of the practiced sailor, and the joy of the constrained freedom in seamanship.

Jesse Steinberg and Michael Stuckart, in "Navigating What is Valuable and Steering a Course in Pursuit of Happiness," the final essay in this section, consider practical, moral, and aesthetic values as they relate to sailing.

They provide a brief taxonomy of what is valuable and then take up Aristotle's notion of "human flourishing" again. They argue that sailing has all the necessary elements for achieving a happy and full life. Indeed, they conclude, "Although it is certainly not the only activity that cultivates virtues, we think that sailing is an especially rich activity in this regard. That is, sailing is remarkably replete with opportunities to be virtuous. Sailing enables and even prompts one to be courageous, careful, curious, knowledgeable, decisive, and clever, and to have a whole host of other virtues."

Part IV shifts from the realms of psychology and values to physics and metaphysics. Sebastian Kuhn's delightful essay, "Do You Have to be (an) Einstein to Understand Sailing," unpacks the notion of relativity and its connection to sailing. "You will find," he writes, "maybe without realizing it, you are making use of 'relativity' in one way or another every time you weigh anchor. Even the General Theory of Relativity, long considered the most arcane of Einstein's ideas, has a direct impact on something as mundane as navigation." Sebastian's conceptual change-ups push one's thought out of the conventional ruts and invite one to consider a bigger picture. For example, the hoary comparison of the slowness of sailing with the speed of power-boating is reformulated by replacing instantaneous speed with average velocity (the total distance between the start and finish position divided by the elapsed time). "By this reckoning," Sebastian writes, "all weekend cruisers, whether laid-back sailors or high-speed motorboaters, have the same average velocity – namely zero! This is because they tend to end up right where they started." Later in the essay, playing with the notion of the reference frame, Sebastian invites us to look at the two sorts of cruiser using the fixed star as the frame. "Compared to that frame, both the most languid sailboat and the most souped-up powerboat move with velocities that are quite impressive – and practically indistinguishable (thirty kilometers per second, or 58,000 knots if you count the sun as the origin of this frame)." Sebastian's reminder that we don't just calculate but that we calculate within a particular frame of reference helps to keep our thinking in perpetual motion. Are there different frames available? What if we used one of those?

In "Paradoxes of Sailing," John D. Norton considers three puzzles about sailing. How is it possible to sail into the wind, and faster than the wind? These are two. The other draws on a common conceit of sailors that a sailboat "makes its own wind." The puzzle then is that, if this is so, why does it need any other wind? Considering these puzzles, John makes some interesting connections with two issues in recent philosophy, one concerning the metaphysics of causation and the other the notion of the thought experiment and the value of thought experiments as a mode of investigating nature. The issues are large and John's conclusions are substantive. His position on thought experiments is particularly interesting. He describes the Platonist view that grasping a thought experiment is like grasping the ideal triangle that is the meaning behind the crude drawing on the chalkboard. We grasp something beyond what is presented to our senses. John, however, sees the thought experiment as no more than a picturesque way of drawing out the implication of assumptions behind its constructions. What assumptions we want to agree to will ultimately be a matter of empirical investigation. Sailing provided the original thought experiment.

In the penultimate essay, "The Necessity of Sailing," Tamar and Nathan Rudavsky look at some of the ways in which sailing has provided philosophers with analogies to explain their views of freedom, fate, and determinism. They move from Aristotle and Maimonides all the way to Nietzsche. It is fascinating to see how philosophy is saturated with sailing metaphors and sailing images, just as ordinary speech is seen to be in Chapter 10. As in earlier essays, themes of freedom, fate, and determinism loom large.

The final essay, "The Channel," by Hilaire Belloc, serves as an epilogue to the volume. It appeared in 1913 as a chapter in the curious collection of travel writings entitled *Hills and Sea*. Belloc's writings about sailing are out of print and somewhat hard to find; they deserve to be better known. Belloc had a lust for life that drove him often to the sea. His views on sailing were "conservative," as were most of his views. He disdained the modern and comfortable and often chose to do things the hard way because only that way allowed him to suck the marrow out of the experience. His nostalgia for a past where life was bigger and more vibrant has something Greek about it. Sailing is a surrogate for him for life in the Golden Age. Raising as he does the suspicion that modern life distracts us with shadows, he is a true philosopher. In this nostalgia and in this choice of surrogate he speaks, I think, to the condition of many of us who sail.

## NOTES

1 Wallace Stevens, "The Place of the Solitaires." In *Harmonium* (New York: Knopf, 1991), p. 60.
2 National Sailing Hall of Fame, *The National Sailing Hall of Fame and Sailing Center* (n.d., http://www.nshof.org/images/booklet15.pdf).
3 Stevens, "The Place of the Solitaires."

# ACKNOWLEDGMENTS

Many people have had a hand in helping me to become a sailor, from the college classmate who first taught me to sail to current friends who share their time and knowledge with me. With their help I have found much pleasure and an added dimension to life. I hope this book, in a small way, pays forward their generosity to me.

Many thanks to Fritz Allhoff, the editor of the *Philosophy for Everyone* series, for his invaluable assistance in putting this volume into proper shape. He has been a most patient and helpful guide.

Thanks are due to my colleague in the Philosophy Department here at Virginia Wesleyan College, Cathal Woods, who made some excellent suggestions for improving the introduction, and to my daughter, Emma Goold, who helped to prepare the manuscript.

Much of my work on the volume was done during a sabbatical from teaching granted me by Virginia Wesleyan College.

PART I

# PASSING THROUGH PAIN AND FEAR IN THE PLACE OF PERPETUAL UNDULATION

CHAPTER I

# SHIPS OF WOOD AND MEN OF IRON

Voyaging the Old-Fashioned Way and Seeking Meaning
in Adversity

 The ship slid down the face of the wave, listing to
port at the trough, shuddering as if she would
break up, then, lurching upright, she lifted once
again to the crest of the next mountain of seawater.
Rain and wind pelted us as we tried to hold a
steady course, but the rain was insignificant in
comparison to the spray caused by the bow
smashing into the sea. Globs of water the size of a
man's fist came speeding toward us, followed by
smaller droplets in a heavy spray. Waves thirty-five
feet high lifted behind and rolled toward our stern
without relief. We pitched, we rolled, we scurried to our tasks with "one
hand for the sailor and one for the ship" to do our duty and not lose our
lives.

No, not a scene from centuries past on a whaler or on a clipper
rounding the Horn; it was a "pleasure" trip on the replica of *HMS Bounty*
that brought me on this perilous journey. I was seventeen years old and
the youngest member of the crew. How does someone that age get to
crew on such a ship? My father piloted the *Bounty* into New York Harbor
after her global voyage to promote the 1962 film *Mutiny on the Bounty*,

*Sailing – Philosophy for Everyone: Catching the Drift of Why We Sail*, First Edition.
Edited by Patrick Goold.
© 2012 John Wiley & Sons, Inc. Published 2012 by John Wiley & Sons, Inc.

starring Marlon Brando and Trevor Howard. The *Bounty* was still owned by MGM Studios and was to spend two years berthed at the Flushing Bay Marina in sight of Shea Stadium just outside the grounds of the 1964–1965 World's Fair in Flushing Meadow. My father and two generations before him were tugboat men in New York Harbor. He advanced to piloting in the northeastern United States and around the world. His accomplishments included being chosen to pilot Queen Elizabeth's royal yacht while she visited America, so he was the first choice for MGM for this prestigious assignment. His influence got me the job.

On arrival in Flushing Bay, the MGM public relations man aboard was disappointed at the lack of wind and the *Bounty*'s listless sails as she approached the dock under the power of her two huge diesel engines. When my father understood MGM's concern, he solved the problem by shifting the *Bounty* into reverse. Stunning photographs were taken of the majestic square rigger on a bright sunny day with all sails set and filled with a breeze. Of course, sailors questioned why there was a wake in front of the ship in the photograph and not behind, but the landlubbers never knew. Ah, the magic of Hollywood!

I had worked on the *Bounty* at the World's Fair when I was sixteen years old. Few visitors came because we were located outside the park grounds and only the truly determined found their way to us. We were supposed to be tour guides but were transformed into maintenance men to repair her decks and spars, going aloft with a brush tied to the wrist of one hand and carrying a bucket of log oil in the other. I was young and fearless and climbed the ratlines without concern. MGM decided not to remain for the second summer of the Fair but to put in at Jacobson's Shipyard in Oyster Bay, Long Island for a winter re-fit. I sailed the *Bounty* there and Hugh Boyd, the ship's boatswain, asked me and another *Bounty* sailor to work weekends to get her into shape.

What a surprise when Boatswain Boyd called me to invite me to sail her to Florida in June of 1965! I could make the journey from New York to Port Everglades, Florida but not the last leg around the Tortugas and up the Gulf coast to St. Petersburg, where a new park was to be built to showcase the ship. I had to return to take my final exams of senior year in high school. As the youngest on board, I received the dubious honor of being designated "the Captain of the Head." That meant that, in addition to my duties aloft, on watch, and at the helm, I was to clean the toilet used by twenty-one crewmen.

Remember that I was not "shanghaied" or pressed into service by a foreign power. I volunteered and was thrilled to accompany the crew, which included some VIPs, such as my watch officer, Julian Roosevelt, a successful businessman and Olympic sailor. What causes modern men and women purposely to leave comfort and security behind to venture out into danger and discomfort? Even a family camping trip can involve inclement weather, insects, faulty equipment, and possibly a close encounter with ferocious animals. Why not stay home and enjoy a DVD of the great outdoors? Some campers mitigate the inconveniences by using air-conditioned motor homes, televisions, and bug zappers. Still, why not just stay home? There is some motivation in us to push the envelope and to experience greater challenges. Most of the time, we seem to seek the greatest comfort level possible and to look for cures for any ailment. Yet, we also eschew modern tools to prove something to ourselves or to others. *Certo ergo sum*? (I struggle, therefore I am?)

I was aware of the struggle and danger when I eagerly accepted the offer to ship out with the *Bounty* crew two hundred miles off the East Coast from New York down to southern Florida. My great-grandfather died in the frigid winter water of Newtown Creek by the East River in New York City. He slipped on ice and fell into the water from his tugboat at night. Some years later, his son, my grandfather, had to abandon his tugboat as the load suddenly shifted on the barge he was towing on a short hawser in the East River, not far from where his father had died. My grandfather, Captain Walter Stillwaggon, yelled to his sleeping deckhand to get off the boat. Without hesitation or the need for greater clarification, the deckhand leaped overboard and was saved. In almost the same spot as his father's and grandfather's maritime accidents, my father, Captain Jim Stillwaggon, then an eighteen-year-old deckhand, had his foot crushed between a tug and barge. He had a successful career in spite of that terrible injury, using an artificial limb, playing a very good game of golf, and even climbing Jacob's Ladders well into his seventies in the Caribbean, Wales, South America, and the Middle East. That provided us children with an important lesson in overcoming adversity and remaining positive.

So, in 1965, I knew the dangers, but they excited rather than discouraged me. The risks presented themselves soon after we left the dock. There was a small ceremony at our departure with the families of some of the sailors on hand to wish us well. Local news reporters filmed the event. The crew could not stop to enjoy the festivities as we took orders from the mates and the boatswain to load up supplies and stow them below. We motored from Oyster Bay on Long Island under the bridges that connect Queens with the Bronx, through the infamous Hell Gate and down the East River to the harbor. As we left Sandy Hook behind, my father completed his piloting of the *Bounty* and boarded a small vessel to return to the safety of terra firma. Almost as if on cue, the swells started to lift and roll our 180-foot-long, 412-gross-ton ship. What power the sea has that even large ships are not immune to its strength and capricious nature!

A heavy wood and metal block was swinging and smashing against the main mast crosstree and shrouds. It had to be belayed so the boatswain looked around for a junior crewman who could spring into action and lash down the heavy block. I was recruited for the task. With a leather string in my teeth, I climbed aloft. Although I was on my guard, the block hit my head with a glancing blow. I was dazed but held on until I felt well enough to grab the pendulous block and lash it to the shroud.

As we lost sight of land, the separation from the security of home and hearth was jolting. A squall had moved in and an ominous look came over all we could see. The June sky looked like winter and the waves built to incredible heights. The wind whistled through the miles of rigging on board our ship. Soon we all regretted the sumptuous breakfast provided by our Greek cook – wet scrambled eggs, spicy sausages, pastries … all you could eat. Between the constant rolling and pitching as we motored southward and the morning feast, seasickness was rampant. I had never before, nor have I ever since, suffered from *mal de mer*. One of the *Mayflower* crew who was on board with us jokingly pointed out that I should not fear dying from seasickness as I was "too sick to die." I drew little comfort from his attempts to cheer me and ate no food for thirty-six hours. Just seeing Boatswain Boyd at dawn eating a green apple as he danced on the deck playing his concertina made me ill again.

I had the four-to-eight watch so I saw dawn and dusk each day. Bow watch was a horror as the bow dug deep into each trough with green water running down the decks. We needed to be aware of the flotsam and jetsam that can stave in a wooden hull like ours. Telephone poles or even a semi-submerged container can put an end to a ship and her sailors in a moment. Steering was even more of a challenge as the *Bounty* slid down thirty-five-foot waves like a surfboard. She was being pushed, not making headway under sail, so her bow pointed ten or twenty degrees port or starboard off course. Mr. Roosevelt, first mate and my watch officer, sternly urged me to "hold the course, helmsman, hold the course steady." I steered this way and that, hoping to average our 175-degree bearing, but it was beyond me. The compass rose was spinning in the binnacle and I was still getting sick.

On the first full day at sea I awoke to the sound of an alarm. It was the claxon blast you hear in movies when an attack is expected. Ours was a fire alarm. That is a sound that can strike fear into the most intrepid heart. Fire at sea! There is no escape route. It is an odd feeling to look all around you and see nothing but a horizon. Instead of providing a sense of vastness, it gave me the opposite impression. It was as if our existence had been reduced to a small disk, like a toy boat left by a child on a round table top. I went to a fire station but learned later that it was not the one assigned to me. That error might have saved my life. My fire station partner, a crewman from the *Mayflower*, passed out as we extinguished the fire. He remained in his cot for five days without moving. We learned later that he had inhaled sulfur fumes from the caulking used to seal the teak deck.

We had three fires in the first three days. Two were from dry-rotted wood that was next to the engine exhaust conduits. The third was electrical, from faulty wiring. We worried each time as sparks landed on wood or as flaming ashes rose up through our hemp lines and canvas sails.

I wasn't privy to the discussions our captain and officers must have had about our misfortunes. Did they consider turning back? How would the owners and organizers react? Would they suspect that our officers had given up prematurely? Did our officers take further risks to prove their courage? I did overhear one such conversation between the first and second mates. It was about the *Mayflower* crewman. They wondered whether he should be left to die on board or be transferred by helicopter to die on shore. His mates from the Mayflower believed he had a sister in Georgia and surely that would be a better place to die with family nearby. That was a dose of grim reality for a seventeen-year-old to hear. Days later, when the man emerged on deck looking well, it was as if Lazarus had returned from the dead.

Imagine the sailors of olden days who had no radio, no inflatable rafts, and no Coast Guard. Turning around would not have been acceptable. Whaling ships out of Bedford and Nantucket left for four-year voyages. There was no opting out for them. When you made your mark on the crew list before shipping out, you were on board come what may. They had little choice and lived in harder times.

Ishmael in *Moby Dick* seemed to voyage for adventure more than fortune or need. For most, though, fear of poverty, the law, or oppression drove young men to the sea. What a difference from us who leave our modern conveniences behind and long to experience what life was like when deprivation was the rule and people were expected to toil endlessly.

We leave our norm of non-stop entertainment and self-satisfying behavior to take on the role of Richard Henry Dana in his experience "before the mast." Do we strive to experience the past as amateur historians or are we atoning for our frivolous modern lifestyle? Are we like the actor who takes up a political cause to prove he can do more than just play make-believe? Does the fact that we endured a risky trial and survived add importance to an otherwise silly existence?

Most people do not climb Mt. Everest, kayak through Oceania, or sail offshore on a replica of an eighteenth-century sailing ship, but many attempt to step out of their secure environments to expand their horizons and test their boundaries. Do we fully understand our motivations in doing such things? Think of the soldier we praise for his or her patriotism. Is there another motivation, though, in addition to love of one's country? Is that person also trying to test his mettle? The soldier wants to know whether he has what it takes to earn his red badge of courage. So many combat veterans say that, when the first bullet whizzes past your face close enough to feel the heat, your mind orders your body to flee the danger. The soldier stays, though, partially through training and discipline but also to prove to himself and to his comrades that he has fortitude.

Most of the crew on the *Bounty* had met only shortly before the departure. Even so, we quickly came together as a team and worked well together. Our officers and boatswain get some of the credit. But there must have been another reason. Perhaps we wanted to prove we were worthy of each other's trust. One example of bravery stunned us. We had finally emerged from a couple of days and nights of stormy weather and had set the fore and aft sails. The engine finally was shut down and the rolling stopped as we heeled over into a comfortable pitch and the seawater turned from green to blue as we entered the Gulf Stream. "All hands on deck" was called out as we tacked from port to starboard and back again hours later. Our peaceful resting in the sunshine was abruptly shattered as a poorly secured sheet slipped from its belaying pin and the main topmast staysail luffed wildly. The boatswain sent us aloft but no one could figure out how to gain control of this large canvas sail. Suddenly, a young sailor leaped from the shrouds, aiming for the flapping staysail. His weight collapsed the sail and he pinned the bulk of it to the main mast, holding on with all his might. Although shocked for a moment, we responded to the boatswain's charge to "help that man!" We left the relative safety of the shrouds for the flimsy-looking monkey ropes that spanned the gap from the shrouds to the mast and, like clumsy trapeze artists, tried to add our weight to his and to secure the sail until the sheet

JACK STILLWAGGON

could be tamed once again. When the job was done, it was pats on his back and cheers all around. There was no boasting on his part and the brave deed was not mentioned again. His act was so selfless that it stands out as unique. What if a blast of wind had lifted the sail just as he jumped? We would have been asking ourselves again whether a sailor had family ashore to whom to deliver the body.

We went back to work knowing that something special had been shared. Were we feeling more like the "men of iron" who came this way before us? There is a sense of achievement that comes from taking risks and persevering. We feel reassured to be accepted by others we admire and respect. General Eisenhower went to the staging area where the first paratroops to land in Normandy were about to embark on their aircraft. He wondered what he could possibly talk about to these men who were headed into grave danger. He asked one of the men whether he liked jumping out of planes. The paratrooper replied, "No sir, I don't. But I like to hang out with fellows who do." This spirit must lie in all of us to one degree or another.

It has been said that "the mass of men lead lives of quiet desperation," yet we strive to break out of the mold that has been made for us and to do more or to be different. We might not like jumping out of planes or climbing a hundred feet above a rolling deck, but may feel that we must do these things to feel truly alive. Now, four days out, we were experiencing the best of the old sailing days. A whale was spotted nearby. Flying fish hopped on board – surprised at their dry landing, I'm sure. We tossed them back and noted that we couldn't be far from the Bahamas. The sun felt warm and dried us out after the first few days of thorough soaking. The food was good and tasty after days of thinking I would never be able to eat again. Life seemed fuller now that we had gone to the edge and made it back. There was time in between watches and meals to just experience life and be glad for it.

Do we value life more when it seems like we might have lost it? For those who have tasted adventure, it is particularly irksome to hear the teenager who has everything say, "I'm bored." Do they need a sea voyage on an ancient vessel to cure their boredom? Whence this modern curse of ennui? Can you imagine the sailor of old who felt fortunate to receive some discarded sail cloth to fashion a pair of trousers, or maybe even mittens to prevent frostbite as he went aloft while rounding Cape Horn? Was he bored? Ha! I don't think those sailors even knew the word. Work consumed much of their waking hours and rum helped them sleep. Their lives might have been miserable for much of the time but the high points probably seemed higher by comparison. Think of the original crew of *HMS Bounty* leaving foggy Britain behind, enduring short rations and flogging underway, but then arriving in paradise. Perfect weather, willing women, and endless feasting! To what extent did that reward counterbalance all the dreariness and suffering of the rest of their lives?

Is that why those seven days on the *Bounty* come back to my memory so clearly? In spite of the danger and discomfort, it was a high point. It stands out and is cherished. You have seen the veterans on parade with their versions of their old uniforms. Often they wear hats that show what unit they belonged to or the location where they served. They have such pride now but, when they were on active duty, most of them could not wait to get out of the service. They counted the days with "twenty-one and a wake up" or kidded a pal who had more time to serve with sayings such as "I'm so short that down looks like up to me." So, why do they shift gears later and remember their service so fondly? They recognize that, in spite of the danger and lack of luxury, those years were a high point. They were involved in something important. They were needed by their teammates and maybe were even recognized for an accomplishment. The negatives are forgotten as the lens of time focuses their memories more favorably and they say, "Those were the days." Do we all selectively reshape our experiences that way? Are the insults and slights allowed to fade and the low points relegated to a dustbin, while the high points are refined so that our victories become more glorious over time? I suppose it is harmless. It seems less a deceit than an artifice to help us to cope.

Being too young to drink legally meant that I stood watch the night we docked in Port Everglades, Florida. The others went into town and celebrated. It was fun to see them return. One group piled out of a taxi, drunk as skunks. I could not figure out why the cab remained where it had stopped until I realized that there was no cabbie. I guess my shipmates had borrowed the cab. Even the boatswain arrived after the 0100h curfew he had set. He apologized for making me overstay my watch. Can you imagine this accomplished sailor who had sailed the seven seas saying sorry to me, the youngest man on board? There were no apologies necessary from the boatswain. I was just seventeen years old so his apology made me feel like one of the men. Maybe I was becoming one of the "men of iron." "Ships of wood and men of iron," as they used to say.

The next day, I packed my duffel bag and stepped ashore. The solid ground felt funny and seemed to roll like a deck at sea. As we assembled on deck to say our goodbyes, the captain presented me with a framed certificate praising me for my able-bodied sailing and sober habits. I was given a one-dollar bill for volunteering, which is Canadian practice and was done because the *Bounty* was built in Nova Scotia.

I was glad to be heading home yet very sad to see the *Bounty* sail away. I watched until the main royal disappeared over the horizon. To end the crucible and part with my shipmates after all we had been through together was a wrenching change.

Still, the journey lives on as part of who I am and what I believe I can do. I had left the safety of home and hearth and endured a trial. I had survived and earned respect from men whom I admired. I had struggled in the face of adversity and valued life a little more than before. Like the rock climber who maintains an inner self-confidence because of having scaled challenging heights, or the marathon runner who completes a race, I was more at peace with myself for reaching new horizons and I expected more from myself from that point onward.

CHAPTER 2

# WINNING PHILOSOPHY

## Developing Patience, Inner Strength, and an Eye for the Good Lanes

In sports the final result is never a sure thing. For competitors and spectators this uncertainty makes every event exciting. This is why we tend to cheer for the underdog. We prefer a close contest with both teams having a chance to win. Being part of a race or game that comes right down to the wire is a thrill. For competitors the uncertainty can be frightening as well as exhilarating. Winning takes inner strength and even courage. The big question for every competitive sailor is how to generate the will to overcome fear and to win.

I have found many effective techniques in my fifty-plus years of racing at every level of sailing. The first step is to avoid worrying about the final outcome, and instead think about the task at hand. I work on one thing at a time and measure my progress along the way. A well-organized practice session gives competitors confidence later during the heat of battle. Before important events I spend time visualizing the race, my boat, my competitors, the surroundings, and the water. This makes me relaxed. If I sense nervousness coming on I go back to my normal pre-race routine. And, if it all goes bad, I have learned to take a deep breath and quietly

*Sailing – Philosophy for Everyone: Catching the Drift of Why We Sail*, First Edition.
Edited by Patrick Goold.

say to myself, "Just for fun let's see how we can turn this around." Unexpected things happen on the race course. Both good and bad experiences are valuable tools in helping to overcome adversity. By thinking hard and being creative, success is always a possibility. In the end, every victory is well earned. All athletes know there are many defeats backing up a championship.

As mentioned, everyone loves cheering for the underdog. Respect is earned when the situation looks helpless but the underdog prevails. Three special events come to mind from over the years as examples of amazing feats in sailing.

Imagine being expected to win the Olympic trials. The qualifying series is seven races with one throw-out against the cream of America's sailors. Race one ends with a disappointing fifth. In race two, the mast goes over the side. Now, five races are left and the odds of winning are looking slim. For many sailors the end would come soon. But not for Buddy Melges, Bill Bentsen, and Bill Allen. With a second string mast and a lot of grit, the trio bounced back by taking five straight firsts. They went on to the Olympics in 1972 but the story did not end there. The trials were sailed on windy San Francisco Bay with the idea of emulating the breezy conditions expected in Kiel, Germany. But there was a surprise. The winds of Kiel went light. How many times have you been at a regatta and heard the words, "The winds aren't normally like this here." Melges and his crew had trained in heavy winds. But somehow the Americans found one zephyr after another to defeat four-time Olympic gold medalist Paul Elvstrom. Melges and crew took home the gold medal. America has never produced a better sailor. Buddy's ability to adapt to unexpected changes sets him apart from all other sailors.

By the age of forty, Ted Turner had won every major ocean race, the America's Cup, and dozens of small boat titles. Turner understood comebacks, having suffered through a miserable summer on the super-slow *Mariner* in 1974 and returned to defend the America's Cup in 1977. But that victory wasn't complete since one race still stood out in his mind – the Fastnet. Aboard his Sparkman & Stephans 61-foot *Tenacious*, Turner assembled a crack crew of seasoned ocean racers. The preceding Cowes Week was windy and *Tenacious* won many of the daily prizes. But the magnitude of the 1979 Fastnet race was not anticipated.

The first three hundred miles to Fastnet Rock, eight miles off the coast of Ireland, were easy. But soon after rounding the rock the wind built to forty, then to fifty, and finally to over a frightening sixty knots. The *Tenacious* felt the fury of the storm. Turner kept the crew focused and calm. It was as if Turner actually thrived on the massive waves and powerful winds. With no visibility, feeling the waves and wind proved to be the solution. Turner mastered the storm, emerging well into the lead to take the first overall prize out of 303 boats. To this day, Turner will tell you it was his most satisfying victory. For me it is a real thrill to have shared both Ted's America's Cup and Fastnet victories.

Being the first American skipper to lose the America's cup brought a lot of criticism Dennis Conner's way, but actually he sailed brilliantly in 1983. The score could easily have been 4–0, advantage *Australia II*. But Conner outfoxed the Aussies time after time. In one race he actually crossed the Australians on port tack. This is something that should never happen in a match race. It is the equivalent of fumbling a football on the opening kickoff and the other team scoring a touchdown.

In the end, Conner failed to cover on the final run of the last race. The error would have ended many careers, but Conner knew he had the ability to make a comeback. He and his syndicate head, Malin Burnham, pioneered corporate sponsorship in sailing. Conner had been beaten by *Australia II* with an innovative wing keel, so he launched a huge research project to develop a fast boat. And they won the next Cup! Overnight Conner became a national hero. Adding to the pressure on Conner was live, worldwide television coverage with onboard cameras. Conner's strongest assets in that campaign were his personal resolve to erase the loss of 1983 and his ability to play the wind shifts. Throughout the 1987 series, he cleverly chose between covering and playing the wind. It was his finest hour.

In each of these three cases, American sailing champions knew they had a chance to overcome adversity. It was not a question of luck, it was a question of resolve. I, too, have learned to come back after sailing disappointing races.

A particular collegiate regatta was going to be intense for me. Only two boats from the Middle Atlantic District would qualify for the Intercollegiate Singlehanded Championship. The elimination series was held on my home waters off the SUNY Maritime College in a new boat, the Laser. This nifty dinghy was new to all of us. I had only sailed the Laser once. At six-foot-two and 180 pounds I was the right size for the boat. But after two races I was in twelfth place out of sixteen boats. Not good! Back at the dock my coach, Graham Hall, said in a very calm way, "you look like you are trying too hard and thinking about qualifying." Hall continued, "you're out of it right now so just go back out there and try to make one improvement at a time." "But what about boat speed?"

GARY JOBSON

I asked. "Oh, don't worry about that, just go have fun!" "Fun?" I thought. Somehow Hall loosened me up. It was at this precise moment that I regained my confidence and my sailing career changed dramatically. I went out and had fun, by winning the next race. In fact, I won the next ten races in a row.

Suddenly, sixteen years of sailing clicked. Looking back through my college logbooks I recorded two thousand races in four years. There were many fundamentals that I refined through competitive drills and lessons learned from mistakes. Every single day I spent time working on boat handling by sailing continuous figure eights, practicing timed runs, and tacking and jibing endlessly. Even to this day I find crisp roll tacks one of the highlights of life. Making figure eights by rounding a set pair of buoys gives you practice jibing, tacking, rounding windward, rounding leeward, and accelerating. Precise maneuvering is an essential asset when you are around other boats. These drills gave me an edge and to this day I savor every roll tack.

At the Intercollegiate National Championship two months later, I again had trouble in the first two races. Now we were racing Lasers on Mission Bay, near San Diego. Observing my problem, Graham Hall suggested just one tactical adjustment: "don't be the first to tack after every start. Wait until you have a clear lane. Use a boat to leeward and ahead to push away traffic." He continued, "think of a running back using a blocker to gain more yardage."

The philosophical shift for me was to be more patient and look for good lanes. For the first time I understood how to use competitors as "blockers." I went on to win ten of the next fourteen races to take the championship.

The most important lesson Graham Hall taught me was to go out on the racecourse and have fun. Another was the importance of good coaching and helping others become successful sailors. Improving is easier if someone helps you. The combination of coaching, practice, and a positive attitude worked well for me.

Taking command is a big responsibility and often lonely. Many people would rather not be in charge. But, for others, leadership is the essence of life. And for many sailors the most rewarding leadership opportunity is aboard a boat. After the fact, a leader can be a hero or a goat. Unfortunately, there is rarely anything in between. Thanks to the experience of racing with many champion skippers over the years and also having had the command myself from time to time, I've learned many valuable lessons in the art of leadership.

To be a good leader, once in charge, be in charge. Trust your instincts! Second-guessing a decision can cause a breakdown in the command structure. The fewer words spoken, the better. Consistency and confidence are essential. Work to avoid arrogance. Plan in advance. Once a plan is decided, execute it with precision. Let everyone on board know your plan. Mistakes are avoided with early preparation. Hold a crew meeting after leaving the dock. Gather everyone on deck so they can easily see and hear the leader. Prompt attendance is mandatory. Talk about safety routine, job assignments, a stated purpose for the day, the anticipated weather, the course to be sailed, and any potential surprises that may occur. Forecasting situations in advance allows the crew to be mentally prepared. By being an oracle of the future, the leader builds confidence that he or she is on the correct course and knows how to handle a troublesome situation. During bad times always remain calm. If the leader is in control, the rest of the crew will follow his or her example.

Communicate clearly! During the crew meeting publicly state every crewmember's job during "all hands." Take the guesswork out of the equation. As I've mentioned earlier, if events become tense, go back to your normal routine. The crew will feel more comfortable.

Deploy your crew carefully! Be sure the right people are resting at the optimum times. Keep a steady pace going and avoid burnout. You cannot have an "all hands" situation every single hour for two days running, for example. It simply will not work. Set up a buddy system on board. In this way two people can share any single task. A common goal brings a crew together. If there is a problem, a second person provides a backup or can help with a solution. Remember the old saying, "many hands make light work."

Keep no secrets! Be open with your crew. It helps to say nice things about the people you sail with. Word will spread. Everyone responds positively to a job well done and the proper acknowledgment. Good leadership is hard. It is learned over time. The best leaders understand all the functions on their boat and the capability of their crews. By setting a common goal and organizing the team by giving specific assignments, the crew will naturally want to work together.

Strike a balance between selling your ideas and being a dictator! Although there is strength in collective wisdom, ruling by committee rarely works. Yacht races and naval battles are won by leaders, not committees. I believe in collective action. Asking for advice ahead of time helps people feel they are part of the decision-making process. But during

GARY JOBSON

the heat of battle there is no time to consult. Take charge! Be authoritative and clear! Hesitation creates uncertainty and undermines confidence. America's Cup champion Dennis Conner often polls his crew before the start of a race about any ideas they might have on the best strategy. But Conner will point out that, once the race starts or after an event has occurred, he doesn't want to hear "we should have." The time to speak up is prior to the event, not after the fact. There is no room for Monday-morning quarterbacking on board a boat.

Striking the right balance will require some creativity at times. I recall a regatta in Maine in which one crewmember, sitting on the windward rail, constantly questioned the decisions of our afterguard. It was a tough series. The currents in Maine are complex and the wind was shifting dramatically. At times we looked great, at other times we did not. The key to doing well is to believe in your convictions and to stick with your game plan. Crisscrossing the racecourse simply puts you further behind. But, after every tack, the crewmember on the windward rail sarcastically questioned every call. "Why did we do that?" or "Well that was a big mistake." Our afterguard elected to ignore the patter. As it turned out, we had a good race, finishing second.

Overnight I thought about the young man on the rail and what to do about him. The next race the wind filled in well before the start. It was going to be a good day. After our crew meeting, but before the preparatory signal, I invited the young rail rider aft and said, "We have three options. We can sail to the right side of the course, up the middle, or on the left side of the course. Since you seemed to have all the answers yesterday, which side should we sail on? And remember – we're in the running for first place for the week, so your decision could make the difference." The young man stuttered a little bit and sweat started to form on his brow, but I just waited. Finally, after two minutes he admitted, "I'm not really qualified to make this call," at which point I said, "Well, when we do make decisions, it would be helpful if you were supportive as opposed to second-guessing." We did not hear a negative word out of him for the remainder of the race.

At the risk of sounding boastful, we won a big Etchells regatta with 1–1–1–2–5–1–4–1 finishes. The next day one of my friends called to offer his Bravo Zulu: "Nice going except for the fifth," he said. It made me chuckle because that was our best, and most important, race. Sometimes when you pop into the lead after a good start or fortunate wind shift winning is easy. Racing when you are well back in the pack is the real challenge and often where regattas are won.

At the start of race five (on the second day), we got off to an adequate start and rounded the windward mark in second. But the wind shifted, and we were late to maneuver into the center of the course. Every boat behind us did take advantage of the wind shift and suddenly we were last. Ouch! To make matters worse, our rival, who was in second in the regatta at that point, was winning the race. My crew, Jud Smith, was brilliant as we approached the leeward turning mark; he declared, "Here's what we are going to do. We are going to round last, and then start the race over." His words were delivered with humor and helped me recover from blowing a good position. By the time we made the turn for the next beat to windward on the five-leg course, our Etchells fleet had caught up to a fleet of thirty-eight J22s sailing ahead of us. J22s are smaller and slower than Etchells. It is hard to sail through a fleet that is slower because they disturb the wind and chop up the waves. And, adding to the confusion, the wind strength was dropping and it was getting very shifty. In other words, there was lots of opportunity to pass some boats.

There is always a tough choice between sailing in disturbed wind and staying on a big lift, or tacking away to sail in clear wind but toward the wrong side of the course. We decided to work the lifts and ignore the boats ahead. It was a good strategy. Within a few minutes we had passed five of the twelve boats in our Etchells fleet. At the next windward mark we jibed immediately and headed downwind. On the run we were able to pass another boat. Meanwhile, our rival got tangled up with the J22 fleet and missed a few wind shifts. One more leg to windward and we moved into fifth while our rival ended up in seventh place. A positive attitude, confusion from another fleet, and weird wind shifts saved the race.

College sailors learn that maintaining a good, consistent average is the key to success. In 2009 and 2010 the winning team at the College Nationals Championship averaged fifth place out of eighteen teams. For me, the real challenge is being able to clear my head when adversity strikes. Imagine being in the top two places in five consecutive races and suddenly being in last. It is easy to be upset and start complaining. That is why Jud's words when we lost the lead were both soothing and helpful. After recovering mentally, the next step is to make a plan.

The best time to plan your strategy during a race is on the prior leg. Think through, in advance, which side of the course has more wind. If you see a boat make a substantial gain, the pattern often repeats itself. Once, in a cat boat regatta on Barnegat Bay in New Jersey, on the last leg to windward, I noticed one boat sail from last into fourth. No one else seemed to see this big gain. About fifteen minutes later a second race was

GARY JOBSON

started and I sailed off in the direction where the big gain was made. Happily, the wind was stronger and there was some favorable current over in this area. We led at the first mark and held on to win. Staying alert paid off for us. More often than not, however, sailing on the closest course to the next mark is the best strategy. In long-distance races, using just one strategy of simply staying on the rhumb line gives good odds of winning.

There is the age-old question of when to split with the fleet and take a flyer. In my experience flyers rarely pay. Ask yourself this question: Should you split with the fleet to make a big advance and risk losing many boats, or chip away at the fleet by trying to pass one boat a time? It's no accident that America's two Olympic medalists in 2008, Anna Tunnicliffe and Zach Railey, won their medals without winning a single race. The lesson learned is to avoid taking big chances.

If you adhere to the philosophy of going for a good, consistent average then I suggest staying with the fleet. Before the Olympic Games, Zach Railey told me his goal was to simply try to pass one boat at a time without taking big risks. The cat boat race was an exception to this rule. I was confident that one side of the course was clearly favored. I had seen it during the previous race. This is when you should be courageous and take a chance with a flyer. Watch for new opportunities and take advantage of them! Anna Tunnicliffe made a flyer pay in the last race of the 2008 Olympics. She worked the right side of the course on the first leg, and was back in eighth out of ten boats. On the next leg she headed left. Over her shoulder she noticed a strong puff well to windward and beyond the lay line. She went with her gut instinct, tacked for the wind, got the puff, and surged into third place at the next mark. The move earned Anna a gold medal.

Maintaining a good attitude during a race is essential. In that Etchells regatta we had two moments that could have turned bad, but a quick acknowledgment of our mistakes calmed our crew down. The first case was jumping the gun at the start. Of course, we did not think we were over, but whoever does? The first step is to get bad thoughts out of your head so you can make a quick recovery. After restarting we noticed that we were on a big port lift, while the rest of the fleet was still sailing on starboard tack. A few minutes later the wind headed and we tacked. Instantly we were back among the leaders. Had we spent time and energy complaining we would never have noticed the wind pattern and would not have made the comeback. A few races later we made the mistake of splitting with our two closest rivals on points. Sure enough we paid dearly as the rivals found better wind and took the lead. Once again Jud simply said, "My mistake." That was it and we went to work to make up ground.

Try to work on one thing at a time. Compare your boat's speed with the other boats around you. Make one adjustment at a time to see what works. One person on the crew should watch what the competition is doing. Make mental notes on who is gaining. When the weather gets sloppy take the attitude that there is opportunity to pass. A good attitude during times of adversity will help you earn that good, consistent average. And sometimes the worst finish in a regatta might just be your best.

At a collegiate National Sailing Championship I noticed how smoothly the teams maneuvered their dinghies. Every dock landing was perfect, roll tacks were crisp, boat speed was at peak performance, and, best of all, attitudes were focused. Is talent like this natural or does it come from within? While almost every college sailor has the fundamentals mastered, I wondered what it takes to achieve that extra margin of excellence that produces champions. A mentor can begin the process.

Inspiration by mentors starts by setting a high example. We need to encourage current sailing stars to reach out and help others. This is the responsibility of success. Give a protégé a reason to work hard by getting them to get goals. Often a brief talk followed by an encouraging letter initiates the process. At this stage, mention that you will be following the aspiring sailor's progress. Occasional checkups will reinforce the message. When the young sailor starts asking questions, you will know that forward progress has begun. The next step is to keep records so lessons learned will be remembered.

Once the first seed is sown, the next step comes from within. A young sailor must start with the desire and then put in a worthy effort. There is no substitute for scheduling and participating in disciplined practice sessions.

Encourage your protégé to ask for help, read about techniques, and experiment on the water. When setting goals, make the priority learning over winning. Use high but attainable short-term goals to measure progress (I define short-term as under two months). Offer case studies as examples of how successful sailors have achieved long-term goals.

Many young sailors give up during times of adversity. They take errors hard. You can help overcome these problems by pointing out specific problems. During a regatta, ask one simple question at a time to allow a sailor to answer for himself what could be done better on the racecourse. Too much input creates confusion. As a mentor, always be calm, as if you expect improvement. This philosophy builds confidence. It's okay to be a cheerleader, but help to flatten out the inevitable rollercoaster ride by not getting too excited when winning or depressed during defeat. Remember that winning is the elimination of errors. Teach sailors to thrive on working out of bad positions after a slow start, making a penalty turn, or being on the wrong side of a wind shift. It takes work to keep one's attitude focused. During the heat of battle, a sailor must be calm and never sweat the small stuff when things go wrong.

There is a fine but dangerous line between helpful coaching and pushing too hard. This problem is frequently found in the Optimist dinghy class. If expectations are too high for early ages, a young sailor may reject sailing. Always balance sailing with other activities. Good grades are the key to opening doors. Make studies a priority. Sailing should never be a young person's only sport. The attributes and lessons learned in other sports are often analogous to sailing. The discipline instilled in a team sport is particularly helpful in sailing with a crew.

Once the seed of desire starts growing, organize a purposeful regatta schedule. Sail both larger and smaller boats to broaden experience. Singlehanded sailing always sharpens your skills. To prepare for maxi racing, for example, I sail Lasers to get me in tune with the wind and water. Sailing on different waters also builds experience. Sailing today has become too specialized. In the long term, variety keeps interest up and builds skills. One type of sailing supports another. Rising sailors exhibit many common attributes. They physically match up well with their boat. During a race, the body is fluid with a boat's motion. Actions are deliberate. Being in good physical condition enhances performance.

Many sailors try to over-sail a race and make mistakes such as tacking too frequently. Teach your sailor to develop a game plan and stick to it. Use common sense. Avoid locking into a match race battle while you are fleet racing. I like to refer to other boats by sail numbers to keep emotions out. It always pays to avoid protests even if it means occasionally giving a little extra room.

Progress may be slow and sailors might even regress sometimes, but keep plugging. As a mentor, if you detect burnout or rejection, it is okay to take a break from sailing, or change boats, crews, or venues. Young sailors should learn to work with the media. Few sailors are good communicators. Learning to be enthusiastic, helpful, and comfortable with the media at an early age will inspire more people to take up sailing.

Help young sailors by opening doors and providing thoughtful encouragement. There are no limits to the skill level sailors can achieve if they have the desire and put in a balanced effort. Look for a young sailor with potential, then help to build the desire and both of you will end up winning.

Winning in sailing takes inner strength. Years of experience help to build confidence. A shortcut to learning is to ask good questions and take notes. If you follow the stories and ideas outlined above, your time on the water will be more successful.

CHAPTER 3

# "HARD A' LEE"

## Why the Work of Sailing Can Be Great Fun

People choose to sail for many reasons, and certainly the physical and intellectual challenge is one of them. One could interpret the pleasure a sailor finds in such a challenge as a throwback to some evolutionary process that favored quick responses to threats or risks. Or the sailor could be read as a real-life existentialist facing the void. Both interpretations add depth to the understanding of sailing as a human endeavor, but both are a bit reductionist and miss the pleasurable dimension of undertaking an engaging physical activity on a beautiful summer day. One need not have one's survival threatened to experience the joy of sailing, and the knowledge one gains from experiences such as sailing exceeds the explanation focused on natural selection. Both ideas can be incorporated into an understanding of sailing as a human endeavor that enriches our inner life beyond simply a sharpening of skills and leadership abilities. The nature of this pursuit lies in the distinction between active engagement with reality and passive experience.

With a nod to Aristotle, I will take the reader on a journey to interpret sailing as the pursuit of "eudaimonia": human flourishing. We prepare the boat for the sail; face the risks of casting off and tacking, the challenge

*Sailing – Philosophy for Everyone: Catching the Drift of Why We Sail*, First Edition.
Edited by Patrick Goold.
© 2012 John Wiley & Sons, Inc. Published 2012 by John Wiley & Sons, Inc.

of sailing close-hauled, and the pleasure of cruising on a broad reach; and finally return to the pier without dashing the boat on the merciless shoreline. Throughout, the sailor gains a kind of self-knowledge about her skill and abilities as well as an appreciation of the relationship between the true and the beautiful as found in the elegance of a well-skippered boat. While the experience of the sublime may have a biological basis, I wish to explore sailing as an activity that leads us to human flourishing.

I have sailed almost exclusively in small craft on inland lakes with family and friends. I have raced in informal afternoon regattas that are about as competitive as a game of touch football in the park. The life lessons I have learned from sailing are drawn from my experiences of these enjoyable afternoons. For those interested in the details, I will be describing my experiences sailing a C-Scow boat, originally designed by Johnson Boat Works of White Bear Lake, Minnesota. The C-Scow is a flat-bottomed boat, about twenty feet long, with a single sail and two bilgeboards. I have also sailed on X-class, E-class, and J-class boats by the same manufacturer; on keelboats; and on the single-handed "Tech" designed by MIT. I prefer the smaller boats to keel boats because they are what I am most accustomed to, because they are more flexible and accessible (I can be in the water within an hour of deciding to sail), and because they test my sailing abilities at the limit to which I aspire. All of these characteristics make the smaller boat more appealing to me, despite the lure of the keel boat, where, as one experienced sailor put it, you won't spill your Mai Tai.

## Preparing the Boat to Sail

You and your mates must judge the wind to be strong enough for a good sail without being unsafe. The ideal wind is steady rather than gusty. If the gusts are strong, you will need to recruit a few more people to provide enough counterbalance for the boat. Recruiting may involve convincing people who have not sailed that they can do it and that *it will be fun!*

Next you should get "provisions," which can include the beverage of one's choice and some snacks. Then complete other preparations – including gathering personal gear, lifejackets, and the sail – and get down the bank to the boat lift. Transfer and stow all the gear, attach the sail to the mast and boom, recruit any last-minute crew, and paddle the boat out to the buoy, the point from which you will cast off.

As these preparations are being made, you must also coach any new sailors on points of safety, which mostly involve wearing one's lifejacket and watching out for the boom, especially before casting off and after mooring at the buoy at the end of the cruise. Finally you are ready to go: raise the sail, bring the boat around to head cross wind, and prepare to cast off.

## Casting Off

This procedure, along with catching the buoy at the end of the cruise, is one of the two tricky times during the sail when experience is especially important. A lot is happening at once: the sail is flapping in the wind, which can make it hard to hear other crew members and is rather alarming to new sailors; the boom can whack an unsuspecting person in the head with little warning; and each member of the crew needs to either know his task or stay out of the way. Once the skipper has brought the boat around to the correct angle to the wind, which takes a bit of effort, the sail will fill with wind and the painter (the line that ties the boat to the buoy) is cast off, allowing the boat to take off. This process can be a bit awkward because the boat is not easily maneuvered with the sail up and still moored to the buoy. If one casts off too early, the boat will drift downwind, possibly all the way onto the rocks. If one casts off too late, the boat may no longer be at the proper angle to the wind and the process must begin again. The crewmember at the painter should give the skipper enough slack to be able to direct the boat properly before letting go. Once the sails fill with wind, the boat should start to move forward. The sailing cruise begins.

## Some Existentialist Reflections

In Lee Werth's existentialist analysis of solo ocean-crossing sailors, he uses the example of Robin Graham, who at age sixteen set out to circumnavigate the globe and recounted his journey in the book *Dove*, named after his boat. Werth draws on Kierkegaard's concept of being "in untruth" as characteristic of "the crowd," those who live their lives as followers. As Werth describes it, "Robin had great difficulty tolerating those who were 'in untruth.' He risked his life too often and was himself too much 'in truth' to easily endure pretence."[1]

I have not experienced "blue water sailing" on the open ocean. I have not taken a solo journey on land or sea that would compare to the journeys Werth considers. But I think that sailing nearly any type of boat lends itself to the possibility of living "in truth." Sailing requires a level of skill that cannot be faked. If one takes a boat out on a sail and is not competent to do so, soon that fact will become apparent to all, including to one's self, even though some may try to blame it on faulty equipment. Many sports demand a fair degree of skill to be enjoyable, but sailing without skill is not only unpleasant but can be dangerous. When the wind and the water have forced the realization that one is out of one's league, the best to hope for is to get back safely and without damaging the boat. Sometimes competence is less about skill than good judgment. Having the ability to choose wisely whether and when to sail, with whom to sail, and under what conditions (environmental and physical) is as important as having the know-how to execute key moves such as coming about (changing the direction of the boat) and landing the boat.

The risk may be much less when going for an afternoon sail on an inland lake than when attempting a solo crossing of an ocean, but it is still there. And that risk provides a moment of truth about one's abilities that one must confront. This is part of what makes sailing a meaningful activity.

## Cruising

Now the fun part begins! After casting off, during which sometimes directions must be uttered directly and tersely, it helps to remind new sailors that we have now reached the fun part. The crew arranges themselves on either side of the boat to distribute the weight evenly. With three or four sailors, everyone can sit on the "upwind" side – the side of the boat that the wind comes across. If numbers are larger, some crew may sit on the "downwind" side, which is less desirable because you must be ready to duck under the sail if the skipper needs to release it suddenly in the event of a large gust. Also, you end up leaning forward into the middle of the boat as it heels over rather than back out over the water, as one does on the upwind side. The crew usually keeps their spot for the length of the tack; that is, until the skipper changes tack (the angle of the boat

CRISTA LEBENS

in relation to the wind, whether upwind or downwind) by either "coming about" or "jibing." But that comes later. Now is the time to crack open a tasty beverage or grab a snack.

If the wind is fairly light, the boat will pick up speed and glide smoothly across the lake. If the wind is strong and gusty, the crew may be in for a wild ride! The boat will heel over and the upwind crewmembers must lean out over the water to counterbalance the weight of the mast and sail against the wind. No Mai Tai under these conditions! Some adventurous types may attempt to stand on the bilgeboard if the wind and the skipper are strong enough to keep the boat up on edge. It's important to remember that this is fun! As the downwind crew leans in under the boom, they will remember why they were advised to wear bathing suits. "C-Scow sailors have soggy buns!" as the bumper sticker says. They'll get their time up top soon enough.

More experienced members of the crew may work lines for bilgeboards, trim the sail, and make other adjustments, and also assist the skipper in looking out for other boats and the occasional swimmer. At this point, in my family, we may decide whether we want to try sailing into the bay of the lake – tricky because the wind shifts and often dies – or whether we want to crisscross the main lake for the length of the sail. Then conversation shifts to the boat, strategies for speeding it up, dreams of a family member buying another boat so we can race, and pondering the style of boat we should get them to buy. Occasionally more serious topics arise, such as "what do you teach in your philosophy classes?" But mostly the conversation is light and enjoyable, renewing family bonds and building friendships.


## The Social Dimensions of Sailing


Another element of risk that ought to be considered in contemporary life is the way in which perception of risk is gendered. Werth, in writing about solo sailors, notes that "A waiting 'cheerleader' is not a bad incentive. Too often, solitary sailing leads to solitary living; few wives can bear to 'only stand and wait.' Even fewer genuinely wish to make ocean passages with their mates."[2] His statement underscores the point that sailing has been, and at the professional level still is, a (white, upper-class) male-dominated sport. It is worth noting that originally sailing was no sport at all, but for centuries a dangerous occupation undertaken not for enjoyment but for trade or military purposes. Sailing as a sport was the realm of the upper classes until the mid-twentieth century. I cannot speak for ocean sailing but, as far as inland lakes go, the availability of affordable boats for day sailing and community clubs that do outreach to school-aged kids make it a more democratic sport.

Recently (in the last summer or so) I asked my sister-in-law if she felt like she was taking a "risk" going sailing with my brother and me. She said she did, and so did I – not a great risk, but enough to make it a bit more exciting than, say, an afternoon bike ride. I found it interesting that my brother did not share that same sense of risk. I'm sure the sail is enjoyable and exciting to him too, but perhaps more as an exercise in skill and less as an experience where something dangerous could happen and someone could get hurt. (I want to emphasize that we are generally careful sailors, especially as we are all now middle-aged.) My point is that the element of risk can be, in part, a subjective thing. The perception of the risk one takes when going out on the water is definitely not the same for everyone. We who sail across the lake on a warm summer afternoon do not confront the void, the very real possibility of one's own death, as does the solo ocean-going sailor. But we face some degree of risk and the moment of truth about one's abilities.

## "Hard a' Lee" or Coming About

Eventually one reaches the opposite shoreline of the lake and it is time to turn the boat around. This is most often done by coming about. To warn the crew, the skipper calls out "ready about!" and the crew prepares to do their respective tasks – adjusting a line, moving, or simply ducking. Then, when everyone is ready, the skipper pushes the tiller (the long handle attached to the rudder that steers the boat) firmly and quickly to the downwind (lee) side of the boat, calling out "hard a' lee" (or "hard to the lee"). This movement turns the boat directly into the wind for a moment and the sail loses power, which slows the boat down a bit, but the pushing motion of the tiller moves the boat past that point to catch the wind on the other side of the sail. The change in direction may be moderate or it may be a switch from sailing mostly into the wind to sailing downwind. If the skipper doesn't push the tiller with enough speed and firmness, the boat will end up "in irons" and begin to drift backward. If the boat swings around too far, a strong wind may catch the sail and capsize the boat

CRISTA LEBENS

without warning. As the ancient Greeks advised, the middle path is the one to follow, and it takes experience to find it.

## Sailing Close-Hauled

The puzzle that non-sailors have about sailing is that it seems to be a lot of work, and often newcomers are told to do things in a rather brusque manner, and to do them correctly or someone might get hurt. Aside from casting off, landing, and coming about, these experiences are most likely to happen when sailing close-hauled, which means that the boat is heading as closely into the wind as possible without losing all power. This tack is not particularly speedy and not particularly enjoyable, but may be necessary to round a mark when racing or simply to return home. It is a good test of one's ability to trim the sail and make other adjustments to maximize the ability to "head up."

If one sails too closely into the wind, one ends up "in irons" with a flapping sail and no forward motion. The pressure of the waves starts to push the boat backward, which can be a disconcerting experience, especially if the shoreline is nearby. The way to get out of this is to "back sail," which means the skipper pushes the tiller downwind, steering backward. This will bring the boat broadside to the wind, and the sail should power up and the boat begin to move forward. It takes confidence to execute a move that seems to be the opposite of what one would do instinctively, and some experience to know when the boat is at the correct angle to the wind. Adjust too soon and you'll end up in irons again, this time possibly closer to shore. It takes experience, trust in one's abilities, and steady nerves. This is *not* the fun part.

## Noticing the "Presence of the Absence"
## (Heavy Sailing Ahead)

The Existentialists sometimes ask what, or who, is not present? I have, for several years, been a member of Hoofers Sailing Club, affiliated with the University of Wisconsin-Madison. Community members are welcome to join. The club makes special efforts to welcome anyone interested in sailing, regardless of experience or ability. To that end the club offers programs to make sailing accessible to low-income kids and persons with disabilities. While I have noticed members who are people of color around the pier, few of those people are African American. This is an absence I want to note. For people to feel comfortable sailing, they must feel comfortable around the water. Typically that means they must be able to swim. I cannot imagine the terror that one would feel standing on a pier without some confidence in one's ability to swim to shore should one accidently fall in the water. And the ability to swim is a classed and raced ability – that is, historically, people of color, especially African Americans, have been banned from many public swimming pools, and not just in the South. Parents often teach their kids the basics of swimming. To take lessons one must put a value on the skill and have access to a pool or a public beach, and one must pay for swimming lessons. The absence of the ability to swim is also passed down from generation to generation. The economics of access to public beaches or pools mean that some people are excluded from a sport such as sailing before they even reach the pier. I say this because I notice the absence of my friends, who have experienced these conditions, and I miss their presence when I go sailing. Sailing, then, is one dimension of the human experience that is not open to them. This bit of analysis is kind of like sailing close-hauled. It is not the most enjoyable part of the trip, but it is necessary if one is to consider sailing as an activity that makes those of us who have access to this experience, in some sense, more human.

## The Broad Reach

No, this is not tough women stretching or anything similar that you may be thinking of. "Broad reach" is the sailing term for a tack where the wind is slightly behind the boat but the boat is not heading completely downwind. This is one of the tacks that makes the boat go the fastest. If speed is what you are going for, this is a fun tack! Depending upon the strength of the wind, the waves may crash over the bow, the boat may heel over enough to allow standing on the upper bilgeboard, and the crew on the downwind side may be anxious to move up. But mostly this is an enjoyable tack where one experiences the pleasure of working with wind and wave to move the boat across a sparkling lake on a pleasant afternoon with one's companions.

CRISTA LEBENS

## Practical Wisdom

Aristotle introduced the concept of *phronesis*: practical wisdom, or wisdom that guides action. John (Michael) Atherton explores the role of *phronesis* in what he calls "outdoor kinetic experiences" (OKEs) and likens it to a kind of body-knowledge. Atherton draws on Peter Todd's concept of ecological rationality to explain knowledge-gathering and decision-making in risky situations: "Ecological rationality involves sampling the environment and making educated guesses under conditions where time is limited and dangers are real ... Move fast or die."[3] Such a skill has a clear evolutionary advantage. Atherton draws out the philosophical implications of such a skill:

> OKEs expand our repertoire of knowledge-gathering skills that we may have previously ignored because in familiar places we may have had time to conduct full inquiries and make robust decisions based on the best information. If our cognitive system is, as Gigerenzer claims, one designed to find multiple ways to know, where we must decide and act quickly and without all relevant information, then OKEs connect us with a neglected aspect of our thinking, our knowledge-gathering abilities, and finally our epistemology.[4]

Epistemology is the study of knowledge – how we acquire it, how we justify it, and so on. Our understanding of knowledge is expanded by the inclusion of this dimension of our knowledge-gathering abilities; that is, the ability to make good decisions under pressure. This is a skill that requires both understanding and practice. In sailing, one can read about good techniques, but one must put that knowledge into practice until it becomes a kind of body-wisdom before one is said to be skilled. Or, as Yogi Berra put it, "In theory there is no difference between theory and practice. In practice there is." The experience of sailing will quickly teach one the difference between theory and practice as well as the need for both.

## Capsizing

On a reach, especially if one is directly perpendicular to the wind, a sudden gust could cause the boat to capsize. This does not happen often and is usually avoidable; however, in sailing a scow, one should be prepared for the possibility – that is, one should be ready to wind up "in the drink." In my experience, capsizing happens in one of two ways. The first is when, while moving slowly, a sudden gust comes up and possibly a line jams or some other malfunction prevents the skipper from responding to avoid the boat capsizing. The second circumstance in which capsizing is likely is when the skipper sails in a high wind, making the boat heel over to the maximum degree. This provides the chance for the crew to ride the bilgeboard, but sometimes the boat heels over just a little too far for the skipper to bring it back. If one wants to maximize speed, this is not good racing form because the boat actually loses momentum, but it is fun. Things happen fast up until the moment you know the boat is going over, and then everything slows down. The wind is no longer driving the boat fast, the sail catches the surface of the water, and eventually the boat comes to a stop with the sail in the water. Regardless of the circumstances that lead to this situation, the first priority is to keep the crew safe from falling or being hit (everyone should have put their lifejackets on before casting off). The second priority is to keep the boat from "turtling," which is where the sail sinks below the surface of the water and the boat ends up completely upside down with the mast pointing into the lake. This makes it more difficult to right the boat and could break the mast.

To right the boat, at least one person must climb on the upper bilgeboard (now perpendicular to the water) and lean out using her weight to counterbalance the weight of the mast. It helps if another person, ideally in another boat, can position himself at the end of the mast, lift it out of the water, and give a push to right the boat. Once the boat is upright, the remaining crew can climb back in and reposition themselves and the provisions and begin to discuss "what happened."

Capsizing is not fun. Though it is a rare occurrence, it is not unheard of. Mostly the crew can take measures to be safe and avoid injury, but when something goes wrong someone may get hurt. While capsizing is not fun, pushing the boat to the edge without capsizing can be a great deal of fun.


## Human Experience

Sailing provides opportunities for learning via engagement in outdoor kinetic experiences, but it also offers more than that. I have had some experience, though not extensive, with sports such as kayaking and cycling. While the latter two sports do require a certain degree of skill and technical know-how, sailing presents a much greater demand on one's abilities, both physical and intellectual. And, I maintain, there is pleasure to be found in that demand. Albert Borgmann, philosopher of technology, examines the meaning of everyday objects in modern life. Drawing on Csikszenmihalyi and Rochberg-Halton's study of the significance of material possessions in contemporary (1970s American) urban life, Borgmann focuses on these authors' analysis of music – specifically, the difference between a stereo and a musical instrument in terms of the meaning and significance people attribute to them as possessions. Borgmann draws a distinction between what he calls a "device" and a "thing":

> The stereo as a device contrasts with the instrument as a thing. A thing, in the sense in which I want to use the term, has an intelligible and accessible character and calls forth skilled and active human engagement. A thing requires practice while a device invites consumption.[5]

One must interact thoughtfully and intentionally with a thing and develop skill in this interaction. Sailing a boat requires such an interaction; it calls forth skilled and active human engagement. At the other end of the spectrum, a powerboat is the epitome, in Borgmann's scheme, of a device calling forth consumption. Paddling a kayak, riding a bike, and hiking fall somewhere in between, but these activities do not call forth the degree of engagement that skippering or even crewing on a sailboat require.

## Returning to the Pier

By this time the crew may be getting a bit tired, or may need reprovisioning. In any case, eventually the cruise must come to an end. As the boat approaches the buoy, the skipper and the crew must assign duties. One crew member must prepare to catch the buoy as the boat moves toward it; another must prepare to lower the sail as soon as the buoy is caught. Other experienced crew may stand ready to raise the bilgeboards, thus reducing the power of the wind to push the boat forward. First-time sailors will be warned to keep low and once again watch out for the boom. The goal is to stop forward movement as close to the buoy as possible to ease the task of catching the buoy while maintaining enough momentum to reach the buoy rather than drifting backward toward the rocky shoreline.

The approach is made from downwind so that the boat can be turned directly into the wind within about ten feet or so of the buoy. This move deliberately puts the boat "in irons," which will slow it down but (one hopes) not so much as to lose momentum entirely. On a light-wind day this can be a relaxed set of maneuvers, but a high-wind day calls for experience and clarity regarding each task. The boat may be moving at a relatively high speed, necessary to keep from drifting downwind, and the skipper must bring the boat about at the right angle so as to be aiming directly into the wind and toward the buoy – not the pier and not the shoreline. On a nice, sunny day, non-sailing family members, friends, and neighbors are likely to be casually observing this sequence of events as they sip cool beverages. The crew member catching the buoy must be able to keep track of it as the boat comes about, and be ready to grab it at the right time, get the painter around it fast, hang on until the boat stops, and then tie a good knot that will hold the boat in place. The crew member lowering the sail must wait until the painter is definitely around the buoy and held securely, then drop the sail as fast as possible to ease up on the pull of the painter held by the other crewmember. Once both these tasks are accomplished, the crew can take a breath and relax for a moment. Friends, family, and neighbors may cheer, depending upon the quality of entertainment provided (which is preferable to their running to the rescue). The sail can be secured or removed, extraneous items can be gathered, and the boat can be left on the buoy for another sail that day or moved to the lift if that is the last sail of the day.

## Pleasure, Elegance, and Truth

Sailing can evoke the connection between truth and beauty, where beauty is a kind of elegance. The well-trimmed sail is not only aesthetically more pleasing than a sail flapping about but results in greater speed. The correct way to trim a sail is also more pleasing to the senses. The smoothly executed come-about is safer and more enjoyable to experience and to observe. The truth of one's skills is demonstrated in the aesthetic qualities of the sailing experience. If one seeks to develop this form of excellence, one will continue to practice this skill. Sailing, then, offers a chance to cultivate habits that lead to eudaimonia, or human flourishing. But, if one wants to be passively entertained, one will quickly turn to a form of activity that "calls forth consumption" rather than engagement. This is actually not a judgment on those who opt for a less demanding form of entertainment. Perhaps it is a question we may ask regarding the quality of our lives. What kind of life permits us to fully engage our human abilities and test our skills in the way that sailing (or practicing a musical instrument) provides? What kind of life leaves us with no more energy than what it takes to be passively entertained? And what kind of life is accessible to whom?

## Final Tasks

Once the boat has been put away on the rack for the night, the sail should be folded up and stored indoors. It should be folded like an accordion, following previous fold lines. This maintains the stiffness of the sail over time. Once the sail and other gear are stored, the cruise is over, but the storytelling has only just begun. Now for the Mai Tai!

## NOTES

1 Lee F. Werth, "The paradox of single-handed sailing (case studies in Existentialism)," *The Journal of American Culture* 10:1 (1992), p. 70.
2 Ibid., p. 69.
3 John Michael Atherton, "Philosophy outdoors: First person physical." In Mike McNamee (Ed.), *Philosophy, Risk and Adventure Sports* (New York: Routledge, 2007), p. 49.
4 Ibid.
5 Albert Borgmann, "The moral significance of the material culture," *Inquiry* 35:3/4 (1992), p. 296.

CHAPTER 4

# SOLO SAILING AS SPIRITUAL PRACTICE

A Phenomenology of Mastery and Failure at Sea

Wisdom is facing "life itself in the face of death itself."[1] Being in peril at sea can be deadly, but it can also be redemptive, a personal process of getting life into proper perspective. The sea is a microcosm of nature's indifference, impartiality, and caprice in regard to human will. How might we come to understand ourselves amid a universe of indifference, impartiality, and caprice? From the autobiographies of sailors who have gone on long offshore voyages by themselves, along with my own personal experiences of sailing, I will try to draw out the essence of the lived experience of facing the sea alone.

## A Phenomenology of Moral Presence at Sea

I would like to suggest that what I call "moral presence" serves as the general form of the lived experience of sailing for most sporting sailors. What is this? Moral presence is an existential counterpoint to the break-down of technical self-reliance at sea, or failures of sporting performance.

*Sailing – Philosophy for Everyone: Catching the Drift of Why We Sail*, First Edition.
Edited by Patrick Goold.

Moral presence is a personal stance in which a willingness to fail when nothing otherwise can be done is implicit in a person's sense of the moment. Making this implicit sense explicit is a manifestation of moral presence, or an assertion of human integrity in the face of despair. Moral presence appears in sailors' lives in three characteristic ways, and it becomes evident in their autobiographical reflections on risk-management and self-worth when they are engaged in their sport. The three ways are:

- Technical finesse
- Cosmic quest
- Personal test

Each will be elaborated by way of illustrations from a number of sailors' lives at sea and their thoughts about their nautical experiences.

First, moral presence may appear as the *technical finesse* of Robin Knox-Johnston, who skillfully avoided possible excesses of technical hubris and won the Golden Globe Race of 1968–1969, the first "solo" and unassisted sailing race around the world. For him, the kind of spirituality that he found at sea always gave rise to pragmatic outcomes, or a "God helps those who help themselves" point of view. As he put it after rounding Cape Horn and taking stock of the readiness of his yacht, *Suhaili*, to make the final run up the Atlantic to the finish line in England,

> The sea and ships are great levellers. There is certainly no room on a small boat for a person who is incompetent or won't pull his own weight ... All share the same risks in a storm, and no earthly influence will select you above the rest to be saved if the ship founders ... Their whole existence depended on their ability to come to terms with the wind and sea, and to use these forces to drive their ship ... It is not surprising that most [seamen] thought more of their counterparts ashore about the cause of these forces, and not in the least surprising to me that so many were superstitious or developed unshakeable religious beliefs, and sometimes both. I have found myself thinking deeply on the matter when out in rough weather on a small boat. It is all very well for someone sitting in an office to explain logically how the waves can build up before the wind, for we have discovered the natural laws that control this, but to a seaman, the explanation of these laws does not always seem sufficient ... the rules are there, the physical laws that we have slowly learned. If we obey them we have a chance of survival.[2]

There is "action through non-action" here, the Taoist concept of *wu-wei*. Moral presence is a similar inner or "spiritual" posture assumed by sailors as they learn to get used to the sea. Sailors may engender a capacity to affirm personal integrity as a hedge against incipient despair in perilous circumstances at sea. If they are lucky, then sailors come to learn that there is much that can be accomplished by taking action balanced by "non-action" after all. Knox-Johnston writes,

> It is no use knowing that your boat is heading towards the eye of a storm and praying to God to see you through it safely. That's not his job. It's your task to steer the boat away from the eye, and you are asking too much if you expect the boat to survive when you deliberately ignore the rules. My own philosophy is developed about the phrase, "The Lord helps those who help themselves." It is no good lying in your bunk, listening to the rising wind and feeling the boat beginning to strain and praying for God to take in reef. No one but a fool would expect anything to happen. One has to get up and reef the sails oneself before the boat's movement will ease ... When everything has been done that you know you can do, you put your trust in your Superior Being, and just hope that what you have done is right ... Because of this belief, throughout the voyage I never really felt I was completely alone, and I think a man would have to be inhumanly confident and self-reliant if he were to make this sort of voyage without a faith in God.[3]

A statement like this one testifies to Knox-Johnston's "detached concern for life itself in the face of death itself," albeit with occasional recourse to religious thoughts and behaviors.[4] The achievement of such wisdom is a spiritual endeavor.

Second, moral presence may invoke a large and purposeful *cosmic quest*, as it did for Bernard Moitessier, who felt driven to circumnavigate the globe as long as his food, water, and stamina allowed, opting out of the Golden Globe of 1968–1969 entirely. If it can be said that Knox-Johnston carried forward a mainly competitive style of sailing as racing, then Moitessier represents a more leisurely style of sailing as cruising. For Moitessier, spirituality meant drawing close to the elemental sea and believing it to be infused with a life-giving mystical force, a power that could be made one's own. For example, there is no better illustration of his resistance to keeping and using high technology on board his yacht, *Joshua*, than his means of communicating his progress during the race.

The staff of London's *Sunday Times* were eager to get as much publicity for their newspaper as possible by featuring frequent stories about

  RICHARD HUTCH

Moitessier's voyage. They offered the Frenchman equipment that he had never before owned. The skipper of *Joshua* came to resent such offers, but mellowed toward key staff once they took into account his views about just how much equipment was needed. Moitessier wrote,

> I stopped resenting the staff of the *Sunday Times* ... Robert, the head of the team, would have liked me to ship a big transmitter with batteries and generator. They offered it gratis ... so [I] could send them two weekly messages. The big cumbersome contraptions were not welcome. [My] peace of mind, and thereby [my] safety was more important, so [I] preferred not to accept them ... Steve, ... from the Press Service, loaded [me] with film, as well as watertight Nikonos cameras ....[5]

While a transmitter and batteries were one thing, a fancy camera was a manageable concession. The problem arose with timing: how would pictures be able to be sent to the newspaper in lieu of radio broadcasts in order for the Press Service to report on the race day by day, week by week? Moitessier reached back into the arsenal of his youth in French colonial Hanoi for a solution; namely, his tried, true, and trusty slingshot, along with a packet of fresh and properly sized wide rubber bands:

> I preferred my old, quiet friend the slingshot to two or three hundred pounds of noisy radio equipment, but [Steve] could feel the "how" and "why" and helped me to find good rubber bands, supplying me with aluminium cans to contain messages I would shoot onto passing ships. A good slingshot is worth all the transmitters in the world! And it is so much better to shift for yourself, with the two hands God gave you and a pair of elastic bands. I will try to send them messages and film for their rag. It would make them so happy ... and me too.[6]

One reads with delight how perplexed and amazed sailors on passing ships were to see Moitessier on his yacht shooting his message- and film-filled cans into the air in the direction of their ships, which then accurately fell on board in one shot and clinked across the deck to be retrieved by crew. News of *Joshua* would then be wired back to London by the captains, and the photographs would be passed on to the nearest British Consul and posted to the *Sunday Times* by diplomatic courier. Moitessier's slingshot was technically efficient but primitive. Moderating any urge to get carried away by modern marine technology was the priority of sustaining a mystical sense of purpose and relationship with the natural elements.

The matter of a camera and film took Moitessier's memory back several years when he sailed from Tahiti to Alicante, Spain with his wife, Françoise: "we never dared take pictures of the sea before the Horn, and least of all our big gale in the Pacific. Not because of danger or fatigue, but because we felt, in a confused sort of way, that it would have been a kind of desecration."[7] He was convinced that destiny controls the moral nature of men and women as does the stars of the horoscope, but also that destiny allows a person a range of options with which to play out one's moral nature in history, from event to event: "Destiny deals the cards, but we play them."[8] He often waxed lyrical about his solitude and likened himself to a seagull:

> I felt such a need to rediscover the wind and the high sea, nothing else counted at that moment ... All *Joshua* and I wanted was to be left alone with ourselves ... You do not ask a tame seagull why it needs to disappear from time to time toward the open ocean. It goes, that's all, and it is as simple as a ray of sunshine, as normal as the blue of the sky.[9]

Moitessier saw himself as a sea mystic in tune with the elemental forces that bathed him in natural wonder.

Third, moral presence may also come in the form of a *personal test* for sailors who are realistically unsure of their skills, but who also are bold enough to embark on an offshore voyage alone in order to do their best in the face of such a challenge. The Australian Kay Cottee lacked self-confidence at the outset, but recouped heaps of it during her circumnavigation of 1988. (This established her as the first woman to complete a single-handed non-stop circumnavigation and the first woman to circumnavigate non-stop west to east, south of the five southernmost capes. She set records for the fastest time for a solo circumnavigation by a woman, the fastest speed for a solo circumnavigation by a woman, the longest period alone at sea by a woman, and the greatest non-stop distance covered by a solo woman.) Nearing Cape Horn is a major emotional, technical, and symbolic event in the life of any solo sailor, more so than approaching and rounding any of the other four capes along the way. Cottee's autobiography comes to a pinnacle of feeling that is mostly sublime in an aesthetical sense, but also physically demanding. Her description of the beauty of the heaving Southern Ocean is perhaps one of the most captivating portrayals of the sea at its elemental best and worst, and a powerful personal epiphany or primordial experience of (in Rudolf Otto's famous phrase) *mysterium tremendum et fascinans.*[10] The *mysterium tremendum et fascinans* is not an ordinary lived experience but an extraordinary event, one that does not immediately make sense as it is beyond rationality and too powerful to contain. *Mysterium* means "mystery" in the sense of the unknown and unknowable; it is the "sacred." *Tremendum* is that aspect of the sacred that induces awe and fear. *Fascinans* is the sacred as evoking fascination, allure, and a sense of the sublime. Like a moth before a flame, a person who undergoes an experience of *mysterium tremendum et fascinans* must reckon with a coincidence of opposites, a paradoxical event that could well create, destroy, and re-make the self all at the same time. Just 585 miles from Cape Horn and in winds of fifty-five knots, Cottee had a personal epiphany:

> It wasn't easy trying to slow down the boat. The further south we went the higher were the seas, as in the south latitudes of the Southern Ocean there is no land mass to break the speed and size of the waves as they hurtle round the globe. By 1600 hours we were under bare poles, towing the sea anchor, still doing a steady 7-plus knots and surfing up to 12 knots on the breakers. I tried setting the storm jib again and backing it with the helm down to put the boat into irons. After all my efforts I remember standing below, looking out of the clear companionway slide and watching the sea anchor, towed behind on the end of 10 metres of chain plus 70 metres of line, bouncing down the face of the next wave after the one we were riding. I estimated the waves to be approximately 20 metres high and breaking with a nice curl. When we were in the troughs I looked up, and despite my fears of being pitchpoled I was captured by the beauty of the aquamarine colours of the sun shining through the peak of the next approaching wave.[11]

Here the *mysterium* presents its more destructive *tremendum* face. Cottee's physical tension at the time was unshakable. With the Horn approaching, she wrote,

> The tension was really getting to me. My shoulders felt stiff and my neck hurt badly since I had put it out a few days ago winching the storm jib up. There were tingles down my spine and my hands continually went numb. I was increasingly worried that I couldn't relax enough to get my neck to click back into place. If I settled into that position, permanent damage could be done. But no show of relaxing tonight, with land only a few miles away.[12]

Cottee's protracted personal epiphany progressed from a sense of destructive power that could not be controlled, even when it became embodied in the contorted vertebrae of her neck, to a fresh sense of excitement, wonder, and personal accomplishment:

> After all the stories I had read about this ocean graveyard, here we were, only a few miles from it. I had thought it would give me a spooky feeling, considering the number of sailors who had been dashed to death on the treacherous black cliffs, or drowned in the mountainous seas. But my prime emotion was excitement and I had a great sense of accomplishment that I had reached what I then perceived to be the major obstacle in the voyage.[13]

Hiding deep within herself was a fear of rounding Cape Horn, but she now was doing it in the light of day and fully conscious of how far beyond that inner fear she was then growing. As a fitting ritual gesture to commemorate the powerful event that had come good, Cottee opened the Cape Horn present that had been given to her by her mother, a bottle of her favorite "Joy" perfume. "I sprayed myself with the lovely scent, then put on some lipstick, before sitting down to a delicious belated lunch of fresh bread with crab and mayonnaise and the remainder of the bottle of Grange."[14]

Cottee used the sea and a fine balance between action and non-action to test herself not only as a self-reliant technical sailor but also as a moral being in formation. Terrifying experience was transformed into fascination. This is a spiritual event, or a means to ultimate personal transformation. She wrote:

> I was very lucky on this particular day because the sun was shining, and as the next huge wave rolled up behind the boat blocking out the sun, the sun shone through the top of it and the colours of the sunlight refracting through the water were just magnificent. I immediately thought that not many people would get to see a sight like it from that angle and how beautiful the waves were. So, after that, the bigger the waves got the more beautiful they became, and that's when I realised you definitely **can** change your thoughts if you put enough practice and conviction into it.[15]

At the end of the day, Cottee's lesson is one of inner growth, or an inner reframing of self-worth as a moral being above all else. Lesson learned, Kay Cottee was on her way home a changed woman, perhaps with a maturity that would allow her to go home but not as she had imagined she would, only to fall again into dependency on others for her self-esteem. She became free from all that.

# Tragic Comedy (or Comic Tragedy): The Paradox of Sailing

The human face of the sport is what makes sailing so compelling. In the end, it could be said that the sport of sailing is drama writ large, a combination of comedy and tragedy all in one. Only around the edges of the drama is the technology of yachts and their equipment a topic worthy of consideration. The comic aspect of the sport would certainly include the often obscenely exorbitant financial costs of state-of-the-art boats, equipment, and, in highly competitive racing, professional crews. For the average weekend sailor, the costs of marina berths, annual haul-outs, regular anti-fouling of the boat's hull, and the not infrequent need for repairs are laughable to outside observers. Some standard jokes in this regard go like this: "Yachting is like standing in a cold shower and tearing up $100 bills," "Yachting is like throwing money into a great hole in the water," and "There are two wonderful days in yachting – the one when you buy the boat and then the day when the boat is finally sold." Indeed, even committed sailors often wonder why in the world they ever got into sailing in the first place and what keeps them "hanging in there." The comic irony of yachting escapes no one, and it always elicits a chuckle.

The tragic dimension of the human drama of sailing takes in all of the existential peril that is faced both by competitive-racing and leisurely cruising sailors. Peril is taken on board and reckoned with miles offshore over the course of time on the high seas, far from effective immediate assistance. Weekend sailing is hardly high drama, though it can become so. For offshore sailors, tragedies can be woven out of the jagged separations of leaving family and friends behind, psychological oscillations between profound solitude and unsettling hallucinations inhabited by companions of varying sorts, real anxieties about the boat striking whales or shipping containers that have fallen off freighters and float just below the surface of the ocean, being unable to control the yacht in wind and waves, and worry about one's mental health and not knowing whether a voyage will succeed or end in tragedy. Whether the human drama of going to the sea in a yacht is more or less comic or tragic must be discerned case by case from reports of sailors themselves. Most single-handed circumnavigators of the globe attest to having been profoundly changed by what they did and all that happened at sea. If sailing is drama writ large, combining comedy and tragedy all at once, then a naïve or short-sighted reliance on the technology of sailing and on an over-reaching will, or hubris, can make a voyage into a fool's paradise.

Perhaps the drama of sailing arises from the worldview of the sailor, a worldview that is more like the pre-modern earth-centered vision of Ptolemy than the modern cosmic outlook of Copernicus and moon-based astronauts. The pre-modern worldview always implied that when human beings found themselves in difficulties appeals could be put to higher powers or God for divine help. In pre-Christian ancient Greek drama, such appeals were represented on stage by a simple technical device called a *deus ex machina*, or "god from a machine." Attached to the set on which dramatic performances would be staged was a small crane. The crane was used to lower props as needed into scenes of the play being acted out below. Included among various props were "gods." They represented the chief divine and semi-divine players of Greek mythology. Representations of Zeus, Prometheus, Demeter, and so on could be attached to the hoist and lowered into dramatic performances, and this was done usually at moments of heightened comic or tragic feeling in the audience. The gods could always be relied on by mere mortals to save the day or condemn them to tragic fates. The stage-bound mortals always happened to find themselves in difficulties that evoked crying and tears of sorrow as well as peals of laughter and joy from onlookers. The result was a catharsis for the audience in the amphitheatre – an emotional release and insight into the drama of being human amid forces beyond one's control.

Do single-handed circumnavigating sailors (and others) persist in hoping that something like a *deus ex machina* will help them to sort out their perilous human dramas at sea? In other words, how might sailors with an otherwise "blind faith" in technology and personal hubris learn to abandon hope that such modern gods will appear and be effective when they think they are most needed? And, so, sailors play their parts on the dramatic stage of the sea. Some soar to heights of technical skill and over-extended hubris, thinking nothing of the difficulties and the dangers, until things begin falling apart and nothing goes exactly according to plan, and when it would be comical if that was all there was to it. Do the "wheels fall off" the *deus ex machina* of technical self-reliance and hubris? Other sea-bound actors venture bravely into the whirlpool of such comedy, where they enter into a maelstrom of desperation that leads to tragedy, perhaps even to death. Such was the tragic fate of Donald Crowhurst, who also set out in the Golden Globe Race of 1968–1969 but who broke down mentally and eventually disappeared. If, somehow, the *deus ex machina* of technology and personal hubris can be restored, if the "wheels" can be put back on again, then sailors can continue to believe that survival may be possible. However, a general sense of futility persists in all of it. Such is the existential nature of the human drama that grips most single-handed sailors, and perhaps grips other sporting people too.

It is not the technological device of the "god machine" itself that is so important, and not the often-vain reach of hubris. The most important thing is the human end served by the *deus ex machina*, whatever form that technological device may take in critical moments at sea. (Does the radio suddenly work again? Does rain replenish empty water tanks? Do flooded bilges pump dry? Does the chopper locate the damaged yacht? Is a long-missing bottle of brandy finally found?) Between tragedy and comedy, the most important thing that is served by technology at sea is the human drama played out to a final catharsis by the sailor. Such a catharsis is a spiritual operation that transforms the seemingly mirror-like waters of the sea into an impregnable "other" in the modern period, neither friend nor foe by dint of its indifference in a person's life. As single-handed sailor and author Jonathan Raban puts it,

> In a secular world, it is this sacral quality of the sea that survives most viv-idly in poetry of our own time. The sea lies on the far margin of society, and it is – as nothing else is – serious and deep. The last line of Derek Walcott's epic narrative poem, Omeros, has Achilles (a West Indian fisherman who, in Alcott's poem as in Homer's *Iliad*, is the prototype of a busy, mortal man) walking away from the end of the story: When he left the beach the sea was still going on.[16]

So, too, lives pass on the backdrop of seemingly timeless nature.

The sea is made to reflect not only its impartial and perilous nature but also all that the sailors have witnessed of themselves out there unaided and mirrored by the water, either liking or worrying about what they observe themselves to be, especially when peril is imminent and the "chips are down." What values arise? Does one develop a capacity to affirm integrity over the temptation to surrender to despair? Bearing such witness to oneself pressed into personal peril in sport is a stepping stone to spiritual insight, or to *wisdom*. Such insight leads to a life in which doing nothing may often be the most effective action to take, action that represents a zenith of human value. This is especially so when the ever-veiled cosmic stakes that underscore human existence are taken into account, terms for living that embrace failure and defeat and, none-theless, make for exhilaration and a revitalization of life come what may.

## NOTES

1  Erik Erikson, *Insight and Responsibility: Lectures on the Ethical Implications of Psychoanalytic Insight* (New York: W. W. Norton, 1964), p. 133.

2  Robin Knox-Johnston, *A World of My Own: The Single-Handed, Non-Stop Circumnavigation of the World in Suhaili* (New York: Morrow, 1969–1970), pp. 172–173.

3  Ibid.

4  Erikson, *Insight and Responsibility*, p. 133.

5  Bernard Moitessier, *The Long Way*, trans. William Rodamur (London: Adlard Coles, Ltd., 1973), p. 5.

6  Ibid., p. 6.

7  Ibid., pp. 26–27.

8  Ibid., p. 33.

9  Ibid., p. 3.

10  Rudolf Otto, *The Idea of the Holy*, trans. John W. Harvey (New York: Oxford University Press, 1958).

11  Kay Cottee, *Kay Cottee, First Lady: A History-Making Voyage Around the World* (South Melbourne, VIC: Macmillan, 1989), p. 192.

12  Ibid., p. 74.

13  Ibid., p. 77.

14  Ibid.

15  Ibid.

16  Jonathan Raban (Ed.), *The Oxford Book of the Sea* (Oxford and New York: Oxford University Press, 1992), p. 32.

# PART 2

# THE MEANING OF THE BOAT
## THREE SCHOOLS OF THOUGHT

CHAPTER 5

# BUDDHA'S BOAT

## The Practice of Zen in Sailing

We sailors can know magical hours. Interludes of peace, freedom, and uncommon joy just seem to happen now and then around sailboats, blessing both experienced and novice sailors. Perhaps you are at the helm of a well-tuned blue-water boat, running with a fresh breeze under a big sky toward a far horizon of the imagination. Or the magic unfolds as you sit in a dinghy on a quiet mooring in a hidden cove, simply waiting for the wind to rise or the tide to change.

For some sailors, however, it is not enough for the magic to "just happen." For them, it is not enough to sail around a pond or across a great ocean for the sheer fun of it, or to race around the buoys for the fellowship and intensity of competition, or to steal a few hours to escape in a sailing dinghy from the dulling routines and distractions of life on land. No, for these few mariners, to sail is to self-consciously seek the mystery dimension of their being, "to rediscover the Time of the Very Beginnings, where each thing is simple."[1] So wrote Bernard Moitessier, the legendary French blue-water sailor-writer, in *The Long Way*, his account of sailing in 1968 on *Joshua* in the first solo, non-stop, round-the-world race. Moitessier, perhaps more vividly than

*Sailing – Philosophy for Everyone: Catching the Drift of Why We Sail*, First Edition.
Edited by Patrick Goold.
© 2012 John Wiley & Sons, Inc. Published 2012 by John Wiley & Sons, Inc.

most, viewed going forth under sail as a meditation, a yoga, a spiritual path liberating him from the "dragon" of civilization. For the Moitessiers among us, sailing may hold the promise of a mystic journey to inner peace in communion with what he called the "singing" of the sea.

Once upon a younger time, I felt a yearning for the mystic, deep sailing magic seemingly made possible only during a long, solitary ocean voyage. Until a few years ago, I imagined myself making a blue-water crossing of the Pacific or, more modestly, signing up for an offshore, week-long cruise with a sailing school, in order to see what happened to me far from land, a thousand miles out, at night, silent and alone in the cockpit at the wheel of a seaworthy sailboat. Would I hear the singing of the sea, as did Moitessier ... and Slocum, and Melville, and Odysseus? Could I become one with the sea's songs, in tune with sublime rhythms rising and falling in a salty symbiosis of myself and the sea?

But these deep-water fantasies are gone from me nowadays. I no longer have the time, will, or resources to captain or crew on a sea-going boat. Even more responsible for my letting go of Odyssean dreams are decades of experience as a practitioner and teacher of Zen Buddhism. Experience and studies in Zen combine to remind me that there are many paths to the boundless, nameless origin of one's self, to awakening in the "Time of the Very Beginnings." Hours upon hours of Zen practice in meditation halls, as well as in a number of the Zen arts such as tea ceremony, assure me that I can taste peace, freedom, and communion in a teacup of a boat, playing with waves on a small patch of shallow water, during an afternoon's brief sail under a haiku sky.

Still, I recognize inklings of my aging self in the words of E. B. White, who wrote in his seventies: "I know well enough that I have lost touch with the wind and, in fact, do not like the wind any more. It jiggles me up, the wind does, and what I really love are windless days, when all is peace."[2] I, too, think of limiting my physical risks, but not to White's point where I fear the moment when the wind presses on my sail. I still welcome what springs up in me with the wind's first wisp of breath on my skin: a cellular gladness, and then gratitude that I am being awakened and moved by something generous and invisible. "Buddha's breath," a friend calls it.

I retired from college teaching about six years ago and moved to Cape Cod with my wife. We looked forward to good sailing on the Cape. Because docking slips and moorings on the Cape are either too expensive or not available for a sea-going boat, we thought that a small boat would precisely fit our situation. We could trailer the boat and launch from the many town landings on the Cape, and go daysailing in protected waters.

I like small boats. My first boat was a Sunfish. But I was getting too old to tolerate a capsizing boat and less inclined to enjoy speed or racing. The motivation to race, to focus my attention and will outward in a competition with others, had eased up and turned inward, almost without me noticing. I needed a boat in which I could hope to finish well in a new inner contest with myself.

So, in this mood I began my retirement on Cape Cod. I felt a nagging urge to approach sailing in a different, more intimate and perhaps more ultimate way, in keeping with this stage of my life. Recalling the ancient Buddhist imagery for the journey to Nirvana, of a raft crossing the currents of ordinary, unsatisfactory life to the distant shore of a fully awakened life, I came about into a new self-narrative of sailing: I needed a Buddha's boat, if by sailing I meant to aim for, and hopefully reach closer to, that far, secret shore in myself.

The search for a Buddha's boat began and ended quickly. I bought a Cape Cod catboat. It suited my obvious need for a stable, small sailboat that would fit on a trailer, not capsize easily, and be appropriately designed for the shallow, protected waters around Cape Cod. I also liked the idea of having only one sail to the boat, so I could sail more simply and alone. For these good reasons, I bought a fourteen-foot gaff-rigged Compass Classic Cat, built at what is now the Pleasant Bay Boat and Spar Company in Orleans, Massachusetts. It has two hundred pounds of ballast in the skeg keel, a seven-foot beam for additional stability, and only ten inches of draft with the centerboard up.

I named it *Garuda*. According to William Snaith,

> Each man uses his boat in his own way to fill certain wants. There are as many roads to Nirvana as boats and men. Nowhere does this show up as precisely as in choosing a name for the darling of his heart ... The choice of a boat's name is the semantic key to his dream.[3]

In Hindu-Buddhist mythology, Garuda is a bird–man hybrid who flies the great god Vishnu back and forth to Heaven, protects the many Buddhas through the eons, and subdues sea dragons by eating them. Luckily, *Garuda* was a happy choice for me as a boat and it has become a very good teacher of a different way of sailing.

I decided to organize my learning to sail solo on *Garuda* along the lines and according to stages I had encountered in learning and teaching other

Zen practices, especially sitting meditation and Zen archery. While the Cape Cod catboat design began over one hundred years ago as a shallow draft workboat mainly for near-shore fishing in protected waters and has evolved into a pleasure craft for a dedicated group of owners and builders,[4] for me it would become a Buddha's boat.

Buddhist tradition holds the view that there are countless ways to the difficult goal of an awakened, flourishing self. Sailing, I believe, can be one of those ways or practices. As such it is best approached as a practice of both *outer work* and *inner work*, a useful division of focus seen in Zen arts such as tea ceremony, swordsmanship, calligraphy, flower arrangement, and meditation itself.

Within both outer and inner aspects of Zen-oriented practices, at every stage of learning and unlearning, we see methods that coordinate two mutually supportive overall aims: *concentrating attention* and *purifying character*, which is the cultivation of specific virtues across an arc of what I call "self-forgetting," the penultimate goal of Zen. Both aims are realized by training body and mind together. Could sailing become a Zen practice deepening and opening my body–mind awareness, while also nurturing virtues such as patience, courage, equanimity, humility, gratitude, reverence, and selflessness?

*Outer work* in a Zen practice of sailing focuses on sailing *technique* and *performance*. Technique includes learning how to sail, the language and terms of sailing, and hours of practice leading to a more intuitive and body-centered habit of maintaining attention to particular tasks, as well as a broader, peripheral awareness of the environment in which sailing occurs. Working on technique ranges from attending to micro-adjustments in body–boat balance and sail shape to scanning other boats, water, wind, and sky to improve one's powers of anticipation in a flexible, open awareness.

With practice regarding how to get things done and how the boat works, the Zen sailor, as would any sailor, will increase her powers of observation and learn to sustain her attention in ways that improve not only her sailing but also her mental, physical, and emotional capacity. She will learn to concentrate on the job at hand in the moment. This often deepens into an absorption in the task that is also a type of *self-forgetting*, developing as her concentration shifts from a stressed problem-solving body–mind orientation to a more relaxed, intuitive one.

Learning to sail is a form of physical learning. Certain senses, without one's noticing at first, become better-tuned to boat response and speed. Which senses are these? One is hearing, because the boat's hull sounds different as it slows or speeds up. Another is touch, because the apparent wind and its direction register on the face, neck, and tiller arm as a pressure that correlates with changes in speed. Finally there is the oft-ignored but vital sense called proprioception, because our inner sensations of bodily position and movement, especially of balance, become sensitive to the boat's tenor – the continuous, often subtle movement and tension of the boat, mainly felt through "the seat of the pants." While tempted by inclination to take a calculating, left-brain approach to learning, sailing in a Zen mood taught me to trust my intuition enough to "just sail" with and in a more open, subtle mind and body. Sailing solo accelerated my learning to sail *Garuda* by simplifying the environment and intensifying self-observation.

Performance, the second level of outer work in a Zen practice, goes beyond a collection of techniques, such as learning how to trim the sails or work the tiller. Performance refers to "putting it all together" into a flowing form, to fashioning a ritual or symphony of sailing practices. Performance includes sequential routines and sub-routines of technique, but also body balancing and cognitive-emotional tuning. The analogy for me is with Zen archery, where formal, ritualized shooting is taught. The rituals of *kyudo* (the Way of the Bow) are known as *kata*, precise body, bow, and arrow routines made up of eight discrete movements or steps in a single, flowing act of establishing body posture, mental concentration, and the bow and arrow for the explosive, sudden of act of shooting. Each of the eight steps includes many technical details and nuances of posture, hand and eye position, and breathing rhythms that are practiced until they become consistent, intuitive, or "natural."

As a ritual, a Zen performance implies a transformation of the person into an actor, one who submits to and acts "without thinking" according to a well-practiced form, who moves "per the form" or "performance" of his art, be it archery, making and drinking tea, or sailing.

A sailing teacher, and the sailor himself, sees what others see outwardly in a sailing performance, but usually with more precision. She looks at technical mastery and fluid performance in a sailor as signs of talent, dedication, patience, and right effort. But sailing becomes Zen sailing for the teacher and the student when they believe that sailing is more than the skillful performance of guiding a wind-driven boat efficiently and safely through water. Zen sailing is grounded in a relation of the sailor with herself, and so the work must now move inward.

The *inner work* of Zen sailing builds upon the outer achievement of acquiring a useful level of technical skills and coordinated performance.

The goal now becomes widely inclusive and deep within: to better bind together the boat, the sailor's self, and the natural world in which they move and have their being. With growing competence in tasks such as hauling up and setting a sail to the wind, there will come a more relaxed attitude, relaxed shoulders and hands, a slower breath, and subconscious motor learning. These are signs of meditative sailing.

Even before stepping into the boat and setting sail, however, a sailor can make himself ready for sailing in a Zen way. Sailing includes preparations for sailing, in which opportunities abound for developing Zen awareness and what we might call the sailor's trance.

In Zen calligraphy, for example, the expert calligrapher may take up to an hour making his black ink by rubbing a solid ink stick round and round on a two-level stone with water in the lower level. What is happening is the preparation of the calligrapher for the action of dipping a bamboo brush in the ink and, in some Zen painting, tracing out shapes of Chinese characters or everyday objects on absorbent rice paper in a lightning flash of intense, flowing, intuitive brush strokes. No touchups are allowed. It is a matter of "one brush stroke, one life." But behind what appears to be a spontaneous act of free expression may lie hundreds and hundreds of practice sessions of the same painting subject.

Similar preparations, by means of simple, repetitive, physical acts that focus the mind's attitude and exercise the body's supple readiness to act expressively, can be found across the spectrum of Zen arts. The archetypal model of this preparation is the attentive counting of breaths in the Zen meditation hall. My own experience is that it takes me about ten minutes of counting breaths before I can achieve a useful state of relaxed alertness and physical loosening of tensions. This seemingly simple skill and capacity came to fruition for me only after years and years of Zen practice. However, by what means I know not, it comes to some in a few minutes of practice.

In sailing *Garuda*, I usually do attentive breathing, slowly lengthening and deepening my exhales, during the ten minutes it takes me to fire up my little Honda outboard engine and motor slowly from my mooring in Arey's Pond to the mouth of the Namequoit River, where I set sail for Pleasant Bay. Sometimes I prepare for sailing just by sitting in the boat at the mooring and doing sitting meditation for ten minutes, or a bit more if need be.

Preparatory rituals before sailing in a Zen mood can involve practical exercises such as cleaning and polishing the boat for ten minutes or so, even if the boat was already clean and Bristol enough. Tony Davis, owner of Arey's Pond Boatyard, uses a set routine before taking new catboat owners or students out for a lesson. His ritual is to go through a preparatory checking of the weather, wind, tide, boat equipment, and sail reefing decisions in a mostly set order. This well-worn routine, he has found, brings him to the relaxed and alert state he needs to teach with presence of mind and to model a correct attitude in sailing.

Right performance or ritual efficacy can be an end in itself for some sailors. But, in sailing as an *inner work* of relating oneself to oneself as one seeks, however indirectly, the plenitude of one's being, sailing rituals become a transitional or liminal zone where we shed our social roles and alter our internal self-narrative. Ritual, somewhat paradoxically if we think of it as limiting and restricting, can help a sailor make the shift toward a freer, more expansive, and more visceral way of being in the world. The demands of sailing well, especially in small boats, entail setting aside the habitual body and mind of the businessman or high school student or professor of philosophy. Sailing well frees the sailor from the constraints of his normal role(s) *by means* of the sailor's role, as he submits to the limits and pressures of his boat and the surprises of wind and water, while suspended in the moment between the earth below and the great sky above.

The Zen sailor comes to the belief that the inner work only now making its appearance in his sailing practice is a "profound and far-reaching contest with himself."[5] Now embedded in what he has learned, yet also going beyond technique and performance, he "will see with other eyes and measure with other measures."[6]

The *first stage of inner work* focuses on becoming aware of, nurturing, and directing an experiential energy or power, called *ki* in Japanese, *ch'i* in Chinese, and by other names elsewhere. Some describe *ki* holistically as an energy matrix or field running through all things and connecting them somehow. But I mean by *ki* something much less metaphysical. By *ki* I know merely what I have experienced myself: a visceral or "nervous" activation accompanying certain breathing exercises inextricably combined with attention to movements in posture. I observe the energy's warmth, strength, or something like magnetism in and around my body. Specifically, my more ordinary experiences of *ki* consist of warmth in my hands, an instant easing like an opening or hollowing in my arms, shoulders, or legs, and a feeling of localized power not dependent on stressing muscles. Put another way, *ki* tends to appear when I am relaxed mentally and physically, focused in a special way on a body part or a stage of breathing in and out, and *expecting ki to appear.*

*Ki* can enter Zen sailing in at least two ways. The most productive way probably comes after a sailor has become comfortable with sailing technique and performance. If you are at the level where both have melted into a flowing, flexible, adaptive ritual of mindful and enjoyable sailing, you have learned a way of staying "in the groove." You experience "flow" in your sailing that is "on a different, more intense, yet easeful level." At that level the sailor does not have to think much about fundamentals and has developed preparatory or performing rituals that do not require constant monitoring. She has reached the stage where she almost automatically moves the tiller to leeward ("into the sail" is my mnemonic) when a jibe threatens, and she tells her crew to move or moves her own body to balance the boat *before* even thinking about it. In this phase of sailing, cultivating *ki* will almost certainly empower the experienced sailor's abilities, increasing endurance, deepening relaxation, sharpening the senses, and helping her to respond precisely to circumstances without reflection or hesitation.

The other, somewhat different, occasion for activating *ki* is in the beginning of learning the outer work of sailing; that is, while learning techniques and the forms of sailing practices. Simple breathing or moving exercises to awaken *ki* can be useful here in relaxing and strengthening a novice sailor who struggles with physical fatigue, mental wandering, nervousness, or frustration. In the case of a sailor facing these hindrances, it is usually best to stop sailing and take ten minutes for breathing and stretching exercises that awaken *ki*; or, even better is to do basic *ki* exercises as preparation before thinking about or getting oneself into the boat.

In teaching Zen meditation to students, I used a basic warm-up set of *ki* movements in a simple standing posture before static sitting called *zazen* (literally, "sitting meditation"). For eight to ten minutes, the students could tune themselves to the right balance of relaxation and tension by concentrating on slowing and deepening their breathing and by easing away from their worries. That was for many the key to sitting effectively on their meditation cushions for thirty-minute sessions of *zazen*.

A brief sketch of a breathing exercise and posture adjustments may be useful at this point. The simplest, most effective breathing exercise is based on a long sigh. While sitting erect or standing comfortably, take in a breath normally, through the nose, but expand your ribs a little more than usual, pause about one second, then slowly exhale through your mouth, letting your shoulders relax and your facial muscles loosen (as in a slight grin). Imagine that your exhaling breath is flying or sailing to the end of the cosmos, if that helps to lengthen it. Repeat this mindful rhythm ten to twenty times, closing your eyes for the first five to ten exhales. Over the next ten or so breaths, gradually open your eyes and take in the visual environment without fixing your gaze too much on one thing.

This exercise usually produces a noticeable, often pleasant relaxation in body and mind. The next step is to keep up the slow, sighing exhale while focusing on one visual object or one sound, such as the sound of your exhale. If your experience is, for example, "looking at the coil of line" or "listening to the *hooooo hum* of my exhale," things are going well.

Now the critical shift: activating awareness of *ki*. On a long exhale, if you are focusing on a visual object, open your eyes a little bit more as if to take in slightly more of the scene, then right away push your inner feeling of breathing pressure lower into your belly until you feel that you are seeing with your whole torso, not just your eyes in your head. That's it! If you are focusing your "self" on a sound or "just listening," let your torso or even your belly hear the sound.

This belly awareness or perception from the belly is one very effective key to activating *ki* energy. Belly awareness brings about a wider zone of sensory perceptions, a panoramic mental awareness, and a lower center of effort in your actions. It calms the nerves. I trust that you will find this new way of awakened acting to be more balanced, intuitive, rooted, and powerful than others, and much less ego-centered. When combined with deeply embedded skill and experience in sailing, drinking tea, or even folding diapers, this new way opens up a new orientation of the self, even if sustained for less than a minute. The sailor, now sailing with his belly, not his head, sails without sailing.

When practice makes this awakening power increasingly available to the sailor, such that it flows softly into the technique and sailing performance of a sailor more and more on self-command, he may begin to glimpse the second, most inward work of the life of Zen sailing: *self-forgetting*. Self-forgetting is the term I prefer to terms such as "egolessness" or "selflessness." Self-forgetting refers to what most often is a process, with nudges, little jumps, and, once in awhile, awesome leaps. In self-forgetting interludes we shed the usual attitude or sense that it is "I" who is sailing this boat. I and the boat are unified, without the habitual sharp physical, emotional, or cognitive separations and distinctions of "normal" experience.

In my view, sometimes too much is said and written of the process leading to and experienced in self-forgetting. Following the tradition in many writings about the Zen arts, a sailor might speak of "awakening to her true Self," "realizing the Buddha-mind," or "achieving *satori*," but I prefer an ascetic, modest silence. Describing the experience of self-forgetting in grand terms that point to or even promise a peak experience is potentially misleading, since a special experience is neither the conclusion nor the goal of a Zen practice.

The silence I keep to is due to the "mystic," ineffable, tacit quality of the experience of self-forgetting. Silence is a way to avoid giving hope that there is any direct, easy path to self-forgetting. Self-forgetting is approached indirectly, not by choosing to be humble and selfless but by anchoring oneself again and again to the disciplines and constraints of technique, performance standards, and energy work on one's body, breath, and *ki*. Paradoxically, the state of self-forgetting, which is characterized by creative improvisation, liberation from ego-driven desires and delusions, and a wide, inclusive awareness, arises most commonly within the mundane, repetitive regularity of practicing mindfully the formalities of sailing and everyday life.

To students of Zen tradition it should come as no surprise that liberation from the ego's control of our conventional self-narrative can come from entering Zen-like training in self-forgetting within and through a formal practice of sailing. Dogen Kigen, the thirteenth-century Japanese Zen master and philosopher, famously wrote that studying Zen is "studying yourself; studying yourself is forgetting yourself; and forgetting yourself is being authenticated by all things."[7] The even more ancient *Dhammapada* applauds this introspection and inner effort at self-mastery in clear terms: "Greater in battle than the man who would conquer a thousand-thousand men, is he who would conquer just one –himself."[8]

The second of Dogen's stages, where "studying yourself is forgetting yourself,"[9] lies at the heart of Zen practice. While "studying yourself" means attending to and noting your reactions to all outer work in sailing, as well as the more inward meditative work of developing *ki* energy, in Zen even this intentional mindfulness eventually is allowed or encouraged to "drop away" in what I am calling self-forgetting.

This "dropping away" of self-scrutiny and interior monologue comes about by means of exhausting even the introspective mood, through long periods of meditation or by hard, sustained physical and mental labor (which can happen in sailing even in a small boat on quiet waters). It can happen in an afternoon suddenly and dramatically, but also in decades of subtle change in dedicated, patient practice. It can be stimulated by a sailing instructor's word that turns your awareness in a new direction or by a puff of wind on your ear. It can be shallow or deep, momentary or lasting for hours. It can make you laugh or weep. You are never the same again, yet you are more your self than before. You have uncovered what Dogen and the earliest Zen tradition call your "original face."

The last stage of Dogen's rubric on Zen training, where "forgetting yourself is being confirmed by all things," is profound and yet simple. "Forgetting yourself" or dropping off narrow ego-oriented attitudes and actions is a kind of emptying of the self; its desires, fears, and delusions; its thirst for control; its hope for the weather to change and the wind to spring up or die back; and its worry about boatyard bills, crew competence, and a short sailing season. Awa Kenzo, the archery teacher in Eugen Herrigel's *Zen in the Art of Archery*, tells Herrigel that at the point of maximum tension, when the bow is fully stretched before loosing the shot, when everything is at stake and the archer waits in a suspension of all striving, he most learn "to wait properly ... by letting go of yourself, by leaving yourself and all things yours behind you so decisively that nothing more is left of you but a purposeless tension."[10]

The "presence" of mind and body in Zen sailing, one's liberation from the ego's grasping for control of experience, and that "purposeless tension" allow boat, water, wave, cloud, and sky to advance and give shape to the sailor's awareness with an unimpeded richness and beauty. All things breathe "yes!" They confirm a Zen-trained sailor in her being.

By not reaching for or clinging to particular expectations of reality while sailing, the sailor is free, with no mind hindrances, and so she acts with creative improvisation in response to what is dynamically real in the moment. Subtly yet firmly, she relies on the skills, habits, routines, and energy developed in hours of mindful sailing practice. Listening to the whispers of his boat and the "shhh" of wind on her original face, she sails in nirvana.

## NOTES

1   Bernard Moitessier, *The Long Way*, trans. William Rodamur (Dobbs Ferry, NY: Sheridan House, 1995), p. 105.
2   E. B. White, "The sea and the wind that blows." In *Essays of E. B. White* (New York: Harper & Row, 1977), p. 207.
3   William Snaith, "On the wind's way." In Christopher Caswell (Ed.), *The Greatest Sailing Stories Ever Told* (Guilford, CT: The Lyons Press, 2004), p. 113.

4   Stan Grayson, *Cape Cod Catboats* (Marblehead, MA: Devereux Books, 2002) is the best book source on the history and rebirth of the Cape Cod catboat.
5   Eugen Herrigel, *Zen in the Art of Archery* (New York: Vintage Books, 1989), pp. 65–66.
6   Ibid.
7   Cited in David Loy, *The Great Awakening: A Buddhist Social Theory* (Boston, MA: Wisdom Publications, 2003), p. 118.
8   Thanissaro Bhikku, *Dhammapada: A Translation* (Barre, MA: Dhamma Dana Publications, 1998), p. 31.
9   Cited in Loy, *The Great Awakening*, p. 118.
10  Herrigel, *Zen in the Art of Archery*, pp. 31–32.

CHAPTER 6

# FREEDOM OF THE SEAS

## The Stoic Sailor

Sailing is, for many of us, about freedom. Casting off the lines to shore is a figurative and sometimes literal release from the oppressor's wrong, the proud man's contumely, the insolence of office, and a thousand other insults to our sense of autonomy. On a passage, with the wind drawing in the sails and the wake lengthening behind us, we feel as much freedom, perhaps, as the human condition allows. The paradox, however, is that sailing necessarily requires subjecting our perceived autonomy to elemental forces far beyond our control, among them winds, weather, tides, and storm.

To a significant extent, the art of seamanship resides in a clear-eyed grasp of our *agency*: understanding the fine lines between what we can control, what we can influence but not control, and the vast world that is beyond our control. The annals of exploration and modern recreational sailing are replete with tales of sailors who came to grief from overestimating their agency. Yet, as many tales can be told of those who lingered on the shore, or puttered safely about the bay, or unnecessarily called the Coast Guard for rescue from failure to appreciate the true scope of their agency.

Many philosophical perspectives speak to agency, but one of the more ancient, and pertinent to the joys and sorrows of seamanship, is the

*Sailing – Philosophy for Everyone: Catching the Drift of Why We Sail*, First Edition.
Edited by Patrick Goold.
© 2012 John Wiley & Sons, Inc. Published 2012 by John Wiley & Sons, Inc.

classical philosophy of Stoicism. Stoicism has a reputation as a cheerless, pessimistic philosophy useful only to those who must endure pain, torture, or the other slings and arrows of outrageous fortune. It has little superficial appeal to those of us living in industrial nations with social safety nets, good health and nutrition, material prosperity, democratic institutions, and the rule of law. But, as William B. Irvine showed in his recent book, *A Guide to the Good Life: The Ancient Art of Stoic Joy*, Stoicism is ultimately concerned with the joy of living.[1] For sailors, Stoicism has much to offer as a means to create and sustain the sense of joy we seek in sailing.

Stoicism was founded by Zeno of Citium in ancient Greece around 300 BCE, but it had its greatest impact several centuries later during the Roman period, when it powerfully shaped the lives and characters of leading Roman philosophers and statesmen such as Cicero (106–43 BCE), Seneca (*circa* 4 BCE–65 CE), Epictetus (*circa* 55–135 CE), and Marcus Aurelius (121–180 CE). Philosophy, for the ancient Stoics, was not a theoretical discipline or body of speculative doctrines. It was a way of life, a practical guide to the art of living. Like Socrates, the Stoics believed that "care of the soul" – virtue, excellence of character – should be our primary concern. In fact, the Stoics believed that virtue is the only thing that is strictly "good," all other so-called goods (pleasure, wealth, reputation, health, relationships, even life itself) being at best "preferred." The ancient Stoics believed that the universe is pervaded and wisely governed by God (the divine Logos); that human souls are "sparks" or "fragments" of God; that all events are inexorably fated to occur as they do; that virtue is the sole human good; that virtue consists in "living according to nature"; and that living according to nature – for rational beings such as ourselves – consists in willing the universal good, having the right motives and intentions, standing strong and unbowed in the face of adversity, and accepting with equanimity and even thankfulness whatever misfortunes life throws in one's path. The Stoics developed a number of practical techniques to achieve virtue and enduring inner peace. Let's look at three of these techniques – cheerful resignation, self-sufficiency, and negative visualization – and their application to sailing and seamanship.

## Cheerful Resignation

As noted above, the ancient Stoics believed that whatever happens is fated to happen by God, the all-wise and benevolent Logos. The Stoics deduced from this that everything happens for the best and that all "discord" is but "harmony not understood." This doesn't mean that nothing bad ever happens to individuals. God's primary concern is with the welfare of the universe as a whole, and what's good for the whole is not necessarily what's good for each of its parts. Can individuals, then, justly complain when they suffer personal tragedy or misfortune? Not at all, for reason – that holy spark of divinity that lies within each of us – requires that we abandon self-centered desires and egocentric perspectives and look at things from the point of view of the universe. From that cosmic, God's-eye perspective, there can be no grounds for murmurings or complaint. Whatever happens to us in this life, good or bad, we must accept cheerfully as part of God's wise and beneficent plan.

In explaining this Stoic attitude of cheerful resignation, Epictetus famously compares life to a play:

> Remember that you are an actor in a play the character of which is determined by the author – if short, then in a short one; if long, then in a long one. If it should be his pleasure that you should enact a poor man, see that you act it well; or a cripple, or a ruler, or a private citizen. For this is your business, to act well the given part; but to choose it belongs to God.[2]

Elsewhere, Epictetus writes:

> True instruction is this – learning to desire that things should happen as they do ... I must die; must I die groaning too? I must be exiled; does anyone keep me from going smiling, and cheerful, and serene? ... "Then I will fetter you." What do you say, man? Fetter me? You will fetter my leg, but not even Zeus himself can get the better of my free will.[3]

The freedom of the seas entails the possibility, even the probability over a long career in sailing, of experiencing storms or other conditions that reduce our scope of action to its lowest point. The boat is hove to, the tiller lashed, all secured above and below, and there seems nothing more one can do but resign oneself to fate. That sense of resignation from the need for physical action can be a tremendous psychological relief. But there is always one thing more we can do, and should: maintain a cheerful composure.

Minnesota schoolteacher Gerry Spiess certainly needed – and exhibited – the Stoic virtues during his epic 1979 crossing of the North Atlantic in his home-made plywood ten-foot sailboat, *Yankee Girl*. Tossed for days in a howling storm, Spiess' tiny boat was repeatedly flooded and was eventually capsized by a rogue wave. Miraculously, Spiess managed to right *Yankee Girl* before the next wave rolled the boat all the way over. As the sun set, an exhausted Spiess slipped back into the hatch and gripped the rails, preparing to face another night of the North Atlantic's fury. "At that moment," he wrote,

> I wanted more than anything to give up – to get away from the agony, to escape the fear. I wanted to close my eyes and open them again and be somewhere else – back home in Minnesota, in safety and security, with my family and friends.
>
>    I bowed my head. I would cry out to God for his help.
>
>    But then, surprisingly, I found myself hesitating …
>
>    God had given me all of the resources I needed to survive this storm and any other that came along. It was up to me to use them – and not to ask for more.
>
>    Instead of pleading for help, I said a prayer of thanks. I was alive, and my boat was whole. That was enough.[4]

One of the most difficult passages on record was that of the *James Caird*, a twenty-two-foot converted lifeboat sailed by Sir Ernest Shackleton, Captain Frank Worsley, and a four-man crew on an eight-hundred-mile voyage through the winter storms of the Southern Ocean, from Elephant Island to South Georgia Island. Under the most trying conditions imaginable, the crew of the *James Caird* struggled against nearly hopeless odds to find and safely land on South Georgia, driven by the need to seek rescue for their twenty-two fellow sailors stranded on Elephant Island. Throughout the ordeal, the crew maintained a disciplined composure and even the ability to laugh, as Worsley recounted in his attempts to fix their broken cooker: "My subsequent antics with the crumpled-up thing that now bears a faint resemblance to a lady's hat that I am endeavoring to trim, sends everyone into yells of laughter, in which, after a while, I cannot help joining too."[5] During the worst moments, attempting to claw off the bleak western cliffs of South Georgia Island against hurricane-force winds, the crew did not give in to despair. Worsley related:

> As we looked at that hellish rock-bound coast, with its roaring breakers, we wondered, impersonally, at which spot our end was to come. The thoughts of the others I did not know – mine were regret for having brought my diary and annoyance that no one would ever know we had got so far. At intervals we lied [to each other], saying: "I think she'll clear it."[6]

Sterling seamanship and a providential wind shift allowed the *Caird* to clear the rocks, and after sixteen days at sea the crew landed safely in a remote inlet. Following an equally epic overland journey to reach a manned whaling station, all of the expedition's sailors were later rescued, in no small part due to the Stoic virtues employed by Shackleton, Worsley, and others, including the virtue of remaining calm and even cheerful in the worst of circumstances.

## Self-Sufficiency

Like Socrates, the Stoics believed that "no evil can happen to a good man." Why? Because only what harms the soul is evil, and nothing can harm the soul except vice, which no good man commits. A good man, therefore, is self-sufficient. His happiness and well-being lie entirely within his own control. All that is good – an upright heart and an invincible will – is within his power. All that is evil – anything that corrupts the soul – can be avoided through an act of will. Thus, "indifferents" such as death, pain, poverty, and loss have no terrors for him. Like the English poet William Earnest Henley, he can proclaim:

> It matters not how strait the gate,
> How charged with punishments the scroll,
> I am the master of my fate:
> I am the captain of my soul.[7]

Even with modern technology and conveniences – EPIRBs, satellite phones, and a full-service boatyard in every port – the ethos of sailing has demanded and will always demand the maximum practical self-sufficiency. A landsman can travel many thousands of miles by automobile without having the slightest idea how to change the oil or a tire, but no sailor on even the shortest passage should be ignorant of how to splice a line, bleed air out of a fuel line, or unclog the head. Stoicism also stresses the virtue of self-sufficiency, but with an emphasis on the psychological: simply, our essential happiness and tranquility should depend as little as possible on the approval or actions of others, and still less on the functioning of plumbing facilities on board.

One of the many reasons sailors go to sea is to enjoy companionship with like-minded souls, and to spend as little time as possible among the harpies of the shore. Yet, the social life on board a small boat can be fraught with tension, misunderstandings, and festering annoyances. Extended cruises can be particularly hard on marriages and family relations, as attested by the number of boats for sale in tropical ports at divorce-rate prices. As Irvine notes, in difficult social situations the Stoic philosophers recommend first reflecting on our own shortcomings and doing what we can to eliminate our own annoying behavior. The Stoics note that becoming annoyed or angry at another's behavior will almost always be more detrimental to us than the behavior itself, and simply make the situation worse. If all else fails, we can always reflect on the brevity of life and the triviality of human differences *sub specie aeternitatis* ("from the standpoint of eternity") and do what we can to maintain the attitude of cheerful tolerance and emotional self-sufficiency so necessary for life on board a small vessel.

## Murphy was an Optimist: Negative Visualization

The third, and perhaps most important, Stoic technique is what William Irvine calls "negative visualization," which is essentially the practice of periodically and systematically imagining what could go wrong in life and the loss of something dear to you (possessions, status, loved ones, life itself). The point of such an exercise is not to develop a morose sense of fatalism but quite the opposite: to free ourselves as much as possible of the fear of loss, and hence to increase the capacity for experiencing joy.

Negative visualization has immediate practical implications for sailors. For example, by imagining a scenario in which we experience sudden loss of auxiliary engine power when docking in a crowded marina, we are prompted to prepare ourselves for that eventuality by having the sails ready to set, the anchor ready to deploy, and a provisional plan for using either to avoid collision or grounding. By imagining the loss of our rudder at sea, we are prompted to prepare ourselves, both to prevent that loss to the extent we can (by proper maintenance and periodic inspections) and also by learning how to jury-rig a replacement if the rudder is someday lost despite our precautions. As sailors, we can take negative visualization one step further and actually *practice* deprivation, for example by shutting off the engine and practicing how to dock under sail, or by learning to navigate by sextant as a backup to the modern electronic navigation instruments at our disposal. As Seneca remarks,

Everyone approaches with more courage a hazard to which he has long squared himself, and resists harsh circumstances by contemplating them in advance. But the man without preparation panics at even the lightest troubles. We must see to it that nothing comes to us unexpectedly, and since novelty makes all things more burdensome, constant meditation will guarantee that you are not a raw recruit for any misfortune.[8]

Perhaps even more important than the physical preparations prompted by negative visualization is the effect on our emotional and mental states. By engaging in systematic contemplation of what could go wrong while sailing, we are far more likely to react calmly, quickly, and therefore effectively to emergencies and difficult situations, even those that we have not specifically contemplated or prepared against. As Seneca writes,

> Unexpected disasters weigh more heavily; novelty adds weight to calamities, and there is no mortal man who has not felt more grief at something that left him in amazement. So we should make sure nothing is unforeseen; we must send our mind ahead to face everything and think not of whatever usually happens but whatever can happen.[9]

At a less practical but no less important level, negative visualization allows us to better appreciate what we do possess and all that has gone right in life's voyage. It is a common human failing to take much for granted (good health, a sound boat, pleasant weather, and so on). It is somewhat paradoxical, but, if we imagine the loss of those things we tend to take for granted, we can truly appreciate them, perhaps for the first time, and take real joy in their presence. Stated differently, by undergoing the difficult emotional work of visualizing the loss of something dear to us or that we take for granted, we can diminish our fear of loss and the crippling effects of fear.

As Marcus Aurelius noted, fear is often rooted in false values and lack of perspective. We fear death, but death is part of nature, causes us no harm (since, as he supposes, there is either a happy afterlife or we don't exist to be harmed), and is necessary for the universal good. We fear loss of creature comforts, power, reputation, pleasure, and youthful good looks, but what are these from the perspective of eternity? Nothing but smoke and bling. All that endures is goodness and truth, for then we participate in something eternal and god-like.

Aside from injury or loss of life, what sailors dread most is to lose their sailboat to storm or reef. The legendary circumnavigator Bernard Moitessier built and lost three boats in his lifetime, including *Joshua*, the steel ketch that he helmed in the first round-the-world, non-stop, single-handed race, in 1968. After seven months of solo racing, Moitessier famously turned back from the finish line in Plymouth, England, and sailed non-stop half again around the world to Tahiti, for a total of thirty-five thousand miles alone under sail. After a decade of activism and further adventures in the South Pacific, Moitessier and *Joshua* were anchored off Cabo San Lucas when an unexpected storm drove a number of boats onto the beach, including *Joshua*. With no funds to salvage his beloved ketch, Moitessier gave the hulk to a friend and for the third time in his life moved on from shipwreck. His life in close communion with the seas had given him the perspective necessary to absorb such losses with something approaching tranquility.

## Agency and Control

The Stoic sailor is distinguished, above all, by an accurate understanding of what seamanship can and cannot accomplish. In 2008, veteran offshore sailor Skip Allen was returning solo from Hawaii on board *Wildflower*, the Wylie 27 he built in 1975, after winning the single-handed TransPac race. For three days he rode out a gale off the coast of California, running before the wind and twenty-five-to-thirty-five-foot waves under stormsail and autopilot, trailing a drogue. The autopilot continued to work flawlessly, but if it failed a broach was inevitable before Allen could regain control of the boat. Exhausted, and with the gale forecasted to strengthen and extend for at least three more days, Allen had a choice: stay with his still-seaworthy boat or radio for rescue from a freighter in the vicinity. He was extremely loathe to abandon his companion of thirty-four years. Still, the sixty-year-old reminded himself that he was responsible not only for his own life but also for taking care of an elderly family member. As Allen described it in an online forum, "I cried, pounded my fist, looked out through the hatch numerous times at the wave mountains, remembered all the good times I had shared with *Wildflower*, and came to a decision."[10] He radioed for rescue. In a final act of seamanship, Allen opened a seawater intake on his beloved boat before leaping onto the freighter's ladder, so that *Wildflower* would sink beneath the waves rather than drift as a menace to navigation.

Allen's story illustrates a key distinction that Stoics make between what is within our control (limited mostly to our goals, reactions, desires, and other internal states) and what is not within our control (pretty much everything else). The latter category can be further divided into things that we can influence but not completely control (for example, how well our crew performs during a sailing race) and things we have little or no influence over (the tide, wind direction, how other racers perform, and so on), resulting in what Irvine calls the "trichotomy of control." Stoics devote most of their mental energy and discipline to the first category (control of our goals, reactions, desires, and internal states), knowing that success in that regard will increase the amount of influence we can bring to bear on external events not within our control. Stoics strive to remain emotionally indifferent to the universe of events completely beyond our control.

As an experienced offshore sailor, Allen was as prepared as possible for the gale, but events beyond his control forced him to make a difficult emotional decision. He focused on what he could control (his goals and desires) and made what was almost certainly the correct judgment in the circumstances: to abandon his vessel. Importantly, though, he continued to influence events to the maximum extent, and even in the act of abandoning *Wildflower* exercised his agency and seamanship to ensure his beloved boat would endanger no others.

Sometimes there is nothing to be done but endure, and it is then that Stoicism can help most. In the 1996 Vendée Globe single-handed race around the world, Raphael Dinelli's boat was capsized and dismasted in hurricane-force winds in the cold Southern Ocean, over five hundred miles from the nearest land. With the boat awash and slowly sinking, liferaft torn away, he stood in the cockpit for twenty-four hours, dancing like a madman to stave off hypothermia. "I wasn't afraid," he remembered. He was angry that death was coming, but knew he "had to keep fighting mentally, because if you don't fight ceaselessly, you're finished."[11]

The next day an Australian long-range search-and-rescue plane dropped him a liferaft, and he clambered it into minutes before his boat finally succumbed to the waves. Inside the raft was a message that Pete Goss, a fellow Vendée Globe racer, was ten hours away, beating upwind in gale-force winds to reach him. Goss was Dinelli's only hope of rescue. A bottle of champagne bobbed to the surface from the wreck, and Dinelli grabbed it with numb fingers. Exposure was taking its toll. He spent the night in the raft, frozen and paralyzed, only the hope of seeing Goss in the morning keeping him alive.

The next morning the plane reappeared and flashed its lights. Dinelli thought, "That's it, Pete Goss must have broken his mast or something, he's not coming, I'll never last another day."[12] But the plane was guiding Goss to the bobbing raft, almost invisible in the immense waves, and ten minutes later Goss' sailboat appeared. Dinelli carefully handed up the bottle of champagne, and Goss heaved the hypothermic sailor aboard. Against all odds, Dinelli had endured.

## Fate, Freedom, and Sailing

Ironically, it is because so much of our lives is "fated" and beyond our control that we have the potential to experience true freedom – a freedom of the mind that, once gained, no man or externality can ever take away from us. Imagine a sailboat coasting along in light winds; the tide turns and the speed over ground slows to zero. Many sailors would curse, fire up the iron genny, and bash against the tidal current, even if in no particular hurry. A Stoic sailor might smile, toss out the anchor, sit in the cockpit reading his Epictetus, and cheerfully wait for the tide to turn again. As Epictetus notes, accepting what is necessary with inner calm is the true secret to freedom and contentment in this storm-tossed world:

> Remember ... that if you attribute freedom to things by nature dependent, and take what belongs to others for your own, you will be hindered, you will lament, you will be disturbed, you will find fault both with gods and men. But if you take for your own only that which is your own ... then no one will ever compel you, no one will restrict you, you will find fault with no one, and you will accuse no one, you will do nothing against your will.[13]

Sailing has an almost unique capacity to teach us patience, and to reward us for practicing the Stoic virtues. We cannot control the winds or tide, sometimes reefs appear off our bow, and always our brief voyage on this planet is over too soon. But, with the help of the Stoic virtues, our seamanship, and a keen understanding of our agency, we can shape a course free of fear and full of joy.

## NOTES

1 William B. Irvine, *A Guide to the Good Life: The Ancient Art of Stoic Joy* (New York: Oxford University Press, 2008).
2 Epictetus, "The Enchiridion." In *Epictetus: The Discourses and Enchiridion*, trans. Thomas Wentworth Higginson (New York: Walter J. Black, 1944), p. 337.

 GREGORY BASSHAM AND TOD BASSHAM

3  Ibid., p. 376.
4  Gerry Spiess, "North Atlantic storm." In Michael Bartlett and Joanne A. Fishman (Eds.), *The Sailing Book* (Westminster, MD: Arbor House, 1982), p. 118.
5  Frank A. Worsley, *Shackleton's Boat Journey* (New York: W. W. Norton & Company, 1977), p. 87.
6  Ibid., p. 144.
7  William Earnest Henley, "Invictus." In Roy Cook (Ed.), *101 Famous Poems* (New York: McGraw-Hill, 2003), p. 95.
8  Seneca, *Selected Letters*, trans. Elaine Fantham (New York: Oxford University Press, 2010), p. 228.
9  Ibid., pp. 188–189.
10  Skip Allen, "*Wildflower* ship log," *Sailing Anarchy Forums* (2003, http://forums.sailinganarchy.com/index.php?showtopic=78146).
11  Raphael Dinelli, "How we met: Pete Goss and Raphael Dinelli: Interviews with Philip Sweeney," *The Independent* (May 18, 1997, http://www.independent.co.uk/arts-entertainment/how-we-met-pete-goss-and raphael-dinelli-1262298.html).
12  Ibid.
13  Epictetus, "The Enchiridion," p. 331.

CHAPTER 7

# SAILORS OF THE THIRD KIND

## Sailing and Self-Becoming in the Shadow of Heraclitus

*It was so old a ship – who knows, who knows?*
*And yet so beautiful, I watched in vain*
*To see the mast burst open with a rose,*
*And the whole deck put on its leaves again.*
J. E. Flecker, "The Old Ships"

*Full fathom five thy father lies;*
*Of his bones are coral made;*
*Those are pearls that were his eyes;*
*Nothing of him that does fade,*
*But doth suffer a sea-change*
*Into something rich and strange.*
Shakespeare, Ariel's Song, *The Tempest*

Several years ago, when I was leaving port on a long voyage of uncertain destination, which has yet to reach its end, an old sailor and mariner, self-confessed one-time smuggler, and engineering mystic growled to me through his bushy horseshoe moustache: "If you ever get to that horizon, give it a good kicking, from me!" I laughed and took a photo of him, standing on the ramshackle Scottish dockside, heavy arms folded, leaning against a large fuel drum between an equally ancient wooden fishing

*Sailing – Philosophy for Everyone: Catching the Drift of Why We Sail*, First Edition.
Edited by Patrick Goold.
© 2012 John Wiley & Sons, Inc. Published 2012 by John Wiley & Sons, Inc.

boat, in fading yellow, blue, and red, and a modern hull of brushed aluminum. He didn't smile as he watched me slip away, but the moment, I felt, was one of mutual recognition and understanding. A good line; but what could it have meant? I think he knew I understood it, which is why he gave it to me. Where was I going? Toward the horizon, certainly. And from that horizon I would raise shorelines, mountains, lights, cities, bays, relationships, skills, struggles, happiness, and near despair. Below the horizon my bow would dip, and my anchor dive, many times. But each destination I raise, every one he raised in his long life at sea, each brief bond of the anchor chain is never the end of the journey. It is never the "home port" at which my cutter sloop and I will remain, and end. For a mariner, for a sailor of the third kind, the horizon is a visible avatar of the source of the process of being itself. To reach it would be a kind of death. For a sailor of the third kind, a day out racing round the cans is all very well, and a trip across the bay with the promise of a pint or good company happy enough. But the bow swung round and pointed to an open horizon on the first hours of a voyage whose destination is more an arbitrary placeholder, a cleat or transient binding point for one end of the first theoretical line of a great circle route: that is a moment of pure joy.

People covet boats, and sail, for many reasons. In this essay I will attempt to sort these sailors into three broad classes. The categories described are generalized and to a certain extent must be caricatures of the real situation. I do not consider that each and every sailor fits neatly into one or other category to the exclusion of the rest, nor do I consider that the characteristics so described are the only ones that may exist. However, the conceit contains, I feel, an approximation of the truth, and is a tool for gaining some understanding of these sailors, and in particular the sailors who most approximate the third. This third will also include those who simply aspire but never have the opportunity to set out toward that unreachable horizon.

First, there are those who become involved with sailing because of its social iconography, a glamorous thread in Western culture and, most especially relevantly for this category, in Western marketing culture. For at least some of these, the mere fact of vague association or involvement is sufficient, sublimated into sailing clothes and shoes, with civilized hands, or a boat owned and polished and prized but rarely used. The endless use of the symbolism of sailing by high-end clothes manufacturers, luxury watchmakers, jewelers, car brands, and other similar products not remotely connected to the practical realities of sailing, has this category of sailor, and aspirant, as its object. The exclusive yacht club is the temple and ultimate showplace for the cultural aspirants of this category, a place wherein the sailors of the second kind might find a welcome, if not a home, and those of the third likely no welcome at all, in the unlikely case that one were to be desired. The hardships and sacrifices of the sea are unlikely to be relished by members of this category, and, while an afternoon's champagne sail along some warm shoreline and a bob at anchor in an idyllic tropical bay may be on the menu, hard-won lonely anchorages alongside rough, uninhabited places are unlikely ever to be experienced or, perhaps, desired. Scars of use on the hands and mind of the sailor, and on the fabric of the boat, are undesirable signs of an experience that is alien to the mandarin cleanness of this world, wherein the realities and passion of sailing are tamed, lacquered over, and reduced to mere ciphers for a culture that is as far from them as are the symbols of heraldry from the events that first gave them meaning. The boat owned by one of this first kind of sailor is likely to be trussed and tethered like a beautiful slave to one or another marina pontoon, with only brief afternoons with impressed guests or direct trips to the next well-chosen showplace. For some of these, the more prestigious the boat – the bigger and more expensive – the better: the boats themselves and the trappings of them are exalted beyond their obvious function to being trophies and symbols of power, reaching their ultimate expression in the mega-yachts, floating pyramids of would-be latter-day pharaohs.

Then there are the sailors of the second kind: those who sail to race. These sailors are no strangers to hardship, and maximum use of the vessel in its most practical form is the name of their game. For the ocean sailors among them, the fastest, shortest possible route, regardless of intensity of prevailing conditions or difficulty of sea-states, often sailing *toward* heavy weather for wind advantage rather than prudently away from it, as might a sailor of the third kind, is the order of the day. Sailing style often subjugates prudence, and what sailors of the third kind would regard as "good seamanship" loses out to the exigencies of speed. Single-handed racers, perforce, often barrel down rough wavescapes at maximum speed asleep with no watch save radar, which is all but ineffective in such conditions, as the radar reflections off the waves, or sea clutter, hide almost everything significant. The use of automatic identification systems, which transmit a boat's position, course, and speed to others in the area, with computerized alarms, has substantially reduced this risk, but it still exists, as many ships and smaller vessels still lack such systems. Tolerances of materials and hull construction are finely calculated compromises whose object is speed and performance over durability and strength in the face of the unexpected, which calculations, as the likes of Pete Goss and Tony Bullimore have found, all too often err on the side of performance. Sail changes on the larger fully manual rigs are often accomplished under severe duress for both crew and boat, perhaps changing a number two to a number three yankee headsail in a rising gale in cold high-latitude waters in the dark, with no bearing away or course deviation to reduce risk or wear and stress on flesh and equipment. There is huge skill and heroic effort and courage involved in these practices, and the money and competition involved in this area of sailing are responsible for driving innovation in many areas, though not always resulting in the most voyage-worthy crafts. Sailors of the second and third kinds share the overriding imperative of practicality, but for those of the second kind this practicality has a single absolute focus: speed, and this speed is not the sole end in itself, but rather is the means to a further end as well. These sailors might take delight in the technical mastery of the latest rig or in the feeling of speed, but ultimately they are in it to compete with others for a definite goal; a social, human prize: prestige. The soul of this goal is land-based, I, as a sailor of the third kind, would argue. At its core is the demonstration, to others, of how short a time the boat can be pushed to remain at sea. The boat becomes a tool for the goal of producing a thrill and exhibiting a skill. The shore-based prize-giving and league tables are the true manifestation of this kind of relationship. Its history is rooted in the land-market demands of commerce. The great tea-clippers are the forerunners of this style of sail.

I once had the experience of sailing with an amateur crew on an amateur one-design round-the-world race. This particular part of it was from Vancouver to Panama City. Somewhere south of the Sea of Cortez, we were nearly becalmed, ghosting along under the lightweight spinnaker at perhaps three or four knots, and uncatchably behind the leader on that leg. Suddenly, fine on the port bow, we spotted massive whaleblows, the size and shape of tall birch trees, around a mile away. Having seen many whales of different species and their blows, it seemed to me the most likely source for these prodigious forms was the blue whale: very rare to see, and the largest species, land or sea, ever to have lived on Earth. I was bouncing with joy and excitement, not least because the day was so calm; we should have been able to see the five or so individuals very clearly in the water. I expected an immediate change of course, to feather by them, at least, if not a diversion to take a more lingering look to honor one of life's great opportunities. I was sorely disappointed. The skipper was not for altering course, not even by the handful of degrees it would have required; and, to my astonishment, of the thirteen remaining crew, not one besides myself wished to pause or alter course. "We are racing," was the universal answer. And, despite my protestations, that was the end of the matter. We did, in the end, ghost past them – perhaps two hundred meters away – on a four-thousand-mile passage, which for those non-sailors among you likely amounted to no difference at all. It is unlikely that such an opportunity will arise again for any one of us then aboard.

At that moment I realized I would never participate in an ocean race again. There have been many other such incidents over the course of my sailing life, but this one stands out as the starkest example of the difference between racers and sailors of the third kind. These two different kinds of sailors, while not always mutually exclusive in a character, are nonetheless quite distinct. I do not disdain these sailors of the second kind. They often accomplish very arduous and remarkable things. I wish them well in their endeavors, but I simply am not, and cannot be, one of them.

So what, then, of the last category? One may borrow, perhaps, a little of the form of words of Immanuel Kant in understanding the difference here. For the sailors of the first and second kind, the boat and the act of sailing are only ever means to some further end: an end that is self-contained and definite, but of a closed, complete, and largely land-based kind – say a prize, or a place on a record, or a favorable impression made. For the sailor of the third kind, the boat itself and its function, the life with it and within it, its relationship to the wind, the land, the ocean and its living beings, the sun, moon, stars, and horizon – that process, focused through the sailor's self, is an end *in itself*. And what is to be found in that end? For these sailors, the act of sailing, especially long-distance living-cruising, represents a kind of singularity in which the beingness of human existence and the being-in of universal existence are as close to unified as it may be possible to be. This will no doubt seem a rather opaque and perhaps suspiciously airy assertion, so I will attempt to clarify.

The branch of philosophy that focuses on the questions "What sorts of things are there? What is real?" is called ontology. It is built on the Greek word *ontos*, which means "being." Ontologists take one of two fundamentally distinct approaches in answering these questions. These approaches may be described as the substantialist and the process views of reality. For the substantialists, who walk in the shadow of the ancient Greek philosopher Parmenides, the world is made up of substantial things that persist and perdure through time, that have events happen

STEVEN HORROBIN

to them, and that cause events, but that are themselves discrete, unitary, unique, and in some fundamental sense unchanging. The ancient philosopher Democritus, the founder of the concept of atoms, defended just such a position. For the processists, followers in the tradition of the Greek philosopher Heraclitus, in a deep sense there are no "things" at all. Every "thing" is simply a passing momentary fluctuation of the universal substance, which is for these philosophers the *only* substance. Every piece of the world, every "thing" that appears stable and solid and unitary and real in itself, is no more real and unitary and stable and solid than the whitecaps that wink above the crests of waves. It is simply a matter of time, and perspective. Consider showing a photograph of whitecaps to one who has never seen waves – they may appear to be solid "things" in the manner of objects. The same may be said if one could only see them in "slow motion" as it were, so their rise and collapse might take days or weeks, years or millennia. It is for this reason that we can name cosmic events such as the Horsehead or Crab Nebulas and speak of them as though they were "things" and not wave-like processes, which is what they are. For the substantialists, the person is, in some fundamental way, a whole and unitary being, with at least one utterly changeless core element that is reidentifiable as such at any moment of its personal history and that does not, in itself, change. For these philosophers, persons are, in some sense, complete beings who interact with the other substances and processes of the world but who ultimately remain above or outside them. The traditional concept of an immortal soul is one way to begin to understand this substantialist view. Sailors of the first and second kinds, so focused upon precise and definite, self-contained and discrete objects and goals are, I feel, more likely to subscribe to a substantialist ontology, whether they know it or not. Wholly open-ended voyaging, with the journey itself as the end, is most likely unappealing to minds committed to this view of the world.

For the processists, the whole of Nature is one vast super-process, and out of this, like everything else, persons arise, as sub-processes of the whole, distinct from it in the way that individual waves are distinct from each other and the ocean's surface but ultimately changeful and restless in their very nature, ultimately and indivisibly part of the whole. For the adherents to this view, the person is never present, whole, and complete in any one moment, and no person is unchanging. To be unchanging is not to be, just as to be a wave without change and movement is meaningless. To be a person is to be a process, and to be a process is to be ever in a state of becoming. For the great seventeenth-century philosopher Spinoza, this process of becoming was in essence a move of the universal super-process toward its own self-realization, with persons achieving greater or lesser moves toward representing, in themselves and their own being, an approximation of the whole. For him, the good was manifest in the direction of movement, within a person, toward the accurate reflection of the whole of nature, in microcosm. In this reflection, in this personal realization, the universe comes to reflect and understand, to re-present its own self. This line of thinking was further clarified in the works of the twentieth-century philosopher Hans Jonas. I would argue that the sailors of the third kind are most likely to be those who, knowingly nor not, live and self-become in the shadow of Heraclitus.

The sea is a rough and violent place, and a boat, properly used in long-distance travel, is a rough and violent being. It is hard on the body and mind and can break people and their relationships. It strips away trivialities and it bonds and exposes the practical, intellectual, and spiritual elements of the self to the open systems of the earth and the wider universe through the tight discipline of the boat's processes. Even tied up to a dock, a sea boat is in a state analogous to a constant saltwater earthquake. Quite apart from the brute mechanical violence of the boat's existence at the juncture of wind, wave, and land – jarring, loosening, and weakening – the salt fingers of the sea extend through atomization into the air and penetrate the hull into every aspect of the boat's systems, requiring constant vigilance, and husbandry from its occupant. Metals laid against each other, by design or accident (a stray screw in the bilge, perhaps), if not equivalent on the galvanic table, form electric currents in the mode of batteries and result in galvanic corrosion, turning the hardest metallic structures to dust. Even stainless steel is not immune to this process. Sacrificial anodes placed at the ends of these sequences to protect them must be constantly maintained, and the circuits that lead to them perpetually checked. The electrical systems of the boat, fuelled by its power systems and batteries, add vigor to this destruction and may, by stray current facilitated by pervasive salt, destroy key parts of the boat's integrity in weeks or days. On deck, fair weather is no refuge as the wind, water, and salt mollify and abrade, and the sun irradiates the sails, plastics, covers, and lines, weakening them constantly and insidiously even through cloud. A long-distance mariner is forced thereby into a constant dance of maintenance, repair, and replacement. Nothing escapes or is immune, and a lack of complete vigilance and constant labor threatens the integrity of the whole. A single failed component, however small,

STEVEN HORROBIN

as every experienced mariner knows, may rapidly compound in non-linear ways and lead to sudden disaster.

There is an old philosophical chestnut known as the Ship of Theseus paradox. Essentially, the conundrum is as follows. Say one has a ship – the ship of Theseus, perhaps – wooden for simplicity, wherein parts wear or rot out and must be replaced piecemeal. At every stage of this process, one is tempted to continue calling this ship by the same name, but gradually it is all changed, until no part of the original remains. Is it still the same ship? A modern wrinkle on this problem of identity, popularized by the philosopher Derek Parfit, is to imagine building a second ship in parallel, alongside the first, from its discarded parts. In the end, which is the "true" ship? Now, a mariner may well be justified in noting to Professor Parfit that the ship built of worn-out and discarded parts will be useless and unable to function as a ship, so perhaps the practical goes some way to resolving this philosophical thought experiment. But of course the question is serious, and interesting. However, it is only really a puzzle to those who accept a substantialist view of reality. The puzzle depends upon the idea that identity consists of a particular set of definite, hard, reidentifiable parts, which constitute the whole, discrete, singular being. By contrast, there is to the process philosopher far less of a conundrum. For, identity to a processist consists only in the particular nature or signature of a process. For a ship to be a particular ship, it needs only to hold the continuous original function and general form of that ship. That it may be true that another ship may be constructed of perhaps not-quite worn-out parts of the original process is no real problem, since a process view of identity does not require that processes do not branch. Indeed, it requires that they do. A whole series of ships constructed in this way would in an important sense be, indeed, the same ship, in very much the way that different owners of different yachts in the same class of yacht – say, a copy of Moitessier's famous *Joshua* – may instantly recognize something of their own vessel in the other, and something of themselves in the other owner. There is a commonality, as they are aspects of a shared local process. This recognition points toward the underlying super-process, from which all processes, or modes of being (as Spinoza would have said), extend, and to which they are inextricably connected. In this way, to a processist, identity is never complete in the way that a substantialist would wish (i.e., unchanging and discrete), and the problem really diminishes, or disappears. The final detail of particularity really comes more from time and place than anything more fundamental: my *Joshua*, at this or that time, was or is here, with me, and not there, where that other *Joshua* was or is, with you. Inevitably these share some of their identity, and more so than they would, say, with a Beneteau Oceanis, and perhaps its owner.

It is no coincidence that the classic form of this conundrum is presented by reference to a ship. There is something about living on the land that gives advantage to the mode of thinking of Parmenides and the substantialists. Simply, it is that the land appears stable and fixed, replete with stable, fixed, unitary, and discrete objects: in a word, substantial. Equally, the opposite is true. The violence of the sea, its accelerated processes, and very fluidity impel the mind toward a more process-oriented view of reality. To a processist the former is, of course, an illusion, supplied by the relative perspective of duration. The processes of the land-based life are simply more stable, less violent relative to the lifespan and daily activities of a person. To see this, one merely needs to add time. The whole continent of Africa, if viewed in a long-term perspective of hundreds, thousands, and millions of years, may easily be seen to be far more fluid, to be in fact not substantial in the traditional mode of solidity and changelessness but rather a boiling mass of process and change, wherein everyday objects, buildings, and even the continent itself melt and flow away as fluidly as do waves on the ocean's surface. In this way a life on the ocean supplies not a complete categorical change but rather a change of perspective, and one arguably toward the underlying reality of things. In respect of the short life of the sailor, the violence of the oceanic life and the threatened, frail processes of his or her boat reveal more closely the underlying reality of the nature of Nature, the total super-process. And the life lived as a long-distance mariner is one in which the being of that mariner blends, perforce, into the being of the violent processes of his or her craft: the days absorbed in the management of passages, and of the management of the fragile confluence that is the boat's own process on the ocean wave.

A salient feature of the voyaging life is its time-consuming nature. A transoceanic passage, which for a passenger on a jetliner may take a matter of hours with little effort at all, will cost a sailing mariner weeks of concentrated effort. I would wager that sailors of the third kind are not likely to be easily bored. For these persons, the time-dilation of the act of sailing has rather the opposite effect that one might suppose: far from making long periods drag, it quickens the perception of the violent, passionate flux of the world. In this way, in all its restless quietnesses, brief intensities, and seeming drudgery, there is something akin to the monastic. But it is not a regulated, calm withdrawal from the world.

STEVEN HORROBIN

Rather, it is a move outward, toward the world in all its wonderful and sometimes dangerous caprice: more anchorite than monk.

Ocean voyaging generates an openness to change: change of weather, change of plans, sudden whales, and changes of life, relationship, status, and fortune – the unexpected that arises swiftly from the blank apparent sameness of the ocean. It mandates sensitivity to subtleties that would otherwise be missed. A wavescape, a cloudscape, some new feature on the water is never merely that but is always to be watched and understood. Each new landfall rises like the lid of a chest holding treasure and threat in unequal and uncertain measure. This watchful unexpectedness alters the mariner's perspective of the world. The relative time of the processes themselves appears foreshortened. All is fluid, and any event, any identity, appears as a fragile nexus, a brief disequilibrium against the constant flow of universal stuff toward equilibrium. This may seem counterintuitive, of course, since the common understanding of equilibrium is one of stability. But the stability of equilibrium, in physics, is absolutely inimical to the requirements of salient, complex processes, such as those that define any living being. All living beings are projections *away* from equilibrium, are highly precarious towers of disequilibrium, held together in a brief relationship by effort and work afforded by free energy from the sun. The boat is a being just like the living body. It is held in high disequilibrium, through constant effort and energy, above the state toward which it would rapidly fall if so allowed. On the ocean, equilibrium is represented all around by that very blank, apparent sameness – a windy surface thinly hiding the sunless, windless abyss, the ever-threatened fall toward darkness, silence, stasis, and death. Above this rides, by the free energy of the wind, a tiny and wildly improbably being, inhabited by, and an extension of, a wildly improbable being whose very improbability is what gives it life and meaning. All the phases of matter are present: a fragment of solid land in the hand, atmospheric gas in the sail, and the keel in a liquid ocean. The sky, the sea, and the land, tides, pressures, and precipitation, the stars, sun, and moon, the universe beyond, the whole history of human endeavor, culture, and technical achievement manifest in the boat's construction. These are fully connected through the act of navigation, and the intimate acquaintance and husbandry of the sailor. They are captured by the hull, keel, and sail, and focused through the mariner's hand at the helm.

The mariner, whose hands bleed daily in working to maintain the nexus of disequilibrium, the complex beauty of the relationship of the boat, mind, and wider universe, is drawn into an intense relationship with these processes. In so doing, such mariners place themselves in a situation closer to, and more open to, an understanding of this naked super-process than most in the human sphere. As Spinoza might have it, they are arguably closer to a kind of universal self-representation. And for that they sail toward the horizon they will never reach.

Or perhaps they are just curmudgeonly misfits who are grumpy about not getting to see whales, or whatever else, as and when they wished!

# PART 3

# BEAUTY AND OTHER AESTHETIC ASPECTS OF THE SAILING EXPERIENCE

CHAPTER 8

# WHAT THE RACE TO MACKINAC MEANS

Seen from the International Space Station through the night sky, the most conspicuous patch of ink-black darkness in the lower United States is the 22,400 square surface miles of Lake Michigan. Lake Superior is larger, but its edges are less defined by electric light, because fewer people live around it. Lake Michigan appears to hang from Canada like a smooth dollop of cool, dark honey from the edge of a jar. If we use this contrast to consider the human condition, we quickly conclude that we hug the shores and seem never to breach them. But, during a few nights every July, the night population on Lake Michigan surges from none to about one person for every seven square miles, in an apparent rush to be off-grid. It is not enough to pierce the sky, but the surface is specked with red, green, and white navigation lights that can only be seen by sailors.

The occasion is a race from Chicago to Mackinac Island, in which about three thousand sailors on about three hundred sailboats cross a starting line near Chicago and use wind to travel three hundred miles north-by-northeast.

*Sailing – Philosophy for Everyone: Catching the Drift of Why We Sail*, First Edition.
Edited by Patrick Goold.
© 2012 John Wiley & Sons, Inc. Published 2012 by John Wiley & Sons, Inc.

To a casual observer watching the sailors prepare their boats, the harbor might seem like a circus grounds; on one end, shimmering stars and starlets in perfect painted luxury porta-homes served by bright-white uniformed entourages; on the other, the hardy, hardened, pockmarked tractor-trailer drivers doing double duty as midway amusement attendees. In the middle, the observer finds an American microcosm: moms and grandmothers, teachers and taxi drivers, frat-boys and fullbacks, cat-lovers and Cubs-fans, sojourners and sportsmen, eggheads and environmentalists, rookies and retirees. One might conclude that sailing can appeal to anyone but that it self-selects: the boats appear to reflect the people and the people seem to reflect the boats.

There are boats that seem like "passenger trains," designed for long work. Engines (sails) will overcome friction and weight to move the train (a boat) down the track (the course) at a relatively predictable speed. Passenger trains can be designed for different duties: some like city work, some like the long haul, some favor volume over comfort, and some favor comfort over speed. The locomotive can be made more efficient or designed to pull more weight, and the cars can be made sleeker or more posh. There are old trains and new ones. Some are brightly painted, others utilitarian. But, architecturally speaking, passenger trains don't differ from each other significantly in form or function. Timing and execution are what separate the good from the bad. Running a passenger train well requires that it is well-known by its engineer, well-serviced by its mechanic, and well-timed by its conductor, and that it keeps moving all along its route. Then, it might reach its destination faster than another passenger train.

There are the "Model Ts." Not Model T, as in old and square, but Model T as in all the same, or one design – Henry Ford's central idea. Sailors seeking competitive purity and parity often rally others with a common interest and select boats that are identical – perfect matches – to race on a level time playing field. Many races, this one included, start and score these fleets without handicap (time allowance for differences) except in the overall fleet. A student studying group think might suggest a thesis to explain the Model T team behavior, where apparently same-age, same-income, same-education, same-sex teams clad in same-colored T-shirts, start at precisely the same moment and race against more same-age, same-income, same-education, same-sex teams on the same boats. It's not so simple; only one Model T finishes first in each Model T fleet. So someone did something very different.

There are the "booster rockets." These are the boats designed to break sailing barriers when the conditions allow; they are super-charged and made practically weightless with exotic composites and vast sail engines. Sailing one means combining the stamina of a young Ethiopian marathoner, the brazenness of a test pilot, and the sleep deprivation of a medical resident. Booster rockets can't take extra crew because they can't afford the weight, and there isn't any place to put them, so there is never a break from intense sailing. Booster rockets are driven to peak performance – to the bleeding edge of safe speeds – almost all the time, but have a narrower window of usefulness and safety margin than a passenger train or a Model T. In extreme conditions or in the hands of the wrong sailors, a booster rocket is a large liability – too powerful and angry to tame and too tiny to protect its occupants. Booster rocket sailors gamble that they'll reach the finish just in time to eject.

There are the "collegiates." Not collegiates as in college sailors, but collegiates as in boats and teams explained with the college athletics metaphor. These are the sailors who make years-long commitments, joining the same teams at the same stadium (sailboat) every season, and who are well-rehearsed and collectively set upon winning the annual tournament (this race). There are small school and large school and Big Ten, Big East, and Ivy League collegiates, usually seen in the size and expense of the program. Collegiate boats are branded and built to attract fan power, and they do. Shore-side, family, friends, and retired teammates track their progress like fans. Collegiate teammates forever identify with the team mascot and the teams take on personas as enduring as the Hoosiers, Aggies, or Badgers.

There are the "retreads." These appear to be tired old boats, scuffed and chalky, skippered by mostly scuffed and chalky sailors. These are the boats that return year after year even though their dated designs and older sails make for long, often slow and labored racing. They might finish well in the competition with the perfect weather conditions, but climate statistics and patterns almost never play in their favor. Retread sailors must be in it for the time together, since the time will inevitably be long. They pack ample food. They bring extra clothes. They seem to be doing the same thing each year, only comparatively slower with time. However, one finds a kind of churning usefulness in this group, new tread each year, so to speak. Notably, aboard the retreads are many if not most of the newly invited: friends, neighbors, nieces, and grandkids whose lives are about to change forever.

This is not a circus, and these are not circus players. A deeper understanding of Mac race sailors requires a closer look at the experience that they share.

The start resembles Chicago Loop traffic, with dense congestion, jostling, horns, shouts, and lane-changes. Each sailor is alert to the positions of jockeying competitors fighting for an express lane. But, as the city skyline falls away, the fleet scatters and stretches out, and the shadows lengthen with the setting sun, the sailor's attention narrows. Awareness shifts from the noise of daily living and the energy of the armada to the mates who will share close quarters and a journey through the longest, darkest darkness in the United States.

This shift of focus toward the center comes clear, often, at the first dinner, regardless of conditions. The day has been spent in trains and cabs, on docks and decks, stringing lines and hauling bags of sails and boxes of food, planning assignments and practicing positions, balancing intense physical outbursts with breaks to breathe and to relish Chicago's extraordinary man-made and natural vistas in every direction. The warm bean casserole hits the gut and concentrates the sailor's attention. It stuns. From a warm belly, one feels a need to balance comfort and dampness, anticipation and fear, nourishment and a tinge of nausea, cold and hot, light and dark, and noise and silence. Flavors pop: a *haute cuisine* of grocery store green beans and dried boxed noodles. Any degree over room temperature is ideal. Everyone wants seconds. The burliest ingest thirds and fourths.

When the bowls are empty and the sun gone, watches begin. Familiar jobs are handed to others, sometimes with relief or even glee, sometimes with trepidation. If you are on the first watch, you signal trust to your crewmates to keep all safe. Invariably you find it impossible to decompress in your berth on the first night. You hear every sound, feel every bounce, and wait for your chance to sail again. If you stay on deck, you learn that the Lake Michigan night is nothing like you expected.

Old-timers will tell you that every night on this lake in this race is different from all others. I can only describe the ones I've seen; I can't guess at the ones that I haven't.

There is the "darkest night," when clouds and fog cover stars and the moon never shows, and when the wind can't coax a drop of luminescence from the water. There is no horizon. There are no neighbors, or, if there are, you can't see them. There are no sounds outside of the whistling in the rig and sails, the water gurgling as it jumps out of hull's way, and the watch crew murmuring. On these nights, the dim glow of instruments, candles, and compasses creates a sphere of visibility that collapses around the crew space as the night matures. Once every few minutes a sailor is compelled to shoot a flashlight toward the masthead just to break

NICHOLAS HAYES

the bubble of light and make sure the sails are still above. All sense of direction is lost, but the compass stays true so everyone strains to watch it. On the darkest nights the crew huddles and talks just enough to keep the boat at speed and on course. Long stretches of silence seem as important to moving forward as is the wind.

There is the "stormy night," when the noise grows until it deafens and the motion worsens until it punishes. The off-watch tends to split up, out of necessity. Since the cabin rocks and rolls and stinks of wet sails and urine, only a few can take it down below. The rest trade their chance at warm and dry to ride a bucking rail, facing cold continuous spray in between dousings from the breakers. The driver and trimmers swerve to avoid the biggest waves, protecting themselves and the boat from the force. The boat strains and pounds and complains loudly. Thoughts go to the design and construction of the keel-bolts and the mast-step and the other places that are bending and twisting. Trust the boat. Trust the people. Trust.

There is the "breathless night," when high pressure somewhere north of Chicago spreads lifelessness into the atmosphere over the lake. Sails go limp and boats slow to a stop and bob, as if the champion racehorse has left the gate at full gallop and come up lame in the first turn. Nobody is more disappointed than the jockey, but his job is now damage control. The difference, of course, is that, while the horse may be hobbled and out of the horse race, the wind might return anytime and the sailing crew is still in the sailboat race. These are the longest nights of all – maddening, worrying, and out of direct control. The team tames a persistent collective frustration, trying to remain focused as if the race might return to full health at any moment. Inevitably it does and the calmest and most patient and balanced crew will be in the best place when the night is over.

There is the "velvet night," the one where the wind is high and firm and the water is smooth and slippery. It takes rare weather to make velvet: just enough nearby isobars to force the wind from one side to the other side of the lake but not enough to force the surface of the lake into protest. On this night every change is perceptible. A slightly stronger puff, an inch of jib-trim, an ounce of pressure on the tiller, the new center of balance when someone off watch turns in a bunk below. Unlike the breathless night, when it's hard to feel anything and everyone whispers, the velvet night fine-tunes everyone's senses. Thus, the crew tends to chat non-stop about the boat, the competition, and the conditions. On a velvet night, the crew goes into tactical and technical high gear, trying new setups, trimmings, or balances to coax the most speed from breeze and boat. Rushes of feedback produce rushes of trial and error to achieve what some call "grooving," that precious time when everyone and everything are in balance.

There is the "brightest night," when the clouds move off with the rain and leave a massive silver moon, the Milky Way, and, for the luckiest, the aurora borealis, to light the way. On this night, every ripple on the surface of the water calls for one second of attention. The sounds of wind and water are crisp and clear, and the sailboat wants all the sail it can handle as it jets down a sparkling runway of moonlight. It wants to take off, and sometimes seems to do it, a few waves at a time. On nights like these, sailors tend to unzip their jackets, to open necks and chests to the crispness, no matter the cold. Small teams execute tacks and jibes with precision and vigor, as if fully and professionally crewed. On-watches often don't want to go off-watch. The arrival of morning goes unnoticed, and the sailors forget to celebrate the new day. They just keep sailing.

Morning brings light and with it finer focus to these people – this space, place, and time. This will be the day that starts and ends sailing; nothing else: no trains, cabs, skylines, or docks. It is the ultimate sailor's day; a rarity understood by everyone aboard as so special that they talk about how many days like it they've enjoyed and how few others will get to experience even one.

I've heard some call this day the "endless one." Depending on your route, it can start and end without a shoreline. Water slips by. Time both speeds up and slows down. As the clock turns, some nap, some eat, some chat, watches go on and off, but the sailing never stops.

Others call it "getting into the rhythm." Sails go up and down with the wind. Trimmers trim and drivers drive to the sensations of speed and power. Teams consider new information about the race and the boat and talk about new ideas and possibilities to make them better. Change is constant but subtle. Everyone is aware of it but nobody acts too quickly. Most eyes look forward, peering into the future, trying to make sense of what might happen.

It is as if everyone on board is in the throes of study at the same time and at the same speed and level of intensity. The core lessons are highly personal, even secret, flavored by nuanced individual perspective, held in the mouth, swirled by the tongue, and swallowed slowly, to ensure that they can be recalled later as something truly grand. Some learn about teamwork over time, a long-winded social experiment, so to speak. Some focus on the competition, trying to decipher what everyone on the boats nearby is thinking and planning. Others are absorbed in nature. A few see God.

For me, this is the "day of hope." Not hope for the race or the boat. Hope for everything. It is the day when I am reminded that I am not in control of anything except myself and that I don't own anything except my time.

It is a day of transcendence and transformation. Sailors will tell you that every person who starts this race will finish as someone new. Perhaps it might be more true to say that a real person appears for a few days. As with boats and races, so it is with sailors; there are recognizable types.

There is the "tweener," the offshore rookie with the smallest sailing vocabulary and the most naivety, but who finds his or her own way to fit in and add value as the race evolves. Tweeners might start slowly but surprise everyone with their contributions, like the eleven-year-old who offers an insightful adult comment at a serious dinner-table discussion. Tweeners are tweeners just once or twice. They provide the rest of the team with a sense of purpose, connection, and pride.

There is the "superhero," mild-mannered and subdued onshore but emerging as a massive force of positive physical and emotional energy on the boat. He exudes strength and optimism, handling sails and winching loads beyond what seems possible. You'll hear this one cheering for the next puff or wave or see him pumping and flexing at the sky. The superhero's suit doesn't come off until the race is over, and then he returns to drab. Superheroes remind the rest of the team that this is something far out of the ordinary.

There is the "teammate," who stays put, working one job non-stop without complaint. But it's more than just consistency, continuity, and dependability. The teammate knows what everyone else is doing, and she knows how her work helps or hinders the others. The teammate is keyed to the dance of the boat and its people and to the adjustments necessary to make it and them more graceful or more fluid or powerful. She selectively shares new ideas and supports them with a strong case, usually with perfect timing. The teammate makes everyone else successful.

There is the "yogi," who strips to shorts, spreads his chest, lengthens his neck and back, and inhales deeply on every puff, grabbing some of the excess energy spilling from the rig. Yogis don't just push and pull lines or sails. The Yogi feels the line and the sail mingling its forces into his own. Yogis can be among the most valuable crewmates, as they often notice subtle wind shifts or hidden favorable currents, long before anyone else. Yogis have the rest of the crew trying to figure out how they stay warm while nearly naked and what they see in the dark or hear in the silence. Perhaps mysticism matters.

There is the "minister," who sits furthest forward on the rail on the stormy night, taking waves for off-watch crewmates, or who clips-in to stand over a steamy stove boiling water for hot cocoa. The minister is calm and reflective while noting the glory in the wind and water even when the wind and water are punishing. The minister tends to all and points out the sublime, the scarcity of velvet, the end of the breathless night, or the rhythm of the endless day. The minister links the sailor to nature.

There is the "salt," whose expression is unchanged no matter the conditions or the situation. The salt has sailed enough to know every boat he is on. When something doesn't feel right, the salt scans the symptoms and knows just the right prescription. When something breaks, the salt knows exactly how to fix it. He has tricks nobody else knows and tools nobody else owns, but a way of speaking plainly, clearly, and slowly so that one day they might.

I have never been on a boat in this race with a "skipper." I'm sure there are some, but I've been lucky to avoid them. My sense is that modern leaders have come to know that leadership is a group concern so they stopped pretending to lead long ago and started actually doing it. It takes a serious group thing like this to challenge us with a workable moral imperative and find real collaboration. It is a matter of assembling skills and perspectives that can work in concert, even as the venue and the program change unpredictably. So, "skippering" in the traditional sense – that is, a director calling shots and the rest doing as directed – is a model that is becoming obsolete on this race. In its place is a flexible group that finds its own organic response and engages both with itself and within the place and time to match whatever nature throws.

Finishing fast in this sailing race means that leaders and teams and nature have come together, regardless of the sailboat that they share, for a couple of very intense days, constructing an experience that deserves its own name too.

There is the "four-in-one." This is the race that stops and starts, figuratively and literally. The first leg is a long open-water sprint to somewhere on the Michigan shoreline, where the weather changes and the second leg begins; the fleet starts a day-long battle to find pockets of shore breeze. A boat can easily win the first leg and lose the second. The third leg begins when the boats make a right-hand turn at a mid-lake light at Gray's Reef to sprint again down a narrowing channel that ends at the Mackinac Bridge. Either shore can be treacherous. A boat can win the first and the second legs and easily lose the third. The fourth leg seems like nothing, but it can be everything. It's the final handful of miles from the bridge to the finish line off the south shore of Mackinac Island. For whatever reason – geography, location, or time of day – this stretch often has its own weather. A boat can easily win the first, second, and third legs and lose the last. In this race, passenger trains can pass booster rockets and retreads can pass passenger trains in the last mile. Winners of a four-in-one often split on whether it was their doing or their destiny. Losers learn large, humbling lessons about work, reward, luck, and injustice.

There is the "crawl," the race that starts and ends slowly and seems to take a lifetime. Stubborn high pressure hangs over the length of the course, leaving boats with little more than a betting game. Will zephyrs of sea or shore breeze favor one place or another? Both advantage and equilibrium are made null by where one happens to be when a puff touches the water. Will nighttime be better near or away from shore? What will Sunday or Monday or Tuesday bring and where shall we try to be when they come? A Model T in a rut is not the same as a Model T on a paved road. This is the race that has crews talking in whispers, trimmers trimming in millimeters, and drivers driving to touch, for hours and hours and hours. Winners sigh, relieved, and welcome everyone else to the finish with a "job well done." Losers that finish win too.

There is the "breakup." This is the race that scares some away. It can start or finish like any other, but somewhere along the way the gods unleash a fury and sailors, at least for a short while, wonder what in hell made them do this. The breakup is so named because when it happens it batters and bruises, and everything and everyone seem scattered about and wide-eyed in its wake. It usually comes with warning, such as lightning and dark clouds on the horizon, but when it hits all the preplanning and organization are both out the window and vital at the same time. Squalls change everything about this experience. Booster rockets become coffins and passenger trains become refuges. Ministers, tweeners, superheroes, yogis, teammates, and even salts are forced to confront their own emotions, the emotions of the others on the boat, and, if they believe in God, His or Hers too. The end is usually understated and contemplative, no matter who wins.

There is the "surf." This is the race that everyone wants, and nobody wants to end. The south-by-southwest breeze is on and strong from the beginning and it never quits. The starting line is less about who gets there first and more about who gets there with their spinnaker drawing and the boat at full speed. After that, all horizons are a mass of color, sailors scanning and coveting the largest, most powerful sails. A stern wave sits just behind every boat, nudging northbound. This is the race where every boat (even the retread) is a thoroughbred and every sailor a jockey. Crews coax the most from every stride. You'll hear them cheering her like a friend asking for a bit more effort. You'll see them petting and slapping her topsides to make sure she's good for more. And then, when the finish line comes and goes and the sails come down, they thank her in unison with a hardy cheer for the ride of a lifetime, surf bums forever.

However the Race to Mackinac unfolds, it unfolds as it wants to and keeps the plot to itself until the very end. But the people are wholly intentional. Newcomers seem to know that, even if they have only one chance at this adventure, it will cement as a vivid and indelible memory. For others, it is a lifelong addiction. There are more than three hundred "old goats," veterans of at least twenty-five races each. A single race can shape an individual's identity. A lifetime of these events can define the identity of a family or many families.

The question is why? Why do these people do it and why does it matter? A classical philosopher might say that we are witnessing a modern hybrid combining a number of philosophic theories. My amateurish interpretation finds overtones of skepticism in the highly charged moments of the gale-force breakup, or in losing a four-in-one after winning the first three legs, or in the endless waiting of the breathless night; and it is hard to miss the themes of enlightenment in the yogi trimming, in the tweener speaking truth, in the design of the booster rocket, or in every glorious minute of the surf.

The deeper answer, I think, lies in the awareness shift itself, which is both obvious and subtle at the same time. Clearly, when one boards a small sailing boat with a few friends and family and heads onto open water, there will be times of deeper contemplation, stressful worry, wild exuberance, and intense dismay. Every sailor knows that the self is both put at ease and put at risk at the same time. In these times, we are becoming aware of something on the edges of our being that we can't see or feel on shore or in the glow of incandescent lights. We have slipped into a place just beyond our physical selves but not too far away; a place where our emotional selves meet the most real and primitive world.

We're pressed into intimate emotional and physical contact with strange and wonderful forces, both massive and minuscule, where we meet, at least for a few days, our relationship with time.

We might become aware of it gradually, first as the fleet spreads apart and then when we taste the first mouthful of bean salad. We might slam into it headfirst, when the night is darkest or stormy; or our ministers, our super-heroes, our yogis, or any other of our teammates might help us into it. It might take a while to get going on a breathless night. It might only take minutes on a velvet night. Almost without exception, it takes complete hold by the day of hope. By then, we have forgotten that we are not onshore. We don't care whose boat or what kind of boat it is, if we are on or off watch, or what we packed. Normal daily happenings don't happen and daily objects lose their purpose.

There is no waiting, because what will happen happens. There is no reminiscing, because what happened happened. There is only one thing.

Everything is now.

The Race to Mackinac usually starts on a Saturday and ends on a Tuesday. Some faster boats finish earlier. If it's a crawl, it might take longer; if it's a surf, shorter. Regardless of on which day the race ends, when it ends, there is wistfulness, a palatable sense of regret and finality that consumes the fleet and the island to which it is moored.

Awareness, perhaps drawn out by the ubiquitous electric lamp, is broadening and diluting again, distracted outward and to all things; the days ahead, the trip home or to the next place, the news of the world. Gear is loaded onto carts and into taxis and eventually into buses and planes. Boats are sent home with skeletal delivery crews. We pay for parking and fall in line with traffic.

Within a day, not more and usually less, everything is back to normal, but normal isn't normal anymore.

Where there is light, everything is tomorrow and yesterday. Having come from the darkest darkness, we long for now again.

CHAPTER 9

# SAILING, FLOW, AND FULFILLMENT

*We have all experienced times when, instead of being buffeted by anonymous forces, we do feel in control of our actions, masters of our own fate. On the rare occasions that it happens, we feel a sense of exhilaration, a deep sense of enjoyment that is long cherished and that becomes a landmark in memory for what life should be like. This is what we mean by* optimal experience. *It is what the sailor holding a tight course feels when the wind whips through her hair, when the boat lunges through the waves like a colt – sails, hull, wind, and sea humming a harmony that vibrates in the sailor's veins.*

Mihály Csíkszentmihályi[1]

Csíkszentmihályi's words are inspiring, and they remind us that the experience of sailing has many great qualities. In this essay I want to focus on one such quality inherent in that range of feelings we associate with an experience described as "flow." Csíkszentmihályi describes flow as a state that arises in people involved in some skilled activity who become fully immersed in it; they reach a state of "intrinsic motivation" and loss of self-awareness; their actions seem to occur spontaneously so

*Sailing – Philosophy for Everyone: Catching the Drift of Why We Sail*, First Edition.
Edited by Patrick Goold.
© 2012 John Wiley & Sons, Inc. Published 2012 by John Wiley & Sons, Inc.

that they seem to become simultaneously a passive witness to their own highly skilled agency. There are skilled movements and maneuvers in sailing in which the equipment becomes, as we say, "an extension of oneself." Under these conditions the sailor has usually reached such a level of proficiency that the state of flow just described may obtain. Moments of flow are relatively rare, and are highly prized by those who know what to look for. Losing oneself in the activity in this way is one of its high points, a point that makes it thereby significant and meaningful. Excellence in sailing confers a kind of fulfillment we rarely attain. It is, for this reason, an ideal worth striving for.

I am going to unpack these concepts – sailing, flow, and fulfillment – but with a twist, for I am going to use as my central case windsurfing. How does it fit with sailing, then? Well, windsurfers refer to what they do as sailing, and to themselves as sailors. Windsurfing shares with yachting features such as the derivation of energy from the relative movement of wind and water, a common vocabulary of sailing terms, some common equipment, and a healthy respect for the elements. Techniques such as the extreme hiking in some catamaran and dinghy sailing classes are reminiscent of what takes place when a windsurfer planes. For my purposes the differences between the windsurfer and the yachtsperson sailing a large sloop do not matter. For, the kind of philosophical exploration I have in mind here of the experience of windsurfing will shed light on an important value of *sailing* insofar as this activity requires skill and concentration and bodily movement that can lead to a state in which one loses oneself in its doing.

## The Key: Losing Oneself

I am standing atop Point Danger, a famous windsurfing site in Victoria, Australia. It consists of a narrow jut of land and reef extending through the breakers. If nature could have designed a windsurfer's playground, this place would be it, with flat water, waves, a bay on one side, and big ocean swells on the other. Its best asset is that on the leeward side of the reef smooth flat conditions prevail even in the biggest swells and the strongest winds, making for ease of entry through the breakers. The wind is cross-shore, twenty-five knots. I rig a 5.0 – in windsurfing this refers to a sail size equivalent to five square meters – and today I am using a 75 liter sailboard, relatively small, but the surf is running at about five feet, so small and light is best. Soon I am down to the water's edge, my heart rate is up, and the adrenalin primes me for what's to come. As I walk the board and rig through knee-deep water, the wind swiftly fills the sail and I quickly ease off my back hand to release the pressure; then I slowly bring it back in to ensure the center of effort of the sail is balanced against the tension in my arms. All is ready. I bring the sail in closer, place my back foot on the board, push off, and I am away. Within seconds the board and rig are at full speed. I hook my harness to the rig and instantly everything is effortless. I am leaning back, the board is planing at twenty knots, and I take aim at the first ramp – a small shoaling wave. Just before takeoff I bear away to ensure maximum lift and thrust, and abruptly I am airborne. The jump is long and high, and I land cleanly and smoothly before the next wave is upon me. I am perfectly powered and perfectly in control.

I am a windsurfer; windsurfing is part of my identity. Its value is, ironically, derived from the fact that, when I am immersed in the activity of sailing itself, I forget who I am, perhaps even that I am a windsurfer. For, especially at those moments of extreme concentration or (physical) effort, nothing but the experience itself is present to my mind. It is as if the memory cords linking me-now, carving across the face of a wave, to all else in the past, have been severed. My future self too seems cut off from the current experience – no room for thoughts about tomorrow's work day. And the focus of my current self on the complexities of the action at hand is total: nothing is left over for thoughts that go beyond it. Action and awareness have become unified, and during that period I forget who I am. For that period at least, I am thereby released from the stresses that come from the intrusion of self-conscious thoughts arising from the tedium of life or its worries.

The description above of sailing at Point Danger is not one of the phenomenology as it occurred then but rather of something salient now from memories of the event. My stream of consciousness at the time contained fewer words; it involved a loss of a sense of self as marked off against the action taking place in the scene described. From beach start to jump, and beyond, my conscious resources were pointed wholly toward the activity. As Csíkszentmihályi has put it,[2] in flow I am in a zone bounded by two alternative possible states: boredom and anxiety. When an activity has ceased to challenge me, I soon lose interest in it, but, when an activity pushes me beyond the limits of my capability, my apprehension disrupts my performance. When bored, my self becomes visible – what am I to do with my self? When anxious, my self, again, becomes

STEVE MATTHEWS

visible – how am I to overcome failure? In the state between these points in the cases of interest I become *in*visible.

## Windsurfing

The experience of flow is itself possible because of years of training. That training is aimed at achieving skilled action in which all the movements and adjustments made while sailing occur spontaneously, non-self-consciously, and without (mental) effort. In cases where the action involves a relation to a piece of substantial equipment, a special condition must obtain: the skilled action requires the equipment and the human person to act in unison. The skis become part of the skier, the racing car and the driver are fused, the violinist and her instrument play as one, and so on. When all is in flow, the windsurfer too does not mark points of distinction between sailor and gear. I am convinced that this point is vital to understanding flow in the case of windsurfing, or any sailing activity in which hiking requires straps, or trapeze, for leverage points to effect a better center of gravity. The more points on the sailor's body there are connected to the equipment, the more he becomes a part of the structure itself. This seems to enhance the sense of the merging of action and awareness.

In order to see how this works, it might be useful at this point to describe the windsurfer's equipment, or "kit," and provide a little more general background that relates it to sailing. Windsurfing is the modification of two kinds of watercraft: the rig of a dinghy and the board of wave surfing. The rig, when set up, comprises a monofilm and dacron-trimmed sail that is "downhauled" to produce a curved aerodynamic shape. When the sail fills, it creates an airfoil for extra power, speed, and stability. The sail is outhauled at the clew, which attaches to the end of a wishbone boom. The rig attaches to the sailboard on a universal joint, so that it then becomes a handheld single piece that moves in any direction. Boards vary in length, width, and volume as appropriate to the style of windsurfing and the conditions. There are now about seven recognized styles, but the fundamental distinction is between short boards and long boards. The former are typically used in wave or freestyle environments; the latter in flat water, for high-speed or slalom sailing.

Learning to windsurf takes skill, persistence, and a strong will to push through the disappointments. That is because it takes near circus-like skills to execute even some of the basic moves well. *The* basic move is something called the carve jibe: a downwind turn through 180 degrees that, when correctly performed in flat water, is a tack involving no loss of momentum or speed. Most windsurfers cannot perform this basic maneuver fully correctly. When it is performed correctly it is pure joy. I have completed thousands of jibes and the sensation that accompanies a (relatively rare!) perfectly executed one performed in high winds is as rewarding now as it ever was.

In the late 1970s, windsurfers began to move from sailing in predominantly flat water and lighter winds to waves and stronger conditions, and this presented a problem: how to stay connected to the board and rig without getting hurt or too tired. The solution: foot straps that unite the body with the board, and a harness that unites the body to the rig (via harness lines attached to the boom). These additions formed the sailor and kit into a more integrated unit. The kit became an extension of the sailor. When learning, one has the sense of riding on the board and controlling it; in straps and harness there is more a sense of simply riding on the water. Let's call this idea "integration." Integration implies three things in relation to performance, psychology, and a philosophical point about what has come to be called "embedded cognition."

## Performance, Psychology, and Embedded Cognition

First, with respect to performance, the straps and harness enable more control and stability, and more speed with control. The sailor is locked into, and so part of, the kit itself. Greater control is available because fewer mental resources are being devoted to staying attached to the kit. In addition, there is the mundane fact that sailing without a harness in strong winds is hard work and the pain of hanging on is a distraction. Csíkszentmihályi lists the steps essential to transform mere physical action from a mechanical process to one in which flow may obtain. Among these he cites the need to be able to concentrate and to make finer and finer distinctions with respect to the perfection of a skill, and that such skill development must be flexible enough to fit differing external conditions. In the present case, one needs equipment and techniques that eliminate "noise" – that is, those things irrelevant to achieving a performance ideal. Integration helps to eliminate noise, and with it in place one is much better located to achieve the final step

STEVE MATTHEWS

Csíkszentmihályi nominates: "to keep raising the stakes if the activity becomes boring"; or, in other words, to keep exploring new challenges as mastery of old ones is gained.[3]

Second, psychologically, the main effects of more closely merging the human body with the sailing gear are greater commitment and confidence. Commitment in this context is both metaphorical and mental. Although a windsurfer can exit the footstraps, or unhook from the harness quite readily, there is no guarantee of escape in all situations. Once hooked in, the windsurfer is then physically bound by those circumstances ("committed") to respond as one with the kit of which they are a part. Learning to sail in straps and harness is, needless to say, a testing and potentially dangerous time, and inevitably all novices at this point experience the dreaded catapult. This occurs when the off-balance sailor loses control of the powered-up sail *to which he or she is attached*, resulting in an often violent centrifugal action. Hence, there is a need for *mental* commitment. Once through these learning stages, however, when body and kit form a single unit, the result is less strain and pain and so more confidence to move up through skill levels.

The third point to follow from integration is one about cognition extending out beyond the mind traditionally conceived. The French philosopher René Descartes was a kind of early cognitive scientist interested in understanding the nature of the mind and its activities. Descartes famously concluded that minds were *essentially* different from the things in the physical world, but it did worry him that the distinction between mind and body was not straightforward. He wrote:

> Nature likewise teaches me by these sensations of pain, hunger, thirst, etc., that I am not only lodged in my body as a pilot in a vessel, but that I am besides so intimately conjoined, and as it were intermixed with it, that my mind and body compose a certain unity.[4]

There is sometimes an emphasis on keeping mind and body well distinct, but in the context of action this is unjustified even in the light of Descartes' own writings. Recent work in the philosophy of mind construes some mental aspects as neither purely in the head nor purely constituted by observable physical movements. Rather, the thesis of embodied cognition is that some mental processes are realized quite literally by involving parts of the body that extend beyond the brain and nervous system. An action, according to this view, is a cognitive act and the body is an essential element of that act.

There is, even more interestingly, a thesis in the philosophy of mind that takes this point further to regard elements of one's environment – such as tools, prostheses, or use-objects generally – as constituting an ineliminable aspect of one's cognitive activities. One version of this has come to be known as the "extended mind" thesis. In this view, a cognitive activity has to be thought of as embedded within a part of the environment that facilitates that activity. The idea, according to Clark and Chalmers, is this:

> The human organism is linked with an external entity in a two-way interaction, creating a *coupled system* that can be seen as a cognitive system in its own right. All the components in the system play an active causal role, and they jointly govern behavior in the same sort of way that cognition usually does. If we remove the external component the system's behavioral competence will drop, just as it would if we removed part of its brain. Our thesis is that this sort of coupled process counts equally well as a cognitive process, whether or not it is wholly in the head.[5]

And so we might import these last considerations into our current question: a windsurfer's kit and a human sailor form a coupled system. Let's just call it a windsurfer. When windsurfing, the first person pronoun "I" extends its reference to include this coupled system. This is part of a normal pattern of language use anyway. For example, after a collision while driving my car I might say, "I hit something on the road today." Similarly, after a day sailing, I might say, "I pulled off a perfect jibe today." The referent of "I" now has windsurfer parts, and that is how I think about it, that is how it feels, and that, with respect to technique, is the best way to conceive of performing all of the windsurfing maneuvers.

Dant and Wheaton have discussed what looks to be a form of the embedded thesis. It is worth comparing their account with what Clark and Chalmers say.

> Unlike, say, formula one racing where there are mechanical controls, the control of the sailboard is wholly achieved by fine-tuning the orientation of the body to the object. At speed, this ability to achieve control must become as if it was intuitive; it must happen without conscious thought so that the equipment becomes like a prosthetic extension of the sailor's body. The sailor must perceive and respond to the environment of wind and water through the equipment of board and sail. Touch and proprioception must work through the various bits of equipment rather than on them.[6]

## Windsurfing and Flow

I arrive at the site full of anticipation. A sea breeze is building, and already –
it's still only midday – there are small white flecks standing out against an
azure sea. At the peak of summer there are only ever a handful of days like
this. The wind is going to be strong and smooth. I rig a 5.4, knowing full
well it will need to be changed down; by four o'clock I'll be in 4.2 territory
since by then the wind will be blowing at over twenty-five knots. I'm rigged
up and at the water's edge. I don't hesitate. I ease the board into the water
and jump on. It's a perfect beach start, and within seconds I'm hooked in,
feet in the straps, and I'm planing. It doesn't take long before the troubles
at breakfast and the traffic snarl encountered on the way to the site are
forgotten; it's as if a lid has snapped shut on the past. Everything moves
into the present. I'm surprised by the strength of the wind and the acceleration reminds me of a fairground ride. I can afford a brief smile, but now
it's time to concentrate. As I emerge out of the chop, the first swells rise up
ahead of me and I have to focus for the first big jump of the day. The start
of the day's sailing is all-important to gauge the temperament of the
elements. I take off, and it's a big jump. Automatically I tuck my back foot
up under my torso and draw the sail down toward the board so that I am
now configured into the shape of an arrow. It's an exhilarating jump and
landing, perfectly executed. By now I am completely consumed by the
need to concentrate. As I continue through the activity, my sense of what
is taking place oscillates between feeling like an active participant and
feeling like a witness to an action taking place under my care.

Csíkszentmihályi has described the components of the phenomenology
of enjoyment gleaned from studies involving "thousands of individuals
from many different walks of life."[7] In simplified form, he says that optimal
experience is possible, conditional on there being a challenging and skilful
task viewed as achievable through an act of control and concentration
with clear goals and feedback. The involvement in the activity has a time-
altering quality, and leaves no room for worries about everyday life so that
concern for the self disappears, yet, he says "paradoxically the sense of self
emerges stronger after the flow experience is over."[8] This last point is a
crucial focus for this essay, and I shall address it in the final section.
I won't consider all of Csíkszentmihályi's components, but it will be
worth considering skill, concentration, goals, and feedback.

The intensity of a flow experience is partly a function of the skill level
required, built from years of effort, together with the merging of action

and awareness. It is a common observation for those in the midst of a highly skilled performance that as soon as one pays attention either to the *collection* of the technical elements of the action or, worse yet, to oneself performing those elements, failure is not far away. This is one reason why some musicians, for example, take beta blocker drugs to screen out the noise of self-consciousness. Flow requires two features that appear in tension: great skills about which one must avoid thinking in a direct way. The hint of paradox is dispelled once we recognize that the skills themselves are "built into" the agent who performs them, much as the complex behavior of a sophisticated machine, such as a jet airliner, is built into it during the design phase. Sometimes this is called muscle memory, but much more is at stake than that suggests. (After all, sleepwalking can occur because of muscle memory.) In flow, automatic action is accompanied by monitoring of the movements as they occur. The monitoring self during the period of flow is "checking" to make sure the action lives up to an ideal it recognizes. So long as the action being performed maintains the ideal – or something that reaches a threshold for it – the self in flow remains volitionally inert, but always ready to step in and make corrections if needed.

I am construing flow as applied to sailing as something essentially phenomenological, and this raises a question about what counts as a single flow-infused experience. One way into the question is to consider the role that one's goals play in deriving the goods that come from the flow experience. Csíkszentmihályi says that "the reason it is possible to achieve such complete involvement in a flow experience is that goals are usually clear, and feedback immediate."[9] He goes on to cite the examples of tennis and chess. Competition games such as these are heavily rule-governed and so goals are very clear. In non-competition windsurfing, and sailing generally, the lack of such rules means that the goals of the activity are subject to the creativity of the participant. Nevertheless, such goals are indeed present. It is useful in the non-competition cases to distinguish between synchronic and diachronic goals. Synchronic (or at-a-time) goals are those for which the end of the activity is perceived within the space of working memory, a period of time no longer than about thirty seconds. Thus, hurtling toward the shoreline, some fifty yards away, I form the intention to jibe at its edge. This now becomes the focus of all attention, and the jibe is duly executed. Diachronic goals (those involving an extended period of time) cannot, in all their specific detail, be fitted into working memory. Thus, my plan to windsurf in and around this particular site for the next few hours is nebulous. There can't

STEVE MATTHEWS

really be any particular piece of feedback from executing the plan that the goal has been reached. So, flow is not a quality that attaches to the diachronic case.

However, it is arguable that flow does not appear to obtain in the case I have described because a vague or nebulous plan can't thereby generate the feedback that would signify the reaching of the goal. However, Csíkszentmihályi discusses cases from solo ocean cruising in which a plan might extend for weeks. He writes:

> Jim Macbeth, who did a study of flow in ocean cruising, comments on the excitement a sailor feels when, after days of anxiously scanning the empty reaches of water, he discerns the outline of the island he had been aiming for ... [one legendary cruiser said,] "I ... experienced a sense of satisfaction coupled with some astonishment that my observations of the very distant sun from an unsteady platform and the use of some simple tables [had] enabled a small island to be found with certainty after an ocean crossing."[10]

What should we say here? Is this just a case of someone deriving a lot of satisfaction from a hard-won goal? Or is there real flow involved here? I think we should be reluctant to claim these as cases of flow. First of all, true flow experiences are relatively rare, but deriving satisfaction from a goal completed is relatively common. Second, the feedback one receives in flow must be directed back into the action with which one is involved, and that feature is absent here. Third, flow experiences involve skilled actions, but in these cases the agent is experiencing the end point of a set of skilled actions. Finally, flow involves the loss of self, yet in the case we just saw the self is present to the self: the ocean cruiser is engaged in some well-earned self-celebration. Now, this is not to underplay the value of self-recognition within the circumstances of a great accomplishment. But it is to underscore a distinction between the components of enjoyment on the one hand and the components of flow on the other.

## Sailing, Flow, and Fulfillment

In this final section I present some brief reflections on the connection between flow and its value. The claim is of course not that sailing is peculiarly enabling of flow. Any activity in which flow may obtain is potentially valuable. And the aim here is not to identify a set of causal factors linking flow with the values it brings. That is a job for psychologists. The task is to identify the conceptual links between flow as described in the context of sailing and some features of human happiness. To do this we need to return to the experience itself. What is it about the structure of agency within flow that makes it a valuable experience?

Csíkszentmihályi says:

> A typical day is full of anxiety and boredom. Flow experiences provide the flashes of intense living against this dull background ... [A] person in flow is completely focused. There is no space in consciousness for distracting thoughts, irrelevant feelings ... When a person's entire being is stretched in the full functioning of body and mind, whatever one does becomes worth doing for its own sake; living becomes its own justification.[11]

Though I would want to qualify this in many ways, it does convey an important insight about human fulfillment and action *as its own end*. Those who become habituated to passive activities – such as watching television, or more generally being a lifeless consumer of leisure – typically do so aiming at hedonic pleasures causally downstream from the activity. If pleasure is the ultimate aim, paradoxically it never really comes. If the mediating source is something as banal as watching television, it too is unlikely to deliver the goal.

Thus, the claim has to be that we derive value from an activity when the activity itself is its own end. Flow activities of course have this quality, and, though speculative, I would want to claim that the level of value at stake varies commensurate with the level of challenge and skill involved in the activity. The main point is that flow activities generate such value because they focus the agent away from herself and "into" the action itself (an embedded cognition), and they can do this with great intensity. Another way to describe the way our selves can become immersed in the action is in terms of *intrinsic motivation*. What does this mean? It needs to be understood in connection with the notion with which we began this essay: losing oneself in the activity.

Csíkszentmihályi quotes the words of a famous long-distance ocean sailor: "So one forgets oneself, one forgets everything, seeing only the play of the boat with the sea, the play of the sea around the boat, leaving aside everything not essential to that game."[12] In moments of flow like these, the motivational structure of the agent might be thought mysterious. Is the concept of an action performed by an agent who forgets herself even intelligible? I think it is. We need a conception of motivated action that is neither that which an animal performs (such as a stalking cat) nor that performed ordinarily by a person focused on what he himself is

STEVE MATTHEWS

doing (e.g., shaking a person's hand while being introduced), but somehow combines elements of both. David Velleman gives a characterization of the difficulty of what we are seeking to describe. He says:

> The more conscious we become of a motive, the more it becomes the object of our thought; and the more it becomes the object of our thought, the less we think from the perspective of its subject; and the less we think from the perspective of the motive's subject, the less engrossed we are in the activities that it motivates.[13]

In flow we are in a state of effortless action while simultaneously remaining completely engrossed in what we are doing. Because we are engrossed, we are not thinking *about* what we are doing, we are just doing it; we are, as they say, "in the zone," a bit like the stalking cat. Yet we seem simultaneously to be *watching* the action, and in flow this is different to becoming conscious either of ourselves or of our motives. Rather, we partially dissociate into a pleasant state of watchful readiness in which the disposition to correct ourselves isn't triggered. Flow states are pleasant partly just because we do not need to correct ourselves. The best sailing days involve great, often highly technical, accomplishments that are effortless.

Velleman also warns of the need to avoid becoming conscious of our motives. And this is a critical part of flow. To put it another way, the trick is to avoid becoming aware of what we are trying to do while we are doing it, since that is an extraneous thought that interferes with the doing. The right motivational structure, then, is a balancing act between the doing itself and an awareness of the doing that omits the reason for it.

In this essay I have applied the concept of flow to windsurfing (sailing). My motive has been to understand how it applies, and the sense in which flow-in-sailing may constitute something of intrinsic worth in a meaningful life. Because sailing at this micro level involves the close connection between sailor and gear, we see that flow is the result of both working as one. This integration idea is essential to the success of flow, because in correctly performed windsurfing maneuvers a single action occurs and is carried out in one seamless "arc," not in two separated movements. I suspect also that integration partly explains the loss of self-awareness that accompanies flow and is integral to what is valuable about that state. In this connection it is worth recalling the concept of embedded cognition – in "prosthetically" enhanced skilled action we lose ourselves into the world, to speak loosely. This has a beautiful, uncanny feeling.

I have characterized the value of flow-in-sailing in terms of the experience itself, as an activity involving intrinsic motivation. The key to this idea is that the activity constitutes its own end, and so the value is always within reach, unlike the many meaningless actions we must perform as mere stepping stones to something else (filling in some tedious form, for example). In flow we are in that valuable state of realizing an ideal we have strived for, while at the same time acting out movements that constitute that very ideal. When contemplating the things that make for a fulfilling life, a sailor may count states of flow among those that significantly contribute to it.

## NOTES

1  Mihály Csíkszentmihályi, *Flow: The Psychology of Optimal Experience* (New York: Harper Collins, 1990), p. 3.
2  Csíkszentmihályi, *Flow*, p. 74.
3  Ibid., p. 97.
4  René Descartes, "Meditation VI." In John Cottingham (Ed. and trans.), *Meditations on First Philosophy: With Selections from the Objections and Replies* (Cambridge: Cambridge University Press, 1996), p. 13.
5  Andy Clark and David Chalmers, "The extended mind," *Analysis* 58:1 (1998), p. 13.
6  Tim Dant and Belinda Wheaton, "Sailing a board: An extreme form of material and embodied interaction?" *Anthropology Today* 23:6 (2007), p. 10.
7  Csíkszentmihályi, *Flow*, p. 4.
8  Ibid., p. 49.
9  Ibid., p. 54.
10  Ibid., p. 55.
11  Mihály Csíkszentmihályi, *Finding Flow: The Psychology of Engagement with Everyday Life* (New York: Basic Books, 1997), pp. 30–32.
12  Csíkszentmihályi, *Flow*, p. 63.
13  David Velleman, "The way of the wanton." In Kim Atkins and Catriona Mackenzie (Eds.), *Practical Identity and Narrative Agency* (New York: Routledge, 2008), p. 180.

JESÚS ILUNDÁIN-AGURRUZA, LUÍSA GAGLIARDINI
GRAÇA, AND JOSÉ ÁNGEL JÁUREGUI-OLAIZ

CHAPTER 10

# ON THE CREST OF THE WAVE

The Sublime, Tempestuous, Graceful, and Existential
Facets of Sailing

## Ahoy!

There is an old French proverb, "he who would go
to sea for pleasure would go to hell for a pastime."
Proverbs let on more than the popular "wisdom"
with which they are often credited. They serve as
heuristic shortcuts to more or less successful
common-sense solutions. They also reveal the
communal psyche of a people and their culture. In
Japan, where the *katana* was the samurai's soul,
the sword terminology and maxims dominate Japanese expressions. In
seafaring nations such as England, Portugal, or Spain, nautical idioms
command the helm. So, while the Japanese speak of the final and decisive
stage of an endeavor as *tsuba-zeriai* (from a phrase meaning a dogged
fight to the end where sword guards – *tsubas* – hook), we say that things
come to the bitter end. We needn't get overly dramatic. We're still moored!

So, let the French saying unfurl for a bit, and allow its implications
to luff in your mind. What does it say about us sailing-obsessed people?
It intimates a certain lunacy, and, indeed, heading out to sea does

*Sailing – Philosophy for Everyone: Catching the Drift of Why We Sail*, First Edition.
Edited by Patrick Goold.
© 2012 John Wiley & Sons, Inc. Published 2012 by John Wiley & Sons, Inc.

require an inclination for the intrepid. It also speaks of women and men of a particular mettle: persons who enjoy themselves when others are taken aback. Additionally, it suggests that whoever coined the saying forswore sailing due to a nasty bout of seasickness (many of us sailors have paid culinary tribute to Neptune at one wave or another, but by and large this is forgotten with the promise of another thrilling close-hauled run).

What's in the offing? Well, we've charted a four-leg course for our essay that explores the rich aesthetic waters of a life on sails, specifically its sublime, tempestuous, graceful, and existential facets. All come aboard!

## The Sublime Poetry of Sail and Wind

Some describe sailing as endless tedium punctuated by moments of sheer panic. Anyone who's sailed enough has lived through both. The middle ground offers a better understanding of the experience, as usually happens in philosophy. Let's look for the center of effort on our conceptual canvas, then.

The natural settings where we may sail and the very emotions these arouse make the notion of "beauty" as inadequate as describing a majestic great white shark as a big sardine. The Greek mercenaries' reaction in *Anabasis*, as their leader Xenophon narrated it, gives a better idea. After fighting their way back home across the Persian desert, they broke into ecstatic cries of "The sea! The sea!" when beholding the azure Aegean Sea. Indeed, that first glimpse of the water after an arduous tribulation, whether through enemy-infested lands or a long week at the office, is a magical moment that takes the wind out of our lungs to put it behind the sails we long for. Once we find ourselves hands on tiller or wheel, we begin to weave the poetry in motion of sailing: a harmonious synergy of water, wind, sail, and hull that transports us to a realm where, as our mate Gagliardini puts it, "we encounter peace, silence, even the infinite." Of course, sailing one's rig in places like the Balearic Islands, the Aegean, or the Algarve Coast, as she has, goes a long way toward finding this kind of transcendence. In everyday life this is as likely as fair days in Cape Horn, but even the most modest of sailboats and the tiniest bay or lake can lead to memorable experiences. The exhilaration sailing can bring has diaphanous mystical overtones. As Ellen MacArthur wrote in her Vendeé Globe log,

This morning as the sun rose the sky went pink in the west, and ... the striking orange glow looked like it hid a million treasures as it peeked out from behind the scattered clouds ... suspended almost as if pre-arranged in the sky ... There were layers and layers of them ... It really is so beautiful ... as I stood in the cockpit I watched *in wonder* ... My eyes began to fill with tears as I marveled at this intense beauty.[1]

Philosophy begins in wonder. And, it's no wonder that poets have lauded the sea's beauty. But, as Joshua Slocum, the first solo circumnavigator (who cried under similar circumstances) makes clear, "Poets have sung of beacon-light and pharos, but did ever poet behold a great light flash up before his path on a dark night in the midst of a choral sea? If so he knew the meaning of his song."[2] We should write of what we know, and sailing enables us to experience some of nature's most amazing facets.

To increase the intensity, we need only point our prow toward the sublime. "It's just awesome!" we gasp – words futilely try to express sailing's wondrous ineffability. The shortest tack is to describe this as *awe*, an emotion that mixes admiration, respect, and intimidation. Even Slocum, a prosaically witty writer, cannot help but wax poetic: "During these days a feeling of awe crept over me ... The ominous, the insignificant, the great, the small, the wonderful, the commonplace – all appeared before my mental vision in magical succession."[3] Of course, sailing can be quite trying: sweltering heat, ice-numbing water, or the bone-jarring battering by waves; however, this is *precisely* what – after the fact – enhances the sublimity of the experience.

Watch for flying jibs and anticipate stinging spray as we stay the course into the sublime! We simplify to a two-reefed Marconi, the illuminating, if complex, rigging that a famous landlubber, Immanuel Kant– overly cautious as ever – deployed to analyze the sublime. These reefs fasten the ideas of transcending boundaries and courting risks. First, there are unassailable restrictions: hulls have maximum attainable speeds; our capacity to imagine is limited. We're awash with the feeling that we can't fathom the sheer size of something like the ocean's immensity. Magellan, his second-in-command Elcano, and their mates surely felt this on encountering the vastness of the misleadingly named Pacific Ocean. Ellen MacArthur expresses the mood well: "all movement, sounds, and thoughts seemed very small against the magnitude of the ocean."[4] Second, the pursuit of danger is another aspect of and way to elicit the sublime – but, unlike a penguin's casual stroll amid hungry polar bears, it should not be foolhardy. After all, reckless sailors are sunken sailors, eventually. The sublime plays with danger amid natural phenomena that have an absolute power over us. Here's our motto for an intellectually badass tattoo: "sublimity, the ultimate playground!"

Structurally, the sublime isn't unlike the two opposing forces of wind on the sail and water on the keel, which push the boat forward as we seek the point of balance. In the case of the sublime, there is a disturbing feeling, elicited either by the realization of the limits of our ability to imagine or sense the greatness of forces that overpower us, or the fear of these forces actually acting upon us. But this is matched by a pleasant emotion: the delight we experience upon realizing that we are equipped to handle these feelings through our skills and reason. One of us, Ilundáin, remembers the roaring excitement of sailing in twenty knots of wind with gusts to thirty, water flirting with the cockpit, and having to stand on the hull's port topside to avoid capsizing. The sublime rides on the point of balance between wave and hull, as emotions drift between the fear that risk arouses and the joy in our skill in meeting the challenge. It's a dynamic, paradoxical process in which harmony results from the power struggle between (our) intelligently harnessed skills and (natural) might – our insignificant "bit o' wood" frolicking in the enormous sea. And the result is exhilarating. Good ol' Slocum again recounts: "These rolling waves thrilled me as they tossed my ship, passing quickly under her keel. This was grand sailing."[5] But, when the forces break the point of balance and go to one extreme or the other, the result is either boredom, that accursed lack of wind, or sheer panic. Out of control and at the mercy of fate, one's skills are irrelevant to cope with either scenario.

Sailing can be beautiful. Better yet, it can be awe-full. Awe is an emotion best reserved for moments of worship. Our sailboat is our altar and the ocean our church. On a boat, we worship best by cultivating our skills and being humbly aware of our limits and the forces we face, else we may have to pray to the sea gods. But we're fast gliding down to our next leg. Brace yourselves. We're about to face…

## Poseidon's Wrath

Amid a nasty storm, Pompeo Magno harangued his sailors: *Navigare necesse est, vivere non est necesse* ("To navigate is necessary, to live is not necessary"). Bringing supplies from Africa to their beloved Rome was essential, even at the risk of their lives. But, to understand those sailors who undertake similar or worse risks not for Rome, glory, riches, or the promise of a warm embrace but the fun of it, we had better interpret the above as "a life without sailing is not (much of) a life." Explaining this "cares to the wind" attitude means cruising far offshore. With gale winds forecast, we recommend life vests for the next few paragraphs. Batten down the hatches!

Luckily our skipper, John Dewey, is an accomplished seaman and philosopher. His notion of an experience anchors sailing's revealing and transformative potential to imbue meaningful, life-enriching insights not only when enjoying the harmony of beauty or sublimity but when the lifeline stanchions live up to their name and sailing becomes utterly terrifying.

Amid the innumerable waves – moments – in our lives, some stand out like mountainous rogue waves. Dewey explains: "Experience in this vital sense is defined by those situations and episodes that we spontaneously refer to as being 'real experiences'; those things of which we say in recalling them, 'that *was* an experience.'"[6] This could be as dramatic as a blown gasket that almost sinks you as the hull fills with water, as José Luis Ugarte recounts about his experiences sailing in the Antarctic,[7] or something banal yet epiphany-worthy such as *that* first Optimist sail that inoculated us with the incurable sailing virus.

Any sailor worth his sextant knows that idyllic waters can turn into a nightmare at Poseidon's whim. As the lips of the waves kiss the gunwale, tongue and all, it doesn't take much to turn this sensual awesomeness into well-justified fear. As Dewey says,

> Then, there is that storm one went through in crossing the Atlantic – a storm that seemed in its fury, as it was experienced, to sum up in itself all that a storm can be, complete in itself, standing out because marked out from what went before and what came after.[8]

This could well have been a description of the tempest Ilundáin's maternal grandmother faced as a little girl ship-bound for Cuba. Even the captain was on his knees praying, as it was pointless to attempt to command the helm. And, being aware that between you and the sea there is but a thin bit of hull is small comfort. Insightfully, skipper Dewey argues that this type of complete and mature experience also has "an element of suffering, in its large sense" because "otherwise there would be no taking in of what preceded."[9] MacArthur evokes this when she describes the sickening feeling of barely missing an iceberg, compounded

FIGURE 10.1    The *Snowgoose* in happier times, before its stormy voyage. Author's copyright.

by the terrifying idea of hitting a boat-sinking ice chunk while surfing down waves at over twenty knots in the southern seas.[10] But, as with the sublime, this enriches both the experience and our lives: we can feel *both* terror and exhilaration.

Aboard his sloop *Snowgoose* (see Figure 10.1), another of us, Jáuregui, found out that the might of a pissed-off sea is nothing to trifle with. The plan was to sail from south of Barcelona to Alicante. In marked disagreement with the forecast, a gale sprung up at night. Murphy was certainly a stowaway: the electronic systems, lights, automatic pilot, *everything* failed (it never rains but it pours). Jáuregui's ill-chosen crewmate was below decks in a drunken stupor (besides the importance of redundancy, Jáuregui learned to better vet enrollees). So, Jáuregui spent the night shining a flashlight on the sails to alert passing merchants of their presence (they were in one of the busiest Mediterranean shipping corridors). Chilled to the bone, desperately trying to control rudder and storm jib, just ahead he saw … well, you'll have to wait to find out (we'll return to this adventure in a bit). But let's say right here that they made it (else there'd be no tale to tell). After reaching port in a sorry shape and kissing the ground à-la-Pope, the welcome was less than comforting: Jáuregui's wife, who didn't yet know of their troubles, snapped, "You guys stink!"

What's the payout of being between the devil and the deep blue sea, other than the stink of fear? For Dewey, an aesthetic experience is *enriching* and not a mere happening. It marks a before and an after. The windfall for us results from how we reflect on our (mis)adventures. An experience is like a Socratic spyglass that gives us a privileged insight into ourselves. Revealingly, the first question that Vendeé Globe veteran and team member of MacArthur's *Kingfisher* project Alain Gautier asked her after she finished second was what she had learned about herself and how she had changed during the regatta.[11] Her discerning reflections are worth many years of armchair pondering. Our tribulations, which test our mettle, can be deep *and* wide sources of self-knowledge and invaluable opportunities to cultivate our character, once we have identified and learned to handle our talents and limitations. And this goes as much post-traverse as before leaving the dock: when Slocum set out he "felt that there could be no turning back, and that [he was] engaging in an adventure the meaning of which [he] thoroughly understood."[12] We need to know *why*.

Being an outdoors activity, hazardous surprises are unavoidable in sailing. Sailors' lives are enhanced precisely because they are willing to face risks in their quest to refine skills that expand the richness of their experiences, be they fun, beautiful, sublime, or scary. These challenges are an intrinsic part of sailing. How they are met reveals much of who we are. "Where, after all, would be the poetry of the sea were there no wild waves?"[13]

## She Moves

Ilundáin's professional deformation as an aesthetician means that he spends countless hours looking at (and lusting after) boats (or anything that floats, actually), whether on docks (the object of many a pilgrimage) or boat magazines (more titillating than any racy centerfold). Although he can justify this as part of his job, he prefers to rationalize it to his wife thus: "If I'm going to lust ... much better if she is a sailboat!"

The union of form and function in a sailboat, which combines to be more than the sum of its parts, is unrivaled among human creations. The contours, perfectly streamlined; the materials, strong and light; the design, simplicity itself, nothing superfluous; and the striking elegance of the boat in motion. Alexander Rost makes the case for this superlative blend:

The necessity for beauty, born from purpose, did not come to the sea by accident. Nature itself had proclaimed it. Wind and waves, and friction and lateral resistance, to mention the technical aspects, were the inescapable factors ... the old philosopher's maxim that nature does not progress in and thus does not tolerate deviations from her logic, was and still is the most important law in the building of yachts.[14]

The feather is the counterpart in the animal kingdom: both are perfectly suited to their task, can offer the visual virtuosity of artworks, and, unsurprisingly, also take advantage of the wind. Literary great Joseph Conrad corroborates this regarding sailboats: "They are the birds of the sea, whose swimming is like flying, and resemble more a natural function than the handling of man-invented appliances."[15] Moreover, in these days of environmental urgency, the very premise of sailboats – motion by means of wind – is more pertinent, even indispensable, than ever. Small surprise, Slocum describes the *Aquidneck*, a boat he once owned, as "a little bark which of all man's handiwork seemed to me nearest to perfection of beauty."[16]

For all its visual appeal, where the sailboat truly stands out is in action. Then *she moves*! And, she enables us to *live* truly unique kinesthetic and existential moments. Here we take aesthetics beyond the wharf of convention.

Consider what sailing feels like: the wind on your face, your tiller or wheel transmitting the pressure of the wind from the sail, the rudder pushing back, the water's lapping noise, your moist (or soaked!) skin, the sea's fragrance. But this physical aspect of sailing belies the fact that sailing experiences, in all their variety, rival religious ones (to echo William James' abundant work on the latter), having as they do just as much awe and a lot less animosity. As Dave Franzell writes, "each type of boat creates its own sailing experience."[17] Indeed, the material conditions – the size, shape, actual materials used – of the boat make possible the "what-it-is-like-to-sail" *that* kind of boat. Cutters, yawls, sloops, ketches, schooners; one mast, two, or more; centerboard or keel; clinker or carvel construction; wood, aluminum, or composite; single-handed or crewed; designed for long offshore hauls, speed, regattas, or casual and coastal cruising – each of these and combinations thereof act like distinct deck light-prisms that kaleidoscopically particularize our experiences.

We could say that a sailor is to his or her sailboat as a snail is to its shell, but the image is hardly inspiring. Let us instead fly a spinnaker and catch more inspiration and depth, and say that there is a symbiosis between body and boat: "The sailor becomes one with his vessel, just as the rider becomes one with his horse."[18] Reading Chichester, Tabarly, Knox-Johnston, Slocum, or MacArthur makes this patent, but Joseph Conrad articulates it best:

> The genuine masters of their craft – I say this confidently from my experience of ships – have thought of nothing but of doing their very best by the vessel under their charge. To forget one's self, to surrender all personal feeling in the service of that fine art, is the only way for a seaman to the faithful discharge of his trust.[19]

This Zen-like focus and dedication to one's charge is no mere attachment: it is held tightly by the capstan that cultivates our skills.

Sailing can be intimidating to newcomers, but for most getting started is easy. "Let's be honest, shall we?" writes Don Casey in the foreword to *Things I Wish I'd Known Before I Started Sailing*,

> Basic sailing requires about as much skill as, say, riding a bicycle. Borrow or rent a small boat and in a hilarious half hour of pulling strings and pushing on that stick thing, you will become skillful enough to be able to sail back to the dock with almost no risk of injury or serious property damage.[20]

However, for some it is not as easy to master "the stick thing" as it is to ride a bike. Just ask Ilundáin's college sailing partner, his brother Jaime. His impressive capsizing record had the head instructor appoint him to the permanent role of ballast.

The challenge lies in getting better at it. There is an ethos that seeks to cultivate excellence and combines sailing's aesthetics and ethics into a *performance*: it's about being the best sailor we can be. MacArthur exhibits the requisite attitude: "I am very much in love with the sport, and I desperately want to be better at it."[21] Improving requires making of it a passion in the full sense: no effort spared, the goal is the continued refinement of abilities while lucidly aware that port is never reached. A most arcane skill is "reading" the invisible wind. *The Princess Bride's* Inigo Montoya asks, when noticing they're quickly being overtaken, "I wonder if he's using the same wind we are using." The wind-games played in regattas are nothing short of wizardry.

Besides boat-handling abilities, navigational skills are crucial once we venture beyond spitting distance from shore. The potential for things to go wrong, as we saw with Jáuregui, is great. Back to his plight! Begging for safe harbor, he saw … the saving red light of what *had* to be, by his calculations, Vinaroz Harbor. Repeatedly radioing the harbormaster – "Vinaroz Harbor, this is *Snowgoose*, do you copy?" – he set a course toward the light. Other than the red beacon light, he could see about as much as a deaf bat. Aware of the rocky bottom, he sounded for depth – twenty feet, fifteen, twelve … way too shallow for comfort. Suddenly, a lucky break in the clouds showed him a cliff towering above him. He realized, frantically pulling all to port, that it was no lighthouse after all … it was the red light of a bordello!

Way back in 1898, Slocum belittled our reliance on technology: "In our newfangled notions of navigation it is supposed that a mariner cannot find his way without [a sea chronometer]."[22] Those were other times. In today's GPS world, knowing how to work the parallel rules and compass rose is one of those underappreciated skills. Until we need them, of course. After all, in life and on water, points of reference and signs are most ambiguous.

## One is Free … on a Boat?

Ready about? Hard a' lee! As we head back to port, we run a leg in which the currents of aesthetics and the existential fuse.

"For the first time in my life I felt totally free."[23] Ellen MacArthur reflects a view endorsed by many: sailing is a vehicle to freedom. But our aspirations of liberty seem to be firmly tied to the cleat of circumstance (and without much pomp). Let's board the play *Rosencrantz and Guildenstern are Dead*, where the pirate flag of fate flies. Sidekick Rosencrantz remarks of the bilge into which he plummets, "Nice bit of planking, that." Chum Guildenstern adds,

> Yes, I am very fond of boats myself. I like the way they're – contained. You don't have to worry about which way you go, or whether you go at all – the question doesn't arise, because you are on a *boat*, aren't you? … I think I'll spend most of my life on boats.

Upon further consideration, he clarifies: "One is free on a boat. For a time. Relatively." Rosencrantz asks, "What's it like?" and Guildenstern replies tersely, "Rough."[24]

Ballast heavy words! Indeed, life is like a boat. One may be ⌐
free. As Guildenstern realizes, we are "free to move, speak, extempo⌐
and yet. We have not been cut loose. Our truancy is defined by one fixed
star, and our drift represents merely a slight change of angle to it."[25] Can
we direct that drift? If you can tie a bowline knot, chances are you've
sailed long enough to realize that onshore and offshore we face imper-
sonal forces that don't give a bosun's whistle what our plans are. Our idea
of free will is fouled – tangled – at both ends of the rope. Our physiology
and psychology entangle the "inside" subjective end with neurological
processes that are tied to objective causal chains and the below-decks –
that is, unconscious – origin of many thought processes and seemingly
spontaneous actions. There isn't room to freely swing a cat here.
Circumstances (social, political, environmental) knot the "outside" end.
Their dynamics, from when and where we are born to complex societal
and natural elements, escape our control in much the same way that we
cannot command winds or currents. We're running with three sheets to
the wind – out of control. This threatens to capsize meaning.

Instead of a mutiny of denial, we propose as a jury-rig to – paradoxically yet sensibly – work with(in) these restrictions. Partially, the bind
results from rigging this as a matter of mutually exclusive extremes:
either free will or determinism, the will is either the lazy guy on this tack
or a working sheet carrying the whole load. Oftentimes we are at the
mercy of the elements: our life's circumstances, inclinations, and talents.
But, sometimes, we can learn how to gain control. This begins by accepting the said limitations and situation and the direction of the wind, then
learning to adjust and work with them. Actually, we need *some* resistance,
for a complete absence of restrictions – pure chance – also throws us
overboard into determinism's unforgiving waters. Thus, while sailing
directly upwind is impossible, we can beat to *any* point should we be
skilled enough. We're not unfettered, but becoming apprised to this gives
us the opportunity to gain a measure of freedom. For a time. Relatively.
As the old saying has it: "You cannot change the direction of the wind,
but you can adjust your sails."

But there's a devil to pay even for this relative freedom. Our ability to
choose is but a capacity to earn and learn, not an inalienable right to a wide
berth of choices. We become free to the extent that we cultivate our talents.
Accordingly, there are better sailors and freer people (than others). The
weatherly (nice) side to this lies in the creative freedom of beautiful performances, which sailing strikingly exemplifies. Coming full circle to run
downwind, the aforementioned sailing skills that enable us to experience

beauty, the sublime, and even the terrifying become relevant again. The discipline and rigor needed to develop our abilities allow us to sail in more challenging conditions *and* to perform beautifully. The economy of movement and the elegance of accomplished sailors' movements are honed by the constraints of training. Here the ethos of discipline and aesthetics blend into a liberating performance in the wake of which we divine the traces of restrained autonomy. Freedom by way of constraint, if you will. By cultivating ways to actually *control* our impulses, movements, and thoughts, we gain a measure to beautifully navigate the "choice" of, and how to get to, our destination.

To dock now, a few words to the wind and the wise. Sailing's crow's nest affords a distinctive, advantageous philosophic perspective on life. Perched on it, we discern and make use of sailing's transformative potential while pointing out the flotsam and jetsam of the mundane. We can spot what's important for a joyful life should our temperament lean toward the naval *and* avoid the gunk threatening to mar our hull. Compared to a safe, lackluster *dry* life, for many sailing is much more than a sport, vehicle, or métier: it is one of the most beautiful, daring, jubilant ways to literally and philosophically sail our existence's familiar *and* uncharted possibilities. Maybe *navigare necesse est* after all.

Godspeed!

## NOTES

1   Ellen MacArthur, *Taking on the World: A Sailor's Extraordinary Solo Race Around the Globe* (New York: McGraw-Hill, 2005), p. 296; emphasis added.
2   Joshua Slocum, *Sailing Alone Around the World* (New York: Dover Publications, 1956), p. 192.
3   Ibid., p. 26.
4   MacArthur, *Taking on the World*, p. 131.
5   Slocum, *Sailing Alone Around the World*, p. 55.
6   John Dewey, *Art as Experience* (New York: Perigee Books, 1980), p. 36.
7   José Luis Ugarte, *El último desafío: La más dura regata de altura, narrada por el único participante español* (Barcelona: Editorial Juventud, 1997), pp. 67–76.
8   Dewey, *Art as Experience*, p. 36.
9   Ibid., p. 41.
10  MacArthur, *Taking on the World: A Sailor's Extraordinary Solo Race Around the Globe*, p. 299.

11  Ibid., p. 20.

12  Slocum, *Sailing Alone Around the World*, p. 11.

13  Ibid., p. 192.

14  Frank Grube and Gerhard Richter (Eds.), *The Big Book of Sailing: The Sailors, the Ships and the Sea* (Hauppauge, NY: Barron's Educational Series, 1978), p. 41.

15  Ibid., p. 10.

16  Slocum, *Sailing Alone Around the World*, p. 3.

17  David Franzel, *Sailing: The Basics* (Guilford, CT: The Lyons Press, 2003), p. 1.

18  Grube and Richter, *The Big Book of Sailing*, p. 6.

19  Ibid., 10.

20  John Vigor, *Things I Wish I'd Known Before I Started Sailing* (Dobbs Ferry, NY: Sheridan House, 2005), p. xiii.

21  MacArthur, *Taking on the World*, p. 319.

22  Slocum, *Sailing Alone Around the World*, p. 15.

23  MacArthur, *Taking on the World*, p. 14.

24  Tom Stoppard, *Rosencrantz and Guildenstern Are Dead* (New York: Grove Press, 1967), pp. 100–101.

25  Ibid., p. 101.

CHAPTER 11

# NAVIGATING WHAT IS VALUABLE AND STEERING A COURSE IN PURSUIT OF HAPPINESS

There are a number of different senses of "value," or of what is worthwhile. Some things are valuable in a practical sense. Given a desire not to run aground, one should steer clear of that shoal. Some things are valuable in a moral sense. One has a moral obligation not to pollute the environment. Some things are more aesthetically valuable than others. A ketch is more attractive than a tug boat. In this essay, we explore the nature of value and how one ought to live one's life through the lens of sailing. After discussing the concept of value and various things that are valuable about sailing and sailboats, we consider what Aristotle had to say about the pursuit of happiness and what it is to flourish. We argue that sailing has all the necessary elements for achieving a fully happy life.

The concept of value is hard to pin down. It's not easy to say exactly what it is to be valuable or to be good. If precise definitions are hard to come by, perhaps we should proceed by thinking about clear examples of valuable things. Just as one can know a boat when one sees one despite being unable to provide a satisfactory definition of "boat," one can tell

*Sailing – Philosophy for Everyone: Catching the Drift of Why We Sail*, First Edition.
Edited by Patrick Goold.
© 2012 John Wiley & Sons, Inc. Published 2012 by John Wiley & Sons, Inc.

what sorts of things are valuable or ought to be pursued even if one can't quite say what "value" is exactly.

We began with such a list. Some things ought to be pursued because they are of practical value. Other things are good because they are beautiful or have aesthetic value. Some things are valuable largely in virtue of the worth that an individual or group puts on them. For example, a coin is just a disc of metal, but it is *worth* something – more than just the same amount of metal shaped into a sphere. And we value certain traits in people such as honesty, patience, kindness, generosity, humor, and intelligence.

Of course, we could go on for days listing things that are valuable. In thinking about the myriad valuable things, a distinction presents itself. Philosophers use the phrases "instrumentally valuable" and "intrinsically valuable." Instrumentally valuable things are valuable because of other values that they promote. Money is an instrument used to buy goods and services, so it has instrumental value in the sense that it is valuable in virtue of the other things that it enables us to obtain. Repainting a sailboat might be wise given the benefits of preserving the boat and enhancing its beauty. So repainting one's boat has instrumental value.

Teak used as a boat-building material is another example of something with instrumental value. It has instrumental value as a wood that resists the deleterious effects of weather and moisture. Teak decks are durable, non-slip surfaces that allow us to move more safely about a boat under adverse conditions, and teak handrails provide safety when we move about. But teak is also a beautiful wood when finished. Most sailors probably give some thought from time to time about whether or not to spend the time on their boats to create the often-admired brightwork that characterizes some sailboats. Of course, many sailors eschew teak handrails and trim for stainless because they see the latter as having more instrumental value. Stainless serves the same purposes, but doesn't require the work to maintain.

Lots of equipment on sailboats has instrumental value. And it's interesting to note that what is seen as having the most instrumental value has changed over time. Not long ago, paper charts, the compass, and perhaps the sextant were essential pieces of valuable equipment for navigating. These were things that were viewed as being quite useful tools. But that's not the case for many sailors today, despite frequent warnings about the consequences of going without them. These objects have been replaced by GPS. And how about autohelm? Clearly the wheel or tiller has instrumental value around the dock. So does a mooring ball. But an autohelm enables the single-handed sailor to work away from the helm or to hold a course when there are other priorities to attend to.

Most sailors probably place greater value on those pieces of equipment that relate more directly to the sailing performance of their boats. This includes everything that works on a boat, from the shape and size of its keel to its prop (is it folding?), its winches (how big are they and are they self-tailing, multi-speed winches?), and so on. It also includes the materials out of which the equipment is made. What fabrics are used in the sails? What is the fiber composition of the halyards and sheets? Of what are the spars made? Are the boat's materials older and heavier or newer and lighter?

While a sailboat and its hardware obviously have instrumental value, it is sailing itself that ultimately attracts people to the sport. With some reason, many sailors disdain power-boaters because of what they don't know. In their minds, after all, power-boaters only need to know how to operate a gearshift, throttle, and steering wheel. Sailors, on the other hand, have to compute wind and water conditions, the direction in which they want to go, the best possible combinations of sail and trim, the sailing characteristics of their particular boat, and myriad other factors to produce the best possible effect in terms of speed, safety, and comfort. Perhaps more than anything else, it is the knowledge required to produce the ideal sailing experience that has such instrumental value to the sailor. It is the harnessing of nature and the maximal use of available technology that is so valued. And, when one's boat enters that groove of which sailors speak, we know that we are close to that beautiful perfection – that marvelous *je ne sais quoi* – that is at the heart of sailing a boat. And this knowledge and these skills provide additional examples of things that are instrumentally valuable.

Perhaps paradoxically, the pleasure and value derived by many sailors actually increase under adverse conditions. Confronting challenging elements increases the need for good decisions. When made correctly, the instrumental value of the act increases. Mastering malfunctioning technology also increases the perceived rewards of sailing. Being self-sufficient, being able to jury-rig a piece of faulty equipment, being able to solve an operational problem all are satisfying to the sailor, are the stuff of sailing lore. They are an important part of sailing culture and are yet further examples of traits that are quite valuable.

So much for instrumental values; what about intrinsic values? These are said to be valuable "in and of themselves." This means that a thing that is intrinsically valuable is good in virtue of it being the very thing that it is and not simply because of the other valuable things it brings. In other words, it is valuable for its own sake. Some philosophers have argued that *pleasure* is an intrinsic value. When we ask why repainting a boat is good or why making sails out of a certain material is good, we appeal to the other valuable things that these bring. But, when we ask why pleasure is good, we don't appeal to other valuable things. Rather, pleasure is good for its own sake. It's good because of the very thing that it is! A philosopher named William Frankena (1908–1994) gave a rather extensive list of things that are intrinsically valuable:

> Life, consciousness, and activity; health and strength; pleasures and satisfactions of all or certain kinds; happiness, beatitude, contentment, etc.; truth ; knowledge and true opinion of various kinds, understanding, wisdom; beauty, harmony, proportion in objects contemplated; aesthetic experience; morally good dispositions or virtues; mutual affection, love, friendship, cooperation; just distribution of goods and evils; harmony and proportion in one's own life; power and experiences of achievement; self-expression; freedom; peace, security; adventure and novelty; good reputation, honor, esteem, etc.[1]

These things appear to be valuable in their own right. They aren't valuable simply because of other valuable things that they bring, but rather are valuable in and of themselves. Interestingly enough, when discussing examples of instrumental values above, some of these intrinsic values came up. The pleasure we get from seeing the teak of our boats shine in the sun, having the knowledge to jury-rig a piece of faulty equipment, and being able to successfully navigate through a tough spot are each examples of things that are valuable in and of themselves. They are good not just for other things but for their own sake too. There are thus plenty of examples of things that are *both* instrumentally and intrinsically valuable. And, as you can probably tell, we think there are an extraordinary number of valuable things having to do with sailing and sailboats.

## What's So Great About Sailing?

With the distinction between instrumental and intrinsic value in hand, let's look more closely at the sorts of things involving sailing and sailboats that are valuable. Of course, many sailors enjoy sailing for its aesthetic value. First, there is the water. We have all seen incredible photographs of the water in various places around the globe, and the magnificent colors it can be. Many of us have seen those colors first-hand. Their beauty at first light, mid-day, and sunset provide sailors with a limitless palette of colors and beauty. Many of us especially enjoy the way that the waves sparkle in the morning or evening, as they reflect the rays of a rising or setting sun. Add the colors of the sun and the terrain, and the aesthetic possibilities are virtually limitless. Clouds, too, are an endless source of aesthetic enjoyment. They come in all sorts of shapes, sizes, and hues, and they convey a multitude of subtle and powerful impressions and moods.

Whether beauty (aesthetic value) is objective or relative is an issue we'll here avoid. Although it's a fascinating question whether beauty is just "in the eye of the beholder," we can't hope to settle this issue in this chapter. It's clear that there is a great deal of variation in the design of sailboats and in the opinions that people have about these assorted boats. As we have said, sailboats are a multifarious lot – they come in various sizes and shapes, they are made of different materials, and so on. In addition, some people find a classic Hinckley or an Island Packet, for example, quite beautiful, while others may opt for the newer designs of Jeanneau or Hanse. One might wonder what constitutes the most aesthetic line of a bow, the shear, or a transom? What makes for a beautiful trunk? The cultural and personal differences in aesthetic judgments are clear, but one thing is certain: there's much to find beautiful in sailboats.

Most sailors, we think, probably attach significant aesthetic value to a sailboat based upon the materials out of which it is constructed. We peruse the wooden boat calendars nostalgically when we take a break from holiday shopping. When was the last time we looked through a calendar dedicated to fiberglass resting at anchor or underway? Of course, one popular sailing magazine does feature "classic plastic" sailboats. But we don't really glamorize boats that aren't wood. No one would seriously compare or prefer gleaming stainless steel to perfectly varnished brightwork.

The sails of a boat obviously have instrumental value (they help to keep the boat moving), but they also have aesthetic value in many cases. This can be true in the case of mainsails and jibs, where perhaps the aesthetic value of a sail is tied to its instrumentality in terms of sail fabrics ranging from the blinding white of new Dacron sails against a blue sky to more exotic fibers whose aesthetic value is tied to their potent instrumentality.

The above thoughts on boat materials raise questions about what might be called "practical value." While many sailors would agree that wooden boats are beautiful boats, they wouldn't want to own one because of the work associated with those boats. One might think that it's better to look at someone else's wooden boat than to own one. Many other sailors opt for the wooden boat; in this case, the practical value of fiberglass is disdained for the aesthetic value of wood. These sailors often spend much of the sailing season with their boats on dry land, working to make their boats more aesthetically pleasing. What they value is owning a beautiful boat, and they derive a great deal of pleasure and satisfaction from the labor expended to keep it that way. Other sailors prefer to be on a lower-maintenance, fiberglass boat. For them, it's more practical. They want to be on the water, sailing. The sailing is more valuable to them. They may still want a full-fledged aesthetic experience, but they want it – and find it – on the water. And this leads us to yet another example of something valuable related to sailing. It's not just the boats that are attractive but also the environment in which people sail. The upshot of all this is that, regardless of what one values, one can derive a great deal of satisfaction and find a tremendous amount of beauty, pleasure, and excitement in sailing. Sailing can be exhilarating and, at other times, relaxing. It can be intellectually or cognitively stimulating and it can be an activity via which to "zone out" and let the cares of life on land wash away. Sailing is indeed a pursuit chock-full of instrumental and intrinsic value.

## Aristotle, Virtues, and Flourishing

In a book called *Nicomachean Ethics*, Aristotle focused on the concept of eudaimonia. This is Greek for "happiness" or, perhaps more accurately, "flourishing." Aristotle argued that, just as caring for an apple tree will help it grow, blossom, and bear fruit, certain ways of living one's life promote flourishing, and thus lead one to live a full and happy life. He claimed that one must *cultivate virtues* in order to flourish in this way. But, you might be wondering, what exactly does he mean by "virtue"? Aristotle thought of virtues as patterns of behavior sort of like character traits. A virtue on this understanding is a tendency to act, desire, and feel in certain ways in certain situations. It is important to emphasize that Aristotle did not think that a virtue is an unthinking habit or tendency that one has. Rather, he thought that being virtuous involves some careful thought and results from a rational cultivation of habits that reflect appropriate response to whatever situation is at hand.[2]

Some examples will help to shed light on his theory. The list of virtues is quite large (and somewhat controversial). These seem like virtues:

being clever, courageous, generous, hard-working, honest, kind, sympathetic, and wise. We might add things like candor, commitment, confidence, determination, enthusiasm, humility, integrity, tact, vigilance, and so on. Aristotle thought that each of the virtues are "golden means" between two vicious (as in "vices") extremes. For example, being generous is to give what is appropriate and not to be overly generous (such that one ends up in the poor house) and not overly miserly. So, each virtue involves responding appropriately to the relevant situation. Of course, whether or not we should characterize someone as kind or honest involves evaluating the person not just on the basis of one action but rather on the basis of how the person behaves over an extended period of time. In order for a person to be viewed as possessing the virtue of honesty, he or she needs to be honest on numerous occasions or, more generally, to have an honest character.

The upshot is this: the trick for leading a full and happy life is to live a virtuous life. The greater the proportion of virtues one exemplifies, the happier one's life will be. Indeed, Aristotle did not think that one just had to be, say, courageous and then one would be happy. Instead, one must cultivate and exemplify as many of the different virtues as one can. The virtuous person, then, is someone who has harmonized each of the virtues. That is, the virtues must be woven into the very fabric of a person's life.

## Is Sailing Virtuous?

The obvious question, then, is whether sailing is virtuous in Aristotelian terms. We think it is on many grounds, but will discuss only a few. Certainly, Aristotle's notion of the virtue of courage applies.

Courage is the mean between being foolhardy and being cowardly. A courageous person thinks, acts, and feels in the "right way" in response to danger. That is, the courageous person is not cowardly or overly concerned with his or her wellbeing. This is one vicious extreme regarding one's response to danger and so we rightly think that being cowardly is a vice. But the courageous person is also not overly unconcerned for his or her wellbeing. Being foolhardy or rash (the other vicious extreme on this scale) is also a vice.

So, the virtuous sailor is neither one who is overly afraid (cowardly) to go out in certain adverse conditions, such as a day when the wind is up a bit more than usual, nor one who is too eager to go sailing when a courageous sailor might wisely opt to stay ashore. This really applies if one is the skipper of a boat, and responsible for its crew and passengers and the boat itself. We all check weather maps before we go out. We check our equipment to make sure that we are properly prepared. We think about the sailing experience and the physical welfare of our guests. These are all factors that can ultimately place us in the position of the golden mean on the continuum between being afraid and being foolhardy. Interestingly, on the same day, it might be foolhardy to go out with one crew and unnecessarily fearful not to go out with another. This last point demonstrates the context sensitivity of what counts as displaying a virtue such as courage.

This all applies more obviously to blue-water sailing, where longer periods of time on the water are involved, where assistance might be less at hand, and where more trying circumstances might be encountered. And, sadly, the threats to sailors' safety are not just natural. There are pirates. So, is it foolhardy to go blue-water cruising or racing? We think of sailors in the Volvo Ocean Race or the Vendée Globe as courageous. Didn't Kipling title one of his books *Captains Courageous*?[3] There are certainly many couples who cruise the world. But would it be fair to label others "afraid" for not wanting to go out in twenty-knot winds if they thought that it was beyond their abilities? Would they be guilty of being cowardly if they didn't go out? Would they be foolhardy if they did?

This essential question becomes more heated when we consider the case of young teens who want to circumnavigate the world solo. They're clearly not cowards, but are they foolhardy or courageous? We give acclaim to the young people who do it but castigate the parents of some youngsters who want to do it. When is young too young? How many people's scales of fear–courage–foolhardiness apply differently to young sailors according to gender? The point is that what is virtuous or vicious depends upon the context one finds oneself in and the sort of person one is – including things like what abilities one has.

Consider another virtue: being hard-working. Weber discussed this at length when he linked the rise of capitalism to the Protestant ethic.[4] If the virtue of work lies between two extremes and one of them is laziness, we assume that the other is something akin to being a workaholic. Is the work of sailing virtuous? Do sail trimming and all of the other forms of work that go into making a sailboat move more efficiently or comfortably constitute an Aristotelian virtue? Haven't many of us heard sailors denigrate power-boating by saying that there is nothing to do except drive? Aren't we saying that we value the work of sailing, and that it makes our sport better? At the same time, we are also aware that we can regulate our workload. On a leisurely sail, we can "set it and forget it" – trim the sails, set the autohelm, and enjoy. If we're racing, that all changes dramatically. Here the workloads can be overwhelming to some. But, as sailors, we have the ability to choose the level of work that we want to perform. The whole point here is that sailing allows one to exemplify various virtues, including being hard-working. And, just like many things in life, one has to work at being a virtuous sailor. Most choose a level of work between being lazy and being a workaholic. The sailor who does it right reaps the rewards of being virtuous.

Aristotle also talks about the virtue of being clever. How many great sailing stories focus upon that virtue – that ability to solve problems with limited resources? As Captain Ron so prophetically said, "If it's gonna happen, it'll happen out there."[5] It seems that power-boaters are more vulnerable to problems when they arise. Sailors seem to revel in the virtue of being able to adapt equipment to solve mechanical misfortune. All sailors are familiar with the idea of using a spinnaker pole as a mast or boom. One of us has had to transform an unused port frame into an alternator bracket. Is it not virtuous to be able to do this? We think it is.

More routinely, isn't navigation largely about being clever? How do we get from point A to point B in the fastest way possible? What is the weather forecast? What tides and currents are there? Where are they? In what direction is the wind blowing and how strong? What sails (and sizes) should be used ideally? Should they be shortened? What are the most efficient points of sail of our particular boat? The best answers combine together to produce the best possible sail. Depending on one's definition of "clever," we think that sailing requires people to be clever and to enjoy being that way.

## Is Sailing More Virtuous Than Other Pursuits?

One might contend that similar points can be made about other pursuits, such as power-boating, playing golf, or bowling. That is, one might think that these other activities similarly require one to cultivate, and allow one to exemplify, virtues – and so it's not clear that sailing is any better than these other pursuits in terms of contributing to a happy life. In response to this, we would urge that sailing requires a much broader range of virtues (if one is going to sail well) compared with these other types of pursuits. For example, one need not be courageous in order to bowl and golfers don't need to be able to cleverly jury-rig their clubs on the links.

In addition, these other pursuits typically don't require the exercise of as great a depth of skill or virtue as is required of sailors. Although being a good bowler requires some hard work and commitment, being a competent sailor requires a great deal more. Golfers might derive satisfaction from seeing beautiful greens, rolling fairways, and clouds on the horizon, but sailing has all of these aesthetic features and more. These differences are undoubtedly attributable to the fact that sailing is so much more complex and rich than these other sorts of activities. And this can be spelled out in terms of the multifaceted nature of the virtues (including cognitive abilities, decision-making, improvisational talents, emotional control, and so on) that need to be developed and executed by the proficient sailor. Lastly, in keeping with the points made above, one might consider the full range of activities in which one might engage, from those most benign to those considered "extreme" by being associated with the thrill of exposing oneself to significant risk. We would suggest that sailing fits nicely into this spectrum as a "golden mean" between these two extremes and so represents an ideal pursuit for cultivating virtues.

## Conclusion

In the preceding sections, we have discussed some of the virtues of sailing. There are clearly numerous others, and we'll leave it to the reader's imagination to think of all the ways in which that sailing can be a virtuous pursuit. Although it is certainly not the only activity that cultivates virtues, we think that sailing is an especially rich activity in this regard. That is, sailing is remarkably replete with opportunities to be virtuous. Sailing enables and even prompts one to be courageous, careful, curious, knowledgeable, decisive, and clever, and to have a whole host of other virtues. Assuming that Aristotle was right that one must be virtuous to be happy, it follows that sailing is a wonderful route to happiness. It's certainly not the only course, but we find sailing to be one of the best for those of us who are fortunate enough to have access to bodies of water suitable for sailing.

## NOTES

1 William Frankena, *Ethics*, second edition (Englewood Cliffs: Prentice Hall, 1973), pp. 87–88.
2 Aristotle, *The Nicomachean Ethics*, trans. David Ross (Oxford: Oxford University Press, 1998).
3 Rudyard Kipling, *Captains Courageous* (Garden City, NY: Doubleday, 1897).
4 Max Weber, *The Protestant Ethic and the Spirit of Capitalism*, trans. Talcott Parsons (New York: Scribner, 1958).
5 John Dwyer, *Captain Ron, dir. Thom Eberhardt* (Burbank, CA: Touchstone Pictures, 1992).

PART 4

# PHYSICS AND METAPHYSICS FOR THE PHILOSOPHICAL SAILOR

CHAPTER 12

# DO YOU HAVE TO BE (AN) EINSTEIN TO UNDERSTAND SAILING?

## Introduction

Albert Einstein (see Figure 12.1) is widely admired as the smartest – and the "coolest" – scientist ever. After all, *Time* magazine elected him the "person of the century" for the 1900s, and practically everyone knows his name (and associates it with "smart"). Among his many endearing traits, his love of sailing ranks right up there as a measure of his greatness. His groundbreaking discoveries, the theories of special and general relativity, revolutionized our understanding of space and time and yielded the universally recognized equation $E = mc^2$. But do *you* have to be an Einstein to get to a full and deep understanding of sailing? I mean this not in the usual sense ("being smart") but quite literally: do the laws of special and general relativity have any bearing on the ancient art (and modern practice) of sailing?

If you restrict yourself to practical matters (how to get from A to B in the fastest and safest way by use of a sailing vessel, or how to win the weeknight race around the cans), Einstein's theories of relativity have little immediate value. Ostensibly, this is so because they mostly concern

*Sailing – Philosophy for Everyone: Catching the Drift of Why We Sail*, First Edition.
Edited by Patrick Goold.

FIGURE 12.1 Einstein in his sloop *Tümmler*, a gift from well-to-do friends that was custom-built for him. Photo used by permission of *Die Yacht*.

themselves with extreme situations – speeds close to the speed of light (not exactly what comes to mind when describing the average cruise) and bizarre aspects of the universe such as black holes and the Big Bang. A closer look, however, reveals that the philosophical underpinnings of Einstein's insights have a lot to do with the basics of sailing. Pondering these underpinnings may not necessarily make you a better sailor but hopefully will provide something worth mulling over while ghosting along in a zephyr (or while eagerly awaiting the return of fair sailing weather in the middle of winter). You will find that, maybe without realizing it, you are making use of "relativity" in one way or another every time you weigh anchor. Even the general theory of relativity, long considered the most arcane of Einstein's ideas, has a direct impact on something as mundane as navigation. In this article, I hope to provide you with some guideposts along the path from everyday concepts familiar to most sailors all the way to Einstein's take on issues such as time, space, and motion.

## Don't Laugh at "Slow" Sailing: Average Versus Instantaneous Motion

A well-known jibe defines sailing as "the art of going slowly nowhere, at great expense and personal discomfort." And, sure enough, if you discount

SEBASTIAN KUHN

tricked-out Open 70s, America's Cup trimarans, and novelties such as the flying moth, most leisure sailors with limited pocketbooks rarely crack the ten-knot barrier. Conversely, our power-boating friends easily reach twenty, thirty, or even forty knots on the water. No wonder they like to poke fun at the comparatively slow progress of a typical sailing cruiser. However, it all depends on your definition of velocity – if you aren't talking about instantaneous speed, but average velocity, we sailors have no reason to feel inferior.

By definition, average velocity takes the total displacement during a given time interval and divides it by the amount of time elapsed. ("Displacement" is a physics term here, not a nautical one. It means the distance between the start and finish position.) By this reckoning, all weekend cruisers, whether laid-back sailors or high-speed motorboaters, have the same average velocity – namely zero! This is because they tend to end up right where they started – in their marina slip or on the boat trailer from which their vessel was launched. In other words, the total distance between start and finish is zero. And zero distance divided by *any* number of elapsed hours yields zero velocity.

If we average over longer and longer time spans, sailors do comparatively better and better with respect to average velocity – few powerboaters venture on long blue-water cruises to distant locales, while many a sailor has traveled "over the horizon" to fulfill a life-long dream. This distinction is not just an accident – the energy source for the propulsion of a sailboat is the ubiquitous wind, which makes possible unlimited travel for years, while the fuel contained in the tank of an ordinary powerboat usually can't get it across a major ocean. (Full-displacement boats such as trawlers come closest in long-distance cruising capability, albeit at the price of nearly "sailing-like" speed.)

Still, whether averaged over long time periods or measured instantaneously, sailboat velocities are hardly in the range that physicists call "relativistic." The most counterintuitive effects of special relativity (time dilation, length contraction, and so on; see below) only become obvious when speeds approach the universal limit of 300,000 km/s (583 million knots) – the speed of light. The speed of even the fastest powerboat pales in comparison. But read on! The connection is real, even if it is more subtle.

## Motion Relative to What? – Galilean Relativity

So far, I have been rather casual in my use of terms such as "distance" and "displacement." As a physicist, I need to define my terms more precisely. Without that, it is not even clear what we mean by our position at a given time, let alone the distance between two positions. (For now, I will pretend that the other variable entering into velocity, elapsed time, is clearly defined – after all, we have high-precision clocks and watches to measure it. But, as we will see later, this is not quite unproblematic either!)

For physicists, the fundamental concept needed here is that of a "reference frame." We can visualize this as an infinite frame, like the frame of a house, made of wooden beams, all rigidly attached at ninety-degree angles to each other. A more abstract concept would simply assume a set of points in space, all with fixed and immutable distances from each other. One of these points is given a special importance – we call it the "origin" of the reference frame, and designate it with "0" distance. Any position in space can then be uniquely designated by giving both its distance from that origin and the direction (relative to the "beams") in which you would have to move to get there.

In one dimension, the nautical equivalent would be a set of mile markers; for example, the ones along the Intracoastal Waterway along the US East Coast, with the origin designated by "mile marker 0" in Portsmouth, Virginia. Snowbirds who want to know where they are during their annual journey south on the Intracoastal Waterway can simply look at the nearest mile marker. In three dimensions, however, things are a little more complicated. For sailors, two dimensions usually suffice, and the system of latitudes and longitudes serves the same purpose as the mile markers in the one-dimensional example (with the origin on the intersection of the Greenwich Meridian and the equator, in the Atlantic south of Ghana). Note that this latter coordinate system is a bit tricky – for instance, you cannot easily calculate the distance between two points simply by knowing their longitudes and latitudes, because you need to take into account the curvature of the surface of our planet. Similarly, it is not obvious what path to follow for the shortest possible distance between two points. If you start from the East Coast of the United States and want to reach a point exactly due east on, say, the European continent, it turns out that following a route due east at constant latitude (the rhumb line) will *not* give you the shortest distance – that's why all transatlantic flights tend to cross over rather northerly places such as Greenland. This complication of ordinary Euclidean geometry by Earth's curved surface has a direct analog in Einstein's general theory of relativity, in which the whole of four-dimensional space-time turns out to be curved (see below).

SEBASTIAN KUHN

It is important to realize that any "fixed" reference frame is only fixed *relative to something else*, and in fact the choice of reference frame is quite arbitrary. For instance, a reference frame "fixed" to the surface of the patch of water on which you happen to sail is obviously of significant importance – after all, without any propulsion by wind or iron genny you will be at rest relative to that reference frame. The faster you want to go relative to the surrounding water, the more force needs to be brought to bear on your vessel. And, as sailors know, it is the motion of the surrounding air relative to *this* reference frame that determines this force. If you want to move in the direction the wind blows you, your speed will depend directly on the wind velocity relative to the water. On any point of sail other than straight downwind, you need the balance of two forces to give you net propulsion in the forward direction (see also Chapter 13). One force is generated by the motion of air relative to your above-water foils (the sails) and the other by the motion of water relative to your underwater foils (keel or centerboard and, to a lesser extent, rudder). Successful propulsion requires that these two relative motions are not the same. If they are, all you get is drag, which will bring the boat to rest relative to both air and sea in short order.

The water surface is just one reference frame to keep in mind while sailing. If you plan to arrive at a certain destination (within some given time frame), you are obliged to pay close attention to the other reference frame we already encountered – the one fixed to the solid surface of Earth. Even if you really don't care where wind and waves carry you, you still need to keep track of where you are relative to this reference frame – if only to avoid shoals or other obstacles to safe navigation. And the number of possible (and relevant) reference systems doesn't stop there – your own boat is an obvious third example, which you automatically invoke when talking about the direction of another vessel ("abeam," "abaft," or "ahead"), or when you tell your crew to "go forward to raise the jib." Finally, if you are a blue-water cruiser from the old school (or just like to keep your options open), you will even have learned to consider the reference frame of the stars, which can help you to navigate on the open ocean. And, compared to *that* frame, both the most languid sailboat and the most souped-up powerboat move with velocities that are quite impressive – and practically indistinguishable (thirty kilometers per second, or 58,000 knots if you count the sun as the origin of this frame). Keep in mind that none of these various reference frames is intrinsically any more correct or fundamental than any other one; they are all equally valid, if not necessarily equally practical, for a given purpose.

Awareness of these reference frames and their relative motion helps to explain many common situations encountered while sailing. Examples abound: While the wind may truly come out of the west, if you are moving due north, it will *appear* to come somewhere from a northwesterly direction relative to your boat, and this relative (apparent) wind direction determines the shape and position of your sails. Vice versa, if you and your boat are floating down a river, with a breeze of exactly the same velocity as that of the water, you will feel completely becalmed – the *relative* wind velocity is zero. So, your velocity relative to the water would be zero, as well, but you would be moving at a good clip over ground. Inversely, if the wind velocity *relative to ground* were zero, you would notice a breeze blowing up the river, and if you wanted to speed up your trip you could even use this breeze to tack back and forth, making way downstream relative to the flow of the river (and therefore be even faster than the river). Conversely, if you have both current and wind against you, even as an excellent sailor you may not be able to make any headway above ground!

In the end, one has to keep at least three or four of these different reference frames in mind to fully understand the magic of sailing. And one should be able to easily convert positions and velocities measured in one system to any of the others. In principle, this problem was solved a long time ago, by Galileo Galilei and other early giants of physics. Not only were they able to derive the laws describing the transformation of positions and velocities from one frame to another (e.g., velocities must be added as vectors) but they also realized an enormously important principle (nowadays called "Galilean relativity"): The laws of nature (for instance, Newton's famous three force laws) do not change no matter which (inertial[1]) reference frame one chooses to describe one's observations. While the velocity measured relative to one frame may turn out to be quite different from that relative to another one, its rate of change (the acceleration) is the same in both of them, and directly proportional to the net force acting. This principle has allowed us to make sense of the world around us, to send space probes to the planets, and to devise many of the wonders of technology. The principle is perfectly adequate to understand the basic laws of sailing (even how to design a faster racing yacht). It has just one small flaw: Unbeknownst (and unknowable) to Galileo and his contemporaries, it is woefully incomplete, and the rules for transforming velocities from one system to another are simply (if subtly) wrong!

SEBASTIAN KUHN

## But There are No Fixed Reference Frames – Special Relativity

The trouble with Galilean relativity is not that it is inherently wrong – quite the opposite: It is not encompassing enough. What Galileo couldn't have known is that the laws governing electric and magnetic interactions (i.e., electromagnetism, which hadn't been discovered yet) must be the same in all reference frames – but they directly contradict the simple rule for the addition of velocities. Let me explain.

Electromagnetic phenomena are of course a constant companion of any mariner, sailing or otherwise. Magnetic compasses have been crucial navigation tools for centuries, and the power of electric currents in the form of lightning strikes has inspired awe and fear in seafarers from the ancient past to this day. Modern sailboats typically make much more comprehensive use of electromagnetic processes (depending on how much money the owner likes to spend on electronics). From the electrical system powering navigation and cabin lights (and windlasses, micro-waves, air conditioners, and other "necessities" of cruising life) to the multiple receivers and emitters of radio waves (VHF, radar, GPS, and cell and satellite phones), electromagnetism seems indispensable for most sailors. However, only in the nineteenth century was a complete and unified understanding of all the different manifestations of electric-ity and magnetism accomplished, with the crowning achievement of the four differential equations now named after Maxwell. Among the aston-ishing consequences of these equations, scientists were able to *predict* that varying electric and magnetic fields should be able to propagate together through vast expanses of space, traveling in the form of electro-magnetic waves (just like water waves travel on the open sea). Even more astonishingly, the speed of propagation for these waves turned out to be a number already fairly well known – 300,000 km/s, the speed of light. This insight not only explained light as just one more electromagnetic phenomenon but also predicted the existence of, and subsequently allowed the generation of, a vast array of other electromagnetic waves – radio, radar, infrared, and ultraviolet up to X-rays and gamma rays. All of these waves were predicted to propagate with the same speed. Subsequent experiments confirmed these ideas with increasing preci-sion, and many ingenious devices (such as the ones mentioned above) are based on them.

There is only one problem. As we've just learned, velocities must always be measured relative to a reference frame, and the result should change if we change reference frames. Surely, if light travels at 300,000 km/s relative to the frame of a fixed star, an observer on Earth (using a ground-based frame) should measure either 300,030 km/s while Earth is moving toward that star (in spring, say) or 299,970 km/s in the opposite case (in fall). This is totally equivalent to the head wind one would experience in our earlier example of a sailboat floating on a fast river during a calm day. But the laws of electromagnetism don't allow such a change of wave velocity with the reference frame – and all experiments devised to find it have failed. No matter where the light comes from, and no matter your own motion, the velocity measured always turns out to be exactly the same: 300,000 km/s. If you don't find that weird, you haven't thought this through. The radio wave carrying a Mayday call arrives at your boat with exactly the same (relative) velocity, whether you are moving at a good clip or are at anchor. The same is true with the light from navigation aids, the radar beam that gets bounced back to you from an obstacle, and any other electromagnetic wave. Even the signals from the GPS satellites that help you to determine your position arrive with that same unchanging velocity, no matter how fast those satellites are moving relative to the ground (in fact, several kilometers per second). This is the same as if a fifteen-knot breeze from the north were to always feel exactly the same to a sailor, whether she were sailing close-hauled, at a beam reach, or downwind! If the laws of physics (including electromagnetism) really are the same in all reference frames, something else has to give. That something turns out to be our very notion of time and space. To understand why, we have to go back to our definition of a reference frame.

Remember the blithe assumption that one can measure positions and distances relative to a reference frame by using "rigid wooden beams" or "fixed markers"? In fact, the first idea is utterly impractical for obvious reasons, while the second has more subtle flaws. Sailors understand more readily than landlubbers the ultimate impermanence of things that seem to be quite solid: Channel markers can be moved or succumb to waves and weather, floating markers can move, sand and clay bottoms can shift, and so on. On a long enough time scale, the inexorable drift of the continental plates means that literally nothing stays in exactly the same place (even if measured from one "fixed" point on Earth to the next). And Earth is the most permanent frame there is – how about the reference frame of the water itself? Currents not only change with time and tides but also vary from one location to the next. What is fixed here relative to what? Does it even make sense to talk about *the* reference frame of the water surface? Ultimately, which method of measuring positions (and times!) can be considered truly reliable?

When Einstein pondered this conundrum, he realized that the apparent *problem* in the laws of electromagnetism actually yielded the (only) solution: Once we *know* that the speed of light (or other electromagnetic waves) is the same under all circumstances, we can use this fact to measure the distance between any two points simply by measuring the time light takes to travel from one to the other. To determine a three-dimensional position in space, in general one needs to measure the distance from (at least) three points with known coordinates. If each of these three points were to send out a short light pulse simultaneously, we would only have to measure the arrival times of these three pulses to fix our position. There is one remaining problem, though: How can we be sure that our own (on-board) clock is exactly synchronized with the clocks that determine the start time of the three light pulses? Otherwise, we couldn't reliably measure the travel time. Well, it turns out you *can't* be sure unless you include a *fourth* sender at yet another position. Admittedly, this is getting a bit complicated, but I hope it makes sense: To determine the four coordinates of a position in space and point in time simultaneously, you need four pieces of independent information – which the arrival time of the four light pulses can provide.

In the early 1900s, when Einstein was developing these theories (while working at a Swiss patent office), this whole arrangement of light senders and receivers would have appeared extremely contrived and utterly impractical – for one, to get good accuracy of position you would have had to measure the elapsed times to a precision of the order of one billionth of a second (one nanosecond)! This is because light travels so insanely fast – by a whole foot in that one nanosecond. Such precision was completely out of reach at the beginning of the twentieth century. Einstein therefore considered this method of measuring position and time as a purely mental exercise – a *Gedankenexperiment*. Amazingly, a hundred years later his method is exactly how most of us measure where we are during our sailing trips (and even on the car ride to the marina)! And all of the complicated calculations necessary can be done by a little electronic box no larger than a transistor radio – the GPS receiver, which requires only a modicum of operator training (as compared to celestial navigation). Of course, the details are quite a bit more complicated than I could possibly explain here, but the basic idea is sound: By measuring the time it takes for electromagnetic waves (radio, in this case) to reach the GPS receiver from any of a number of satellites that are constantly sending them out, we can not only calculate our position (and plot it on an electronic chart) but also calculate the actual time of day (your GPS knows it a lot better than your beautiful brass clock down below!).

But Einstein's idea goes way beyond a convenient new navigation method – he realized that this method (and assuming a fixed velocity of light) are the *only* reliable way to synchronize clocks and measure distances. This has profound consequences that lead to all the confusing paradoxes that come with his special theory of relativity: First, the length of an object contracts if measured from a reference frame in which it moves. For example, your boat, as measured from shore, is shorter than its nominal overall length, if only by one trillionth of one-thirty-second of an inch (assuming a seventy-seven-foot yacht moving at eight knots). Second, time appears to pass more slowly for a clock that is moving relative to the observer (time dilation). After a twenty-four-hour day of sailing at those same eight knots, even the most perfect onboard clock will show eight trillionths of a second less elapsed time than an onshore one. Third, the notion of two things happening simultaneously no longer can be assumed to be universal. Ultimately, this last consequence is the biggest jolt to our understanding. It is also the reason why the other two only appear to be paradoxical.

To understand this, imagine yourself exactly at the middle point between two GPS satellites (let's pretend for now that they are at rest relative to Earth, which is of course far from true). Both of them send out a radio pulse at exactly the same time. If you are at anchor, you will receive those two waves at exactly the same (later time), and, since you (or, rather, your GPS receiver) know about the relative position of your boat and those satellites and the constant speed of radio waves, you can indeed conclude that they must have been emitted simultaneously. However, what happens if you are making eight knots toward one satellite and away from the other? Since it takes a little while (a fraction of a second) for the radio waves to reach your position, you will have moved away from the point exactly in the middle of the two satellites and will have moved closer to one than the other by the time you receive the pulses. However, since you must assume that the speed of radio waves is still 300,000 km/s in either direction, you will have to conclude that the satellite ahead of you emitted its signal a smidgen earlier than the one behind you. And you are not wrong with that conclusion! The whole notion of simultaneity depends on your reference frame, and a moving boat has a different one from a boat at anchor.

SEBASTIAN KUHN

Of course, I hasten to add that all of these seemingly paradoxical consequences are miniscule in magnitude unless your boat is going close to the speed of light, so you can safely ignore them while cruising. However, without careful consideration of special relativity, your GPS system wouldn't work. And there are other consequences of Einstein's discovery: The mass ($m$) of an object is not a constant, but depends on its state of motion and, more generally, its energy ($E$): $m = E/c^2$. (If you remember a little algebra, you will quickly realize that this equation has the exact same meaning as the famous one quoted in the introduction.) Again, the increase resulting from this relationship to the mass of a five-ton yacht underway is so miniscule to be entirely negligible. However, only recently a group of physicists made the stunning discovery that, quite apart from nuclear power and other more well-known applications of this famous equation, even such mundane devices as lead batteries (ubiquitous in today's yachts) would not work, or at least not as well without these relativistic effects.[2]

## General Relativity – Can it Really Matter?

It took Einstein only a few years to develop his special theory of relativity. However, his greatest achievement (and arguably the greatest achievement of any single scientist, ever), the general theory, occupied him for a decade. To this day, many people (though fewer and fewer physicists) consider this ultimate theory of gravity to be beautiful but thoroughly mysterious and utterly irrelevant for daily life (including sailing). But, once again, it turns out that, while its consequences are miniscule, they are not exactly null, and they are becoming more and more measurable. As philosopher-sailors, we shouldn't be content ignoring something just because it is incredibly small – maybe we should be more like obsessive racers, who will fret over the tiniest barnacle adhering to the otherwise slick underbody of their sailing machines. The plain truth is that even the special theory of relativity has shortcomings.

I alluded to one problem already earlier: the ambiguous nature of notions such as distance and direction if your reference frame is not strictly rectilinear and orthogonal ("flat" in geometry parlance). As sailors, we are familiar with one such coordinate system, that of longitudes and latitudes on the surface of the (emphatically not flat) Earth. We have already discussed some of the non-intuitive consequences of measuring positions and directions using these coordinates. We could of course avoid these problems by using an ordinary, three-dimensional (rectilinear or Cartesian) coordinate system instead – breaking down any position into distances and directions measured relative to the center of the Earth. Such a system would regain the ordinary definitions of direction and distance for the price of awkwardness – you could not even tell immediately whether any position given within this system was on the surface of planet Earth or hundreds of meters in the air (or below the water).

What the general theory of relativity tells us, though, is that the very space itself that we take for granted (and time with it) cannot be described in terms of a purely flat geometry, even if we try. Space-time is intrinsically warped or curved by the presence of mass and energy. It is this warping that leads to all the well-known effects of gravity (e.g., falling and buoyancy) as well as the more exotic consequences of Einstein's theory – black holes and Big Bang cosmology. And it has consequences for our very notion of distance and direction that cannot be cured by changing to a different coordinate system.

As an example, consider two ships starting out simultaneously (with the same speed) from the equator, separated by sixty nautical miles and moving exactly parallel toward the north (along fixed lines of longitude – say 0 and 1 degrees). Our everyday notion of parallel lines would imply that these two vessels will never be in danger of collision – but, unfortunately, on a curved space (Earth's surface) this isn't true: both will eventually reach the North Pole (ignoring intervening land masses) and therefore arrive at the same point at the same time – the definition of a collision. Similarly, light rays from one and the same distant star can bend left and right around a massive object (say, a galaxy cluster) that they have to pass on their way to an observer on Earth. This can lead to that same star appearing at two different points in the sky at once, an effect called "gravitational lensing." (For an illustration, think of two ships starting in different directions from the South Pole and reuniting at the North Pole.) Yet both light rays (and both ships) simply follow the shortest possible path in a curved geometry – what we would normally call a straight line.

And it is not only space that is affected by this "irreducible" curvature; time also becomes warped in a sense. For instance, it turns out that time elapses (slightly) more slowly close to a massive object than further away from it. Again, the effect is small, but with an ultraprecise pair of clocks it has recently been demonstrated for a change of only one foot in height

SEBASTIAN KUHN

above Earth (the massive object in this case). As a consequence, I can rightfully claim that you will age ever so slightly more quickly while aloft on your mast than down in the cockpit – although only by one trillionth of a second for each quarter hour. And, once again, it turns out that the effect is big enough to be corrected for when using GPS satellites – thousands of miles above our heads – to fix our position on Earth, where time is elapsing just a tad more slowly. So, in the end, it turns out that Einstein does have something to tell us about our favorite pastime – maybe one of the reasons he enjoyed sailing.

## NOTES

1 Technically, inertial reference frames are those special frames where an object at rest will remain at rest as long as no force acts on it. Most (or all) of the frames we have considered so far are not exactly inertial ones – which explains the sloshing back and forth of water in the bilge or of the tides on the ocean. However, this distinction is of minor practical importance for our purposes, and turns out to be illusory anyway in light of the general theory of relativity.

2 If you want to know the details: The increase in mass of the electrons in lead atoms due to their very high motional energy as they swirl around the nucleus leads to stronger binding, which in turn increases significantly the energy released by moving these electrons from cathode to anode – in other words, the battery voltage.

JOHN D. NORTON

CHAPTER 13

# PARADOXES OF SAILING

## The Physics of Sailing and the Import of Thought Experiments

Paradoxes have long been a driving force in philosophy. They compel us to think more clearly about what we otherwise take for granted. In antiquity, Zeno insisted that a runner could never complete the course because he'd first need to go half way, and then half way again, and so on indefinitely. Zeno also argued that matter could not be infinitely divisible, else it would be made of parts of no size at all. Even infinitely many nothings combined still measure nothing. These simple thoughts have forced us to develop ever more careful and sophisticated accounts of space, time, motion, continuity, and measure. And modern versions of these paradoxes continue to vex us.

This engine of paradox has continued to power us to this day. Relatively recently, Einstein fretted over a puzzle. How was it possible that all inertially moving observers would find the same speed for light? Surely if one of them was chasing rapidly after the light that observer would find the light slowed. But Einstein's investigations into electricity and magnetism assured him that the light would not slow. He resolved this paradox with one of the most influential conceptual analyses of the twentieth century. He imagined clocks, synchronized by light signals, and concluded that

*Sailing – Philosophy for Everyone: Catching the Drift of Why We Sail*, First Edition.
Edited by Patrick Goold.
© 2012 John Wiley & Sons, Inc. Published 2012 by John Wiley & Sons, Inc.

whether two events are judged simultaneous will depend upon the motion of the observer judging.

What is distinctive about these philosophical paradoxes is that they are not mere expressions of practical limitations. The difficulties they expose lie within the very ideas themselves. Zeno's worry was not that a real runner might fail to complete a long race because of tiredness. His concern related to the very idea of any runner, no matter how accomplished or idealized, completing any race, no matter how short. The difficulty lies in the ideas of space, time, and motion. In his paradox of measure, Zeno was not concerned that we might never find a real knife capable of slicing matter indefinitely finely. His concern was that matter must be such that infinite division lies beyond even the sharpest knife, whose edge has been honed to the perfection of an ideal mathematical point.

Now let us consider sailing. There are many difficult technical problems associated with sailing. If a sailboat is to be even minimally serviceable, its design must conform to an engineering lore that has grown through the centuries. In general, the problems this tradition solves do not rise to the level of paradox. However, there are some puzzles attached to sailing that are more fundamental than a particular engineering challenge. In this essay I will consider three. They do not have the importance of the paradoxes of Zeno and Einstein. Indeed, as I shall try to show, their diagnosis and resolution is a short and, I hope, entertaining diversion. However, they are foundational paradoxes, for they challenge no particular sailboat but the very idea of sailboats powered by the wind. They are:

- If a sailboat is powered by the wind, how can it sail into the wind?
- If a sailboat is powered by the wind, how can it sail faster than the wind?
- If a sailboat "makes its own wind" when it moves, why does it need any other wind?

The first two will be familiar to sailors, most of whom will have made their peace with them. The third is less straightforward. That sailboats "make their own wind" is commonly said by sailors, but few explicitly pursue the thought to its paradoxical end. We shall do so now.

While profound philosophical morals will not be found in these paradoxes, I will suggest that they connect nicely to two issues in recent philosophy. The first two paradoxes will lead us directly into a conundrum concerning causal metaphysics. The third will lead us to ponder an intriguing mode of investigation of nature, the thought experiment.

Here are the first two paradoxes again, spelled out in greater detail. They are treated together since they involve essentially the same issues.

1. The cause of a sailboat's motion is the motion of the wind.
2. The effect of a cause cannot be greater than or contrary to the cause.
3. Therefore, a wind-powered sailboat cannot sail faster than the wind or into the wind.

But this conclusion is contradicted by the reality:

4. Real sailboats routinely sail into the wind, and sailboats designed for speed can sail faster than the wind.

Those who are not sailors will likely find the argumentation leading to the conclusion (point three) convincing, at least initially. Its plausibility depends upon a limited experience of what the wind can do. It calls to mind dry leaves blown about by wind. The wind may lift them, but it will not move them faster than or contrary to its own motion. The conclusion is also correct for some cases of sailing, such as old-fashioned square-rigged sailing ships running before the wind. Then their sails function like big bags catching the wind. The boat will be blown in the direction of the wind, near enough, and, as long as it sails in that direction, the ship will never move faster than the wind.

However, the conclusion is incorrect for almost any sailboat that can align its sails in a fore–aft direction. This is especially so for the most common type of small sailboat now used recreationally. A Bermuda-rigged sailboat has a single mast with two triangular sails, a jib and a mainsail, oriented in the fore–aft direction. Such sailboats routinely sail into the wind, and, if designed for speed, easily sail faster than the wind when sailing across the wind.

Where the above analysis (points one to three) fails for such boats is that it mischaracterizes the causal processes. The motion of the wind is not the immediate cause of the motion of the boat. A more immediate cause is the force with which the wind presses on the sails. For even light winds, this force can be considerable. In what are called "moderate breezes" on the Beaufort scale of wind (thirteen to seventeen miles per hour), the wind generates pressures of around one pound per square foot on the sails. Small modern sailboats, under twenty feet in length, can carry two hundred square feet of sail, and older designs often carried significantly more.[1] So, the wind exerts a considerable force of many hundreds

JOHN D. NORTON

of pounds on the sails. This force now acts independently of the motion of the wind that produced it. A few hundred pounds of force pressing on the sails will lead the sailboat to heel over, just as if someone were to attach a rope to the center of effort of the sail and pull it.

Some of this force can be directed toward the bow of the boat and drives it over the water. How much boat speed results from a given force depends almost entirely on the design of the boat's hull and, as a result, the resistance the water provides to its motion. Once that forward-directed force is fixed, so is the motion of the hull. It makes no difference if the force comes from the press of the wind, oars, and paddles or a motor-powered propeller. The force contains no coded record of the speed of the wind that produced it for the sailboat to read covertly and respect!

A small boat of the familiar monohull design can easily be driven up to a maximum speed that cannot be passed by greater forces generated by sails. For small boats this maximum speed is commonly less than the speed of the wind. But that is purely an accident of the hull design. If the hull is designed for speed, nothing prevents the boat achieving speeds greater than the wind. Two-hulled catamarans present considerably less resistance that monohull boats. If sailing across the wind, they do not lose the press of the wind when they move fast. Then, well-designed catamarans are easily able to sail faster than the wind. The wind can provide considerable force; their hulls provide little resistance, so off they go!

To see how a sailboat can gain against the wind, we need to consider the different "points of sail" of a sailboat. These are the different ways in which a sailboat can proceed in relation to the wind. They are shown in Figure 13.1.

When a sailboat is on a run, the wind blows directly from its stern. Then the sails function like bags just catching the wind. On this point of sail the fastest the boat can move is the speed of the wind. As the boat approaches the speed of the wind, the boat's motion cancels out the speed of the wind, so that the wind felt on the boat by the sails diminishes. When the boat is close to the speed of the wind, the air on deck becomes calm. The experience is not unlike being carried by the wind in a balloon. One's speed over the ground may be quite high, but in the balloon's basket the air will be still.

All this changes when the boat sails across the wind on a beam reach. On this point of sail, the sails are let out so that they deflect the wind toward the rear of the boat. The resulting pressure on the sails yields a force, "$F_{wind}$," pointed diagonally forward, as shown in the first diagram of Figure 13.2.

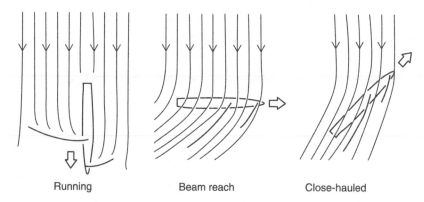

Running      Beam reach      Close-hauled

FIGURE 13.1   Points of sail. Author's copyright.

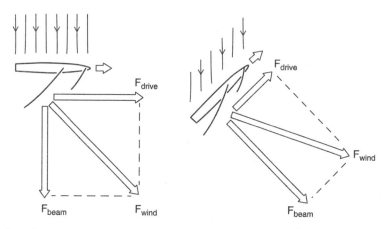

FIGURE 13.2   Resolution of forces on the sail. Author's copyright.

If the boat's hull was simply a tub, then this force would move the boat in that diagonal direction. However, an essential part of hull design is to make it as resistant as possible to sideways motion. This is usually effected with a centerboard in small boats and a broad, flat keel in bigger boats. The force on the sails, $F_{wind}$, can be divided into two components, as shown in Figure 13.2. One, "$F_{drive}$," is parallel to the boat's motion, and the other, "$F_{beam}$," is perpendicular to it. The high resistance to sideways motion means that the sideways force, $F_{beam}$, produces little or no motion, whereas the low resistance to forward motion means the forward force, $F_{drive}$, produces motion forward. Hence the boat is driven across the wind.

    JOHN D. NORTON

Only a small modification to the above analysis shows how sailboats can sail into the wind. When a sailboat is close-hauled, as shown in the second diagram of Figure 13.2, the wind still produces a force on the sails. That force, $F_{wind}$, can once again be decomposed into two parts, $F_{drive}$ and $F_{beam}$. Since the sails are now pulled in closer to the centerline of the boat, the component $F_{drive}$ is smaller in relation to $F_{beam}$. However, the hull will still prevent $F_{beam}$ producing sideways motion, so that $F_{drive}$ will drive the boat forward.

This forward motion will now gain against the wind. It is common for Bermuda-rigged sailboats to be able to sail at 45 degrees to the wind. As a result, if a close-hauled sailboat tacks repeatedly – that is, zig-zags across the wind – it can follow a track whose average course points directly into the wind.

In sum, the first two paradoxes are resolved by denying the second premise, that the motion of the wind, as a cause of the motion of the boat, cannot have an effect greater than or contrary to itself. When powering a sailboat, the motion of the wind can produce faster motions in the sailboat and motions directed against the wind.

To a philosopher, what is important in this last analysis is the centrality of causal notions. In the abstract, it seemed entirely unremarkable to expect that the effect of a cause cannot be greater than or contrary to the cause. Yet this simple causal truism was wrong and generated the first two paradoxes.

We see here in miniature one of the dominant and, in my view, most important facts about our investigations into causation. At any moment in history, we have held to a repertoire of facts about causation that we believed to be necessities. They are assertions that, shielded from deeper reflection and a broader exposure to experience, seem unassailable. However, when we think more and learn more about the world, we find we must abandon them.

Until the seventeenth century, it was widely accepted on Aristotle's authority that a final cause, the goal toward which a process moved, was as important as the efficient cause, that which initiated the process. In that century, the advent of mechanical philosophy was premised on the denunciation of final causes. However, we had by no means then "got it right." The century's hero, Isaac Newton, felt he had such an unassailable grasp on causation that he could, in 1692, denounce causal action at a distance as "so great an absurdity, that I believe no man, who has in philosophical matters a competent faculty of thinking, can ever fall into it."[2] Yet, by the nineteenth century, Newton's gravitation was widely accepted to be precisely this, unmediated action at a distance. In that century, the notion of causation was stripped down to its barest essentials.

It came to be equated with determinism, the simple fact that the present state fixes the future. This pure and apparently secure notion of causation fell. It was overturned with the advent of modern quantum theory in the 1920s. According to that theory, the present cannot fix the future. The best we can have are probabilities for a range of different futures.

These are just a few episodes in the history of our failure to grasp what causality demands. It is important that we see just what this failure has been. It has not been our failure to discern what has always concerned causal thinking: how it is that things in the world are connected. The little history just unfolded is a story of our coming to understand better and better how things are connected. The failures of the story were our efforts to discern ahead of science what sorts of connections new science must reveal.

How are we to interpret this long history of failure? There are causality optimists who think that the best response to failure is to try and try again. Eventually, they hope, we will hit upon the true causal principles that govern the world and all possible sciences. My own view is rather different and represents a minority view among theorists of causation.[3] It is that we need to learn that efforts to legislate causal principles ahead of experience are doomed to failure at the hands of new investigations.

As a result, I believe that the familiar causal talk is very different from what it seems. One could be forgiven for imagining that science is exploring a realm governed by some general law of causality that rules from the metaphysical heights above all sciences and to which all sciences must defer. In my view, something like the reverse is correct. Science is revealing to us deeper truths about the interconnectedness of things in the world than we could have ever imagined. In order to facilitate our understanding of it, we graft causal talk onto those discoveries. The repeated cycle of the failure and revival of causal talk is really a history of the elasticity of causal terms and our eagerness to apply them to whatever science may deliver. We do not have and will never have a factual principle of causality to which all sciences, known and as yet unknown, must conform.

Sailors commonly remark that sailboats create their own wind. The effect is a familiar one. If you pedal a bicycle at 10 mph on a calm day, you will find yourself pedaling into a 10 mph headwind created by your motion. Exactly the same thing happens with a sailboat. A sailboat travelling at 10 mph is sailing into a 10 mph wind it has created. Of course, sailors never see this headwind in isolation. The wind they see, the apparent wind, is always the vector sum of the created wind and the true wind. So, if the sailboat is on a beam reach in 10 mph winds, the two winds combine to yield a 14 mph wind coming at an angle of 45 degrees

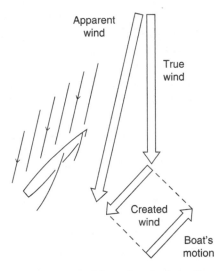

FIGURE 13.3  True and apparent wind for a close-hauled sailboat. Author's copyright.

to the bow. The two velocities are at right angles and so must be summed by Pythagoras' theorem:

$$(\text{apparent wind speed})^2 = (\text{true wind speed})^2 + (\text{created wind speed})^2$$

Figure 13.3 shows how the true wind and apparent wind are combined when a sailboat is close-hauled. It will be important for later discussion to note that the effect of the created wind is to move the direction of the apparent wind closer to the bow.

Thus far we have no paradox. By their motions, sailboats create wind. Our quest is for paradoxes and there does seem to be an intriguing paradox lurking in shadows. It arises from the essential difference between the cases of a bicycle and a sailboat. A bicycle is powered by your muscles; a sailboat is powered by the very thing created, the wind. Here is the paradox:

5. A moving sailboat creates its own wind.
6. A moving sailboat is powered by the wind.
7. Therefore, a moving sailboat is in part self-powered and is thus, in part, a perpetual-motion machine.

But this conclusion is contradicted by the following:

8. Perpetual-motion machines (self-powered devices) are impossible.

The concern is that a sailboat is, in part, realizing a device whose impossibility underlies one of the most important laws of physics, the conservation of energy. For it appears to be achieving just what perpetual-motion-machine makers have long sought. Their goal is a device that derives the power to run from its own internal operations. They have tried many designs. For example, they have equipped an electric car with a generator so that as the car moves the generator is turned. The generator produces electricity that, supposedly, now fully powers the car's electric motor. This simple design and its thousand and one variants have all failed. Is a sailboat the thousand and second variant that has finally succeeded?

It is not too hard to see that the traditional design of a sailboat acquires no added motive force from the created wind. Qualitatively, the result comes from combining effects that work in opposing directions. The force that drives the sailboat comes from the speed of the wind over the sails. So, an increase in the speed of the wind over the sails will increase the force on the sails. It doesn't matter whether the wind is the true wind or the apparent wind. Sails cannot distinguish the two. The force on the sails is determined by the speed of the wind at the sails, however it arises.

If that were the only effect, then we would be well on our way to realizing the paradox just sketched. However, there is a counteracting effect. As Figure 13.3 shows, the effect of adding the created wind to the true wind is to move the direction of the wind closer to the bow. As a result, the angle between the wind direction and the sails decreases; the wind now comes closer to blowing parallel to the sails' surfaces. This diminished angle reduces the wind-generated force on the sails in two ways. First, the volume of air scooped up by the sails diminishes since the profile of the sails facing the wind is smaller. Second, the force-generating deflection of the wind is now passes through a smaller angle. Figuratively, the wind strikes a more glancing blow onto the sails and thus exerts a weaker force on them.

These effects have been described only qualitatively. However, when they are combined, the effects that diminish the force overwhelm the one that increases it, so that the net effect is a loss of motive force. To see quantitatively that this is so, one needs to construct a careful mathematical model of the interaction of the wind with the sails. The result follows after some elaborate juggling of trigonometric functions. I will not reproduce them here, since the details of the calculations are tedious and not any more illuminating than the reciting of the qualitative effects above.

One can, however, get a sense that the apparent wind cannot drive a sailboat merely by recalling an experience familiar to every sailor. Imagine the sailboat sitting becalmed in completely dead air. If the boat is given a small push, perhaps from a paddle or a hand on a dock, it will move forward. That motion will create wind. However, the wind will blow straight down the centerline of the boat and, therefore, will be unusable by the sails as a way of generating any forward-directed motive force. The boat will gently slow to a halt, just as the generator–dynamo self-powered car cannot sustain an initial push.

What this last analysis shows is that a particular design of sailboat, the common Bermuda rig, is unable to realize the perpetual-motion machine of the paradox. Does that settle the matter? Might another design fare better? Might an improved design of sailboat be able to extract energy from the created wind and thus realize a perpetual-motion machine? Here the decision is not so straightforward. The normal response to a proposal for a perpetual-motion machine is that it is impossible because it would violate the law of conservation of energy. However, in addition it is customary to complete the refutation by pinpointing where the design fails. The generator–electric motor car, for example, fails because the slightest loss of energy due to friction means that the generator cannot supply as much energy as the electric motor demands.

What complicates the question is that a sailboat has an external source of energy, the kinetic energy of the true wind, as well as the possibility of the internally created energy of the created wind. Any analysis must disentangle the two. If a sailboat generates more energy when it is moving faster and thus experiences a greater apparent wind, which is the source of the extra energy? Is it merely more energy harvested licitly from the kinetic energy of the true wind? Or are we generating more energy from the created wind in violation of the law of the conservation of energy?

What we should like to develop is a general sense that the created-wind perpetual-motion machine will always be defeated by internally counter-acting effects. The greater apparent wind will deliver greater energy, but all gains will be lost by some other effect that essentially arises in connection with the created wind. To see that things will always work out this way is hard if we examine the functioning of any real sailboat or even any real wind-powered device. For all such devices are beset by many inefficiencies, such as frictional energy losses or incomplete extractions of wind energy. If a boat functions better when sailing into the wind, is

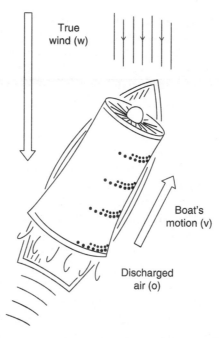

True
wind (w)

Boat's
motion (v)

Discharged
air (o)

**FIGURE 13.4** Wind-turbine-powered boat. Velocities with respect to water. Author's copyright.

it truly because of some sort of perpetual-motion effect, or is it simply the result of the reduction of inefficiencies?

The way to escape this problem is to consider an imaginary, wind-powered boat in which all the inefficiencies are idealized away. In this thought experiment, we consider a device that is perfectly efficient in extracting energy from the wind and is beset by no dissipative processes. For concreteness, we will imagine that our boat extracts energy from the wind with a large system of wind turbines and that this energy then powers its propeller. Any idealized system capable of extracting all the energy from the wind could be used; the turbine system is used simply because it is easy to visualize and compute. Its operation is shown in Figure 13.4.

The boat sails at vector velocity $\mathbf{v}$ into a true wind with vector velocity $\mathbf{w}$. The wind turbines are perfectly efficient, so that the wind turbine extracts all the kinetic energy of the wind that enters its throat. This means that the wind enters the turbine throat at velocity $\mathbf{w}$ and, as the boat moves off, it discharges a wake of entirely quiescent air; that is, air with zero velocity.

JOHN D. NORTON

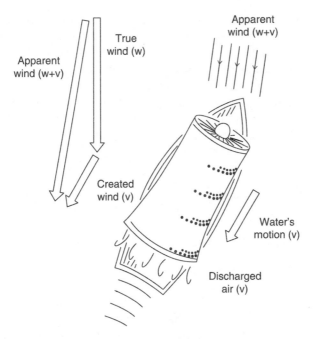

FIGURE 13.5 Wind-turbine-powered boat. Velocities with respect to boat.
Author's copyright.

How does this moving boat appear to a sailor on its deck? We merely add a velocity **v** to each of the velocities, with the result shown in Figure 13.5. The boat is now at rest and the water beneath the boat moves at velocity **v** toward the stern. The air discharged by the wind turbine is at rest with respect to the water, so it also moves at **v** toward the stern. Finally, the air entering the turbine moves at an apparent velocity of **w + v**. This added velocity **v** is the wind created by the boat's motion.

We use these velocities to compute the energy the turbine extracts from the wind, for the turbine has no way of distinguishing true from apparent wind. All it knows is that it scoops up air at velocity **w + v** and discharges it at **v**. It turns out that the resulting energy extraction is greater than the kinetic energy of the true wind passing through the turbine (see the Appendix for the calculations). We interpret the extra energy as supplied by the created wind and write:

$$\text{Total energy extracted} = \text{Kinetic energy from true wind} + \text{Kinetic energy from created wind} \tag{1}$$

If this were the entirety of the analysis, then we would have achieved a device that generates energy from nothing. However, it is not. The total energy of (1) is not available to power the boat. There is a consumption of energy that arises inescapably as part of the operation of the wind turbine. In order to extract energy from the wind, the turbine must take rapidly moving air and slow it down. That means that the turbine must apply a force to the wind. This is an ineliminable resistance force against which the boat must work. Moving against this force consumes energy. It turns out that this energy consumption matches exactly the extra, created energy:

$$\frac{\text{Energy consumed in moving}}{\text{against resistance force}} = \frac{\text{Kinetic energy}}{\text{from created wind}} \tag{2}$$

Combining (1) and (2), we recover

$$\text{Net energy extracted} = \text{Kinetic energy from true wind} \tag{3}$$

Hence, the extra energy we thought we had gained from the created wind is exactly consumed as the energy needed move the boat against the wind. That is, the net energy extracted is just the kinetic energy extracted from the true wind. The boat is not a perpetual-motion machine that is powered even in part by its own self-created energy.

In sum, we learn for the highly idealized wind-powered boat of the thought experiment that it can extract energy from the wind created by its own motion. However, exactly that extra energy is consumed by an inescapable counteracting effect. The result seems quite general. There is nothing in the thought experiment that specifically requires a wind turbine to extract the energy. Any device will be subject to essentially the same analysis. Making the boat more realistic by removing the idealization of perfect efficiency and no dissipative frictional effects will not help. It will carry us further from the possibility of a perpetual-motion machine. We now develop the sense that extracting net energy from the created wind is an appealing but impossible illusion.

For a philosopher interested in epistemology – the study of how we get to know things – this last conclusion is fascinating. The thought experiment has taught us something important about the operation of wind-powered vehicles like sailboats that is much harder to recover from experiment. We could have conducted a series of tests on a variety of sailboats to see whether we could gain net energy from the created wind. Presumably each test would have told us that we could not, in that case.

JOHN D. NORTON

However we would always have been left wondering whether our failure to extract net energy from the created wind merely resulted from our lack of ingenuity in finding the clever design of boat that could do it. The thought experiment, however, indicates that our failure is a matter of principle. The quest for a better design can end.

Merely thinking about examples so idealized as to be unrealizable gives us a more secure and more general understanding of physical possibility than real experiments. How is that possible? This is the central problem of the epistemology of thought experiments. This problem has attracted a flourishing philosophical literature. I'll mention two extreme views in this literature. One is defended by my colleague Jim Brown of the University of Toronto[4] and the other by me.

Brown is a Platonist and he urges that something in the right sort of thought experiment enables us to tap into a Platonic realm in which the laws of nature reside. The thought experiment lets us "see" the laws in a way that mere material experiments cannot. If this seems far-fetched, it might be helpful to recall the case that is the model for Platonic thought, mathematics. Draw an equilateral triangle – one with three equal sides – on a piece of paper and measure its angles. To within the accuracy of measurement, you will find that the angles are the same. Repeat the exercise for several more triangles. The results will be the same. That is no surprise. You fully expected it to be so, to the extent that any slight differences in your measurements would be dismissed as errors. But how did you get this knowledge that trumps actual experience? It is because thought affords you a deeper understanding of triangles than mere measurement can bring. Your mind can grasp the ideal triangles of the Platonic realm of which the triangles you drew are but poor imitations.

My view is the opposite of Brown's. It is deflationary and finds nothing epistemically remarkable in thought experiments. While they certainly have great rhetorical powers, epistemically they can do nothing more than ordinary argumentation. They are, I maintain, merely picturesque argumentation. As a result, you get nothing more out of a thought experiment than what you put into it as assumptions and what can be wrestled from those assumptions by deductive or inductive argumentation. In the thought experiment concerning wind-powered boats, what was assumed was the Newtonian mechanics of frictionless fluids. That theory conforms to the conservation of energy. As a result, it was a foregone conclusion that it would not allow the creation of energy from nothing. The only novelty was to see precisely how the theory blocked its creation. We did not learn anything that transcended the assumptions made. Had we made different assumptions, such as some concocted mechanics that did not respect energy conservation, we could have arrived at a thought experiment that vindicates the free creation of energy.

To see how Brown and I have sought to settle our differences and for an entry into the literature on thought experiments, see James Brown, "Why thought experiments transcend empiricism" and James Norton, "Why thought experiments do not transcend empiricism."[5]

## Appendix: Analysis of the Wind-Powered Boat

Air will enter the inlet of the turbine with cross-sectional area[6] $A_{in}$ at density $r_{in}$ and velocity $\mathbf{w} + \mathbf{v}$. It is discharged at the outlet with cross-sectional area $A_{out}$ at density $r_{out}$ and velocity $\mathbf{v}$. Conservation of mass requires

$$r_{in}A_{in}\cdot(w+v) = r_{out}A_{out}\cdot v \tag{A0}$$

Considering velocities in the boat frame of reference, the turbine scoops up air with energy density $(1/2)\, r_{in}\,|\mathbf{w}+\mathbf{v}|^2$ at a volumetric rate $A_{in}\cdot(\mathbf{w}+\mathbf{v})$, and discharges air with energy density $(1/2)\, r_{out}\,|\mathbf{v}|^2$ at a volumetric rate $A_{out}\cdot\mathbf{v}$. Hence, the total power – that is, the total rate at which energy is delivered by the turbine – is

$$P_{total} = (1/2)r_{in}\left|w+v\right|^2 A_{in}\cdot(w+v) - (1/2)r_{out}\left|v\right|^2 A_{out}\cdot v$$

Applying equation (A0), this becomes[7]

$$P_{total} = (1/2)r_{in}\left|w\right|^2 \left(A_{in}\cdot(w+v)\right) + r_{in}(w\cdot v)\left(A_{in}\cdot(w+v)\right) \tag{A1}$$

This equation corresponds to equation (1) of the main text. The first term represents the rate of delivery of kinetic energy by the true wind. The true wind, moving at speed $|\mathbf{w}|$, has kinetic energy density at the inlet of $(1/2)\, r_{in}\,|\mathbf{w}|^2$ and arrives at a volumetric rate $(A_{in}\cdot(\mathbf{w}+\mathbf{v}))$. The second term is the energy delivered by the created wind, which has an apparent energy density at the inlet of $r_{in}\,(\mathbf{w}\cdot\mathbf{v})$.

To operate, the turbine scoops up air with a momentum density $r_{in}$ $(\mathbf{w}+\mathbf{v})$ and discharges air with the reduced momentum density $r_{out}\mathbf{v}$. To slow the air, the turbine must apply a force to the air equal to the rate of change of momentum:

$$F_{resistance} = r_{in}\,(w+v)\left(A_{in}\cdot(w+v)\right) - r_{out}v(A_{out}\cdot v)$$

Applying (A0), this expression reduces to

$$F_{resistance} = r_{in} w \left( A_{in} \cdot (w + v) \right)$$

Since the boat moves at velocity **v**, energy is consumed in working against this force at the rate

$$P_{resistance} = F_{resistance} \cdot v = r_{in} w \cdot v \left( A_{in} \cdot (w + v) \right) \tag{A2}$$

This corresponds to equation (2) of the main text. The net power available is just the difference

$$P_{net} = P_{total} - P_{resistance} = (1/2) r_{in} |w|^2 \left( A_{in} \cdot (w + v) \right) \tag{A3}$$

This equation corresponds to equation (3) of the main text.

## NOTES

1  Norman L. Skene, *Elements of Yacht Design* (Dobbs Ferry, NY: Sheridan House, 2001), p. 92.
2  Isaac Newton, "Four letters to Richard Bentley." In Milton K. Munitz (Ed.), *Theories of the Universe* (New York: Free Press, 1957), pp. 211–219.
3  See John D. Norton, "Causation as folk science," *Philosophers' Imprint* 3:4 (2003, http://quod.lib.umich.edu/p/phimp/3521354.0003.004). Reprinted in Huw Price and Richard Corry (Eds.), *Causation and the Constitution of Reality: Russell's Republic Revisited* (Oxford: Oxford University Press, 2007), pp. 11–44. See also John D. Norton, "Do the causal principles of modern physics contradict causal anti-fundamentalism?" In Peter K. Machamer and Gereon Wolters (Eds.), *Thinking about Causes: From Greek Philosophy to Modern Physics* (Pittsburgh, PA: University of Pittsburgh Press, 2007).
4  James R. Brown, "Why thought experiments transcend empiricism." In Christopher Hitchcock (Ed.), *Contemporary Debates in the Philosophy of Science* (Malden, MA: Blackwell, 2004), pp. 23–43.
5  Brown, "Why thought experiments transcend empiricism," pp. 23–43 and John D. Norton, "Why thought experiments do not transcend empiricism." In Hitchcock (Ed.), *Contemporary Debates in the Philosophy of Science*, pp. 44–66.
6  The vector $A_{in}$ has a magnitude equal to the cross-sectional area of the inlet and a direction normal to the cross-section. The same is true for $A_{out}$.
7  Using $(1/2) \left[ |w + v|^2 - |v|^2 \right] = (1/2) \left[ |w|^2 + 2\, w \cdot v + |v|^2 - |v|^2 \right] = (1/2) |w|^2 + w \cdot v$.

TAMAR M. RUDAVSKY AND NATHANIEL
RUDAVSKY-BRODY

CHAPTER 14

# THE NECESSITY OF SAILING

## Of Gods, Fate, and the Sea

The shallow rocks and unpredictable winds of the Aegean make for some of the world's most dangerous sailing. The sea routes connecting Greek cities with their colonies, from the shores of the Black Sea to Sicily and further to the remote edges of the Mediterranean, were long and perilous. Before the Greeks learned to philosophize they learned to fear the sea. They knew the uncertainty of the winds and of the gods, neither of which were to be trusted.

From this uncertainty were born the twins philosophy and theology. Theology is the study of the gods, and if gods controlled the sea perhaps there were ways to appease them. Perhaps there were ways in which the uncertain forces of the world could be controlled, or at least encouraged. Philosophy, the study of the self, postulates that another way to master external forces is to master oneself, one's mind. If the highest good was a state of mind, then the dangers of the external world counted for very little. The question kept coming back to individual freedom. If the gods willed a storm at sea, did that mean they willed the traveler's destruction, and that death was inevitable? If a fortune teller foresaw a bad end at sea, could the individual

*Sailing – Philosophy for Everyone: Catching the Drift of Why We Sail*, First Edition.
Edited by Patrick Goold.
© 2012 John Wiley & Sons, Inc. Published 2012 by John Wiley & Sons, Inc.

choose to go another way? Could the inner freedom of the philosopher render one impervious to the sea?

The distinction between an inner philosophical freedom and an outer freedom in the world would last as long as the ancient world. Only with the victory of a single God – and the monotheistic philosophers recognized the same God, even if their Jewish, Christian, and Muslim co-religionists did not – would inside and outside meld the two freedoms into one. So the questions were rearranged. What was the difference between postulating a god who knew all shipwrecks in advance (like the ancient fortune teller) and recognizing one who caused shipwrecks as part of his natural ordering of the world? How much freedom, how much room to maneuver do individuals have in shaping their destiny in a world ordered by such an all-knowing or all-powerful God? If choosing to live a just life was the only personal freedom, what were the risks for a just man setting sail for a distant port?

With the regularization of travel, stricter safety standards, and modern shipbuilding in the eighteenth and nineteenth centuries, sea travel lost much of its menacing power to drive humans to God or to philosophy. But the sea took on further meaning, signifying the world of explorers pushing forward to new horizons. Nietzsche was one of the last of the great sea philosophers. He spent most of his life on the coast, fascinated by sailing. For Nietzsche, the sea provided a palpable image for the inner struggles and inner freedoms of the "new individual." In this brief essay, we explore three moments in the history of philosophy that exemplify human struggles with sailing. Our story begins with the ancient obsession with foretelling sea journeys and then turns to medieval grappling with God's foreknowledge. We end with Nietzsche's enthralled use of sailing toward open horizons as an image for human freedom.

## Of Greek Gods, the Judaeo-Christian God, and the Sea

The Greek gods that we know were given their form by Hesiod and Homer. Hesiod, in the rich farmlands of Boetia of the eighth century, took a dim view of sailing. "If the desire for stormy seagoing seizes upon you," he sings to his brother, then at least sail during

> the timely season for men to voyage.
> You will not

break up your ship, nor will the sea drown
its people, unless
Poseidon, the shaker of earth,
of his own volition,
or Zeus, the king of the immortals wishes
to destroy it,
for with these rests authority for all outcomes,
good or evil.
At that time the breezes can be judges
and the sea is not trouble[1]

Sailing, for this singer of harvests and sowings, is the lot of traders who take to the waves to escape debt or earn riches. Hesiod's gods, whose intricate family relations he describes elsewhere, have little personal to offer. Zeus sends a hard-blowing south wind and heavy rain in autumn and good weather in early summer. He and Poseidon destroy a ship at will. Their temperaments are natural forces, responsible for all things and accountable to none, against which Hesiod can only counsel wariness and good timing. How far from the gods of Homer, who pick and choose their mortal loves. Of course, Hesiod is singing advice for a farmer whose greatest act of heroism was to bribe local judges into giving him more than his share of his father's land. In the end he can only council caution. "You will find it hard to escape coming to grief," he sings, "and even so, men in their short-sightedness do undertake it; for acquisition means life to miserable mortals; but it is an awful thing to die among the waves."[2]

While Hesiod's gods restricted themselves to autumn gales and nourishing spring rains, they lived intensely human private lives among themselves. The first Greeks to reject such a cosmos we call the pre-Socratic philosophers. Among them, Pherecydes of Syros discussed the creation of the world and its first principles, the transmigration of souls, and other topics we can only guess at, since his great book, the *Heptamychos*, comes down to us in fragments. He is also said to have constructed a sundial and predicted eclipses. Pythagoras of Samos taught about the mystical properties of numbers and founded a religious sect that made important discoveries in mathematics. Both were also said to have predicted shipwrecks as well as earthquakes, storms, and the outcomes of battles. And, since Pythagoras' students were sworn to keep his teachings secret, the first one to spill the beans perished in a shipwreck. Or so the story goes. Don't dismiss this as mere legend. The pre-Socratics were intoxicated with their new ideas and the force of the world they were trying to explain.

  TAMAR M. RUDAVSKY AND NATHANIEL RUDAVSKY-BRODY

It is hardly surprising that some should have perished by those forces and others have co-opted them, seduced by their powers.

One of the best challenges to the old gods is said to have occurred at Samothrace, the island where the famous statue of Winged Victory (now at the Louvre) once reigned over the harbor. Under her wings, travelers arrived to visit the sanctuary of the great gods. These were deep gods – deep in time, since they were worshiped before the Greeks settled their lands, and also deep in the earth, since the Greeks assimilated them to chthonic deities: gods of the soil and underworld. They were known as protectors of sailors, and their cult flourished for centuries before and after the flourishing of the Greek world.

This story comes down to us in the writings of Cicero, a later Roman philosopher:

> While Diagoras, who is called the atheist, being at Samothrace, one of his friends showed him several pictures of people who had endured very dangerous storms; "See," says he, "you who deny a providence, how many have been saved by their prayers to the Gods." "Aye," says Diagoras, "I see those who were saved, but where are those painted who were shipwrecked?"[3]

Diagoras was a sophist, a contemporary of Socrates. He had a reputation for getting into trouble, both for denying the gods and for more mundane political reasons.

Also with Diagoras we see the end of the mystical. Another time when his ship was caught in a storm the sailors wanted to throw him overboard, believing his impiety had called misfortune down on them. "What about the other ships caught in the same storm?" the thinker asked them "if they believed Diagoras was also aboard those ships?"[4]

We turn finally to "the philosopher," Aristotle, the most influential philosopher in the ancient world. In his logical work, *On Interpretation*, Aristotle uses the example of a sea battle to show that, while logical propositions about the present must necessarily be either true or false, propositions about future events are logically open, since the world is not determined. Though he seems to be talking only about logic, he is in fact criticizing fortune telling. His true intentions become clear when he says, "events will not take place or fail to take place because it was stated that they would or would not take place, nor is this any more the case if the prediction dates back 10,000 years."[5] In this important passage (one that would be dissected by generations of medieval philosophers), Aristotle tries to salvage human freedom by arguing that the future is truly indeterminate – although it is necessarily the case that a sea-fight battle will either occur or not, neither possibility is necessary until the future actually unfolds.

Consider further Aristotle's famous conclusion about man's happiness. A generation earlier, the Athenian statesman Solon had warned the king Croesus, "Count no man happy until he is dead." Aristotle transformed that into "he who is happy ... is active in accordance with complete virtue and is sufficiently equipped with external goods, not for some chance period but throughout a complete life."[6] Philosophy may provide protection against the uncertainties of life, but only for the mind. Accidents still determine the span of life and the ultimate trajectory of happiness. A few centuries later, the Roman Cicero would put the two (fortune telling and the sea) together in his treatise *On Fate*, in which he considers propositions such as "If anyone is born at the rising of the dog-star, he will not die at sea."[7]

But soon, a far greater death was announced on a calm sea. The sailor Thamus heard a voice call across the water as he passed the island of Paxi off the west coast of Greece: "When you reach Palodes, take care to proclaim that the Great God Pan is dead."[8] The occasion for such a lament, according to Christian commentators, was the coming of Jesus of Nazareth: a new god had come to take the place of all the old ones.

The Acts of the Apostles tells how Paul was arrested and sent to Rome as a prisoner for the emperor, guarded by the centurion Julius. Midway across the Mediterranean, rough seas forced them to take shelter in a harbor on the southern coast of Crete, but the sailors were impatient to sail. Paul warned them to wait for spring. Nevertheless, the crew pushed off, and a storm tossed them about fiercely for fourteen days. In the end it was Paul who rallied spirits with comforting words and sound advice. He encouraged them to eat bread because they would need strength to attempt a beaching on unknown shores. At last, too, a prophecy:

> Paul stood up among them and said, "You should have taken my advice, gentlemen, not to sail from Crete; then you would have avoided this damage and loss. But now I urge you not to lose heart; not a single life will be lost, only the ship. For last night there stood by me an angel of the God whose I am and whom I worship. 'Do not be afraid, Paul,' he said; 'it is ordained that you shall appear before the emperor; and be assured, God has granted you the lives of all who are sailing with you.' So keep up your courage."[9]

God had his sights on the long view – bringing Paul to Rome. These sailors were saved because Paul was on board. Perhaps this was the first message of Christianity, a god who saved all who came in contact with his grace. Still, the sailors could have spared themselves some trouble had they listened to Paul's first warning. With the advent of Christianity, the gods of the Greek world were dying. Of course, Christianity took much from the Jews as well, and with the spread of Islam the three religions developed together in a newly monotheistic world. From now on the gods were one God, accidents were God's will, fate was God's knowledge. But the sea was the same sea.

## A Ship Bound for India

David ben Maimon found himself in the Sudanese port of 'Aydhāb with nothing to buy. In spring of the year 1169 he had sailed up the Nile from Fustat ("old Cairo") to Qūs, on the edge of the desert. He and his travel companion had been separated from their caravan and had crossed the desert alone, a foolhardy risk; they reached 'Aydhāb only after "disastrous" hardships. "God had willed that we be saved." Yet in the city there was nothing to buy except indigo. "So I thought about what I had endured in the desert; then it appeared to me an easy thing to embark on a sea voyage. I took Mansur as my travel companion."[10] David decided to trust his fate to sea, to the monsoon winds, the India passage.

David was writing to his brother, and the letter was fortuitously preserved in the *Cairo Genizeh*, where Cairo's Jewish community discarded their used documents. When this treasure trove was rediscovered in 1896, the lives of Cairo's medieval Jews were opened up for us in amazing detail. Many were traders, sailing to every shore of the Mediterranean. They also joined in the India trade, navigating the seasonal monsoon winds from the Red Sea, the Persian Gulf, and the southern coast of Arabia to India's Malabar coast and Sri Lanka. The stakes were luxury goods, precious stones, spices, gold, ivory, metalwork, and fine fabrics; raw materials – iron and copper and tin, and hardwoods; and foodstuffs – wheat, rice, and cheese. Many were learned, and a few were scholars.

But David's brother was more than another learned merchant. He was Moses ben Maimon, known as Maimonides, the most important Jewish philosopher of the Middle Ages. In 1169 he was still young, but soon he would be recognized as leader of Egypt's Jews. Later he would be appointed court physician to Saladin's son and successor, al-Afdad. Ever since the family had arrived in the East as refugees from war-torn Andalusia, David had supported his brother's studies.

Now poised between the desert and the sea, David reassured his brother that God would look out for the family's finances. He asked him to comfort "the little one," his wife: his ship was to embark around Ramadan. He did not return. Eight years later the philosopher Maimonides recalled his grief in a letter:

> The most terrible blow which befell me ... was the death of the most perfect and righteous man, who was drowned while traveling in the Indian Ocean. For nearly a year after I received the sad news, I lay ill on my bed struggling with fever and despair. Eight years have since passed, and I still mourn, for there is no consolation. What can console me? ... My one joy was to see him. Now my joy has been changed into darkness; he has gone to his eternal home, and has left me prostrated in a strange land.[11]

Left to support both families, Maimonides began practicing medicine professionally, an activity that would leave him exhausted and short of time all his life. Still, his reputation as a religious thinker grew as he took on the philosophical dilemmas of his Islamic masters, Averroes, Avicenna, al-Farabi, and ibn-Bajja. These thinkers were steeped in Aristotle and had worked hard to make Greek philosophy compatible with their monotheistic religion. Maimonides was to devote much of his life to the same dilemma.

In the third book of his monumental *Guide to the Perplexed*, he asks a very direct question: when a ship founders, why does a just man drown? First he summarizes and rejects five theories held by his predecessors. Epicurus and his followers denied that God had any role in the world. Aristotle believed that divine providence extends only to the realm of the celestial spheres, not to the terrestrial world. The Islamic Ash'arites claimed that every event in the world is predestined by God, denying any contingency. The Islamic Mu'tazilites believed in limited free will for humans. Finally, traditional Jewish law accorded humans perfect freedom, while at the same time insisting that everything that happens them is the result of God's justice. In this last view, God is absolutely just, and all calamities are deserved. Does it suggest that Maimonides' brother deserved to die at sea?

The philosopher rejects these five opinions, and describes his own: "Divine providence watches only over the individuals belonging to the human species ... but regarding all the other animals, and all the more, the plants and other things, my opinion is that of Aristotle."[12] Although providence in the terrestrial world extends to all and only human beings, it does not necessarily reflect divine retribution or reward. For Aristotle, a storm was part of the natural order, but the deaths of those on a ship that foundered were caused by to chance and undeserved. Both the Mu'tazilites and Ash'arites would have agreed that the deaths were undeserved, but the result of divine will. According to Jewish law, the drownings were deserved, but we cannot understand the ways of God. Maimonides agrees with Aristotle that the foundering of a ship is "due to pure chance." In his view, divine providence is consequent upon the perfection of human intellect, and intervenes only in the decision to board the ship:

> The fact that the people in the ship went on board and that the people in the house were sitting in it is, according to our opinion, not due to chance but to divine will in accordance with the deserts of those people as determined by his judgments, the rule of which cannot be determined by our intellects.[13]

Maimonides' successors contested his position. Yet the summation of his argument, which some philosophers have found problematic or even naive, turns out to be deeply moving. David, when he arrived in 'Aydhāb, chose to go on to India. The traditional question for the untutored reader is how God could let a just man like David die undeservedly. David's choice to embark upon a sailing ship represents not only the perils of sailing and the chance of shipwreck but also a struggle with the very fatalistic powers of the sea. That very choice, not just the drowning itself, must be accounted for in a theory of divine providence. Even if it implicates God, the fateful choice must be given meaning, so that David's death and then his life have meaning in a world of merchant scholars where religious study and contemplation were the highest goods – all the while accepting from the philosophers that we live in a chaotic natural world.

## Beyond the Pillars of Hercules

So far we have been unkind to the sea. We have dragged up shipwrecks and skirted storms, and reported deaths both foretold and unexpected. Sailing itself connotes death, destruction, and the power of the gods and of God. But the sea has other moods: calm as a breeze fluttering the leaves of a plane tree on a summer day, an image familiar to Greeks; whipped up by the terse gusts of a sunny morning; gray and expansive. For every traveler who felt the weight of uncertainty as he boarded his ship, another was filled with the promise of fresh mornings under sail. Such a one was Ulysses, the conniving hero who ended up in the eighth circle of Dante's hell for crimes of fraud. At Dante's wish, the hero recounts his own death.[14] After returning to Ithaka from his wanderings, not even his love for Penelope could calm Ulysses' lust for adventure: "So I set forth on the open deep with but a single ship and that handful of shipmates who had not deserted me."[15] Ulysses and his companions sailed west, through the straits of Gibraltar, the very pillars Hercules had placed as a western barrier to human travel. None who passed these pillars had ever returned. There, to raise the spirits of his rowers, he gave a famous speech:

> Oh brothers, I said, who in the course
> of a hundred thousand perils, at last
> have reached the west, to such brief wakefulness
> of our senses as remains to us
> do not deny yourselves the chance to know –
> following the sun – the world where no one lives.
> Consider how your souls were sown:
> you were not made to live like brutes or beasts
> but to pursue virtue and knowledge.[16]

Reinvigorated, they sailed southwest across the Atlantic for five months until a mountain loomed before them: Purgatory. But a whirlwind rose up, capsizing their ship, and "the sea closed over us."[17] Dante seems to have invented this story himself, maybe inspired by the Visconti brothers, who passed Gibraltar in 1291 in search of India, and disappeared. It makes a nice counterpoint to the travelers we have seen terrified of a bad end at sea. Ulysses, challenging heaven and earth, faces the sea head on. Adventure for him arises out of the passion for knowledge and discovery.

It took Columbus to discover land across the western ocean and return. For Friedrich Nietzsche, writing in the nineteenth century, the sea carried a double message that reflected the theme of discovery. To question the Christian metaphysics and morality that weighed on Europe was to set off on a voyage to the unknown. Columbus' voyages to the New World became a symbol for this daring philosopher.

  TAMAR M. RUDAVSKY AND NATHANIEL RUDAVSKY-BRODY

"Finally the horizon seems clear again," Nietzsche announced in *The Gay Science*, a work written to prepare his readers for his destruction of Western morality. "Finally our ships may set out again, set out to face any danger; every daring of the lover of knowledge is allowed again; the sea, *our* sea, lies open again; maybe there has never been such an 'open sea.'"[18]

Nietzsche's works are replete with references to the sea, to sailing to new horizons, to destroying the old gods in order to usher in a new moral order. "We have left the land behind and boarded the ship! We have burned our bridges – more than that, we have demolished the land behind us," he tells us in *The Gay Science*.[19] In this work, a "madman," presumably a spokesperson for Nietzsche himself, comes running to the marketplace one morning decrying the death of God. But the crowds do not want to hear him, do not have the patience to listen to his words, and they mock him. Finally the madman grows silent and announces, "I come too early ... it is not the right time for me, yet," reiterating Nietzsche's own view that most people are simply not ready to hear and accept his message.[20] Nietzsche realizes that such a journey is not for everyone. It is the journey of a lifetime, not of impetuous youth. As a young man, he had already noted that

to dare to launch out on the sea of doubt without compass or guide is death and destruction for undeveloped heads; most are struck down by storms, few discover new lands. From the midst of this immeasurable ocean of ideas one will often long to be back on firm land.[21]

Live dangerously, Nietzsche exhorts us: "Build your cities by Vesuvius! Send your ships into unexplored seas!"[22] In other words, be prepared to take risks.

In *Thus Spake Zarathustra*, written toward the end of his life, Nietzsche returns to the motif of sailing into uncharted seas as an exhortation to follow the words of Zarathustra the prophet. "Ah, this sombre, sad sea, below me! Ah, this sombre nocturnal vexation! Ah, fate and sea! To you must I now GO DOWN!" says Zarathustra as he begins his journey to share his wisdom with those on Earth.[23] His message is addressed "To you, the daring venturers and adventurers, and whoever hath embarked with cunning sails upon frightful seas, – To you the enigma-intoxicated, the twilight-enjoyers, whose souls are allured by flutes to every treacherous gulf."[24] In other words, to those who are willing to take risks, to embark upon rough waters without fear, Zarathustra offers the promise of a new code of values, a trans-valuation of morality, a replacement of the "old" tablets of the law for "new" tablets. This trans-valuation, or replacement, is itself described in sea-worthy language:

> O my brethren, when I enjoined you to break up the good, and the tables of the good, then only did I embark man on his high seas.
> And now only cometh unto him the great terror, the great outlook, the great sickness, the great nausea, the great sea-sickness.
> False shores and false securities did the good teach you; in the lies of the good were ye born and bred. Everything hath been radically contorted and distorted by the good.
> But he who discovered the country of "man," discovered also the country of "man's future." Now shall ye be sailors for me, brave, patient!
> Keep yourselves up betimes, my brethren, learn to keep yourselves up! The sea stormeth: many seek to raise themselves again by you.[25]

With these powerful words, Nietzsche connects the raw energy of the sea and the danger of sailing to distant shores with the denial of fate, and the rejection of conventional morality. Only the brave sea-worthy individual can discover new lands and, in so doing, create a new covenant.

With the words of Zarathustra, we are not so far from Aristotle, who also tried to mitigate the hazards of life by denying their force in the face of a philosophical life, nor from Maimonides, who made contemplation the only way to include oneself under divine providence. But, when Nietzsche snatches fate from the force of the sea and the will of the gods and places it in the hands of the individual, he makes contemplation and philosophy the way to freedom, not because they protect one from the shocks of adversity but because they can be used to forge a path through it. The gods have died, humans push forward in their small boats on a new quest, but the sea is still the same sea.

## NOTES

1 Hesiod, *The Works and Days; Theogony The Shield of Herakles*, trans. Richmond Lattimore (Ann Arbor, MI: Ann Arbor Paperbacks, 1991), ll. 665 ff.
2 Ibid., ll. 683 ff.
3 Cicero, *Cicero's Treatise on the Nature of the Gods*, trans. Charles D. Yonge (London: G. Bell, 1878), pp. 137–138.
4 Ibid., p. 138.
5 Aristotle, *Complete Works of Aristotle: The Revised Oxford Translation*, vol. 1, ed. and trans. Jonathan Barnes (Oxford: Oxford University Press, 1974), 18b38.

6  Aristotle, *Complete Works of Aristotle*, 1101a10.
7  Cicero, *Cicero's Treatise on the Nature of the Gods*, p. 138.
8  Plutarch, "The Obsolescence of Oracles," *Moralia*, book 5:17.
9  Acts 27:21–25.
10  Solomon D. Goitein (Ed. and trans.), *Letters of Medieval Jewish Traders* (Princeton, NJ: Princeton University Press, 1973).
11  Moses Maimonides, *A Maimonides Reader*, ed. Isadore Twersky (New York: Behrman House, 1972), pp. 4–5.
12  Moses Maimonides, *The Guide of the Perplexed*, ed. and trans. Shlomo Pines (Chicago, IL: Chicago University Press, 1963), p. 471.
13  Ibid., p. 472.
14  Dante Aligheiri, *Inferno*, trans. Robert Hollander and Jean Hollander (New York: Doubleday, 2000), Canto 26, p. 483.
15  Ibid.
16  Ibid.
17  Ibid.
18  Friedrich Nietzsche, *The Gay Science*, ed. Bernard Williams, trans. Josephine Nauckhoff (Cambridge, UK: Cambridge University Press, 2001), p. 199.
19  Ibid., p. 124.
20  Ibid.
21  Julian Young, *Friedrich Nietzsche: A Philosophical Biography* (Cambridge, UK: Cambridge University Press, 2010), p. 35.
22  Friedrich Nietzsche, *The Gay Science*, p. 283.
23  Friedrich Nietzsche, *Thus Spake Zarathustra*, trans. Thomas Common (New York: Modern Library, 1921), p. 45.
24  Ibid., p. 46.
25  Ibid., p. 56.

CHAPTER 15

# THE CHANNEL

## An Old Drama by which the Soul of a Healthy Man is Kept Alive[1]

Friends of mind, friends all, and you also, publishers, colonials and critics, do you know that particular experience for which I am trying to find words? Do you know that glamour in the mind which arises and transforms our thought when we see the things that the men who made us saw – the things of a long time ago, the origins? I think everybody knows that glamour, but very few people know where to find it.

Every man knows that he has in him the power for such revelations and every man wonders in what strange place he may come upon them. There are men also (very rich) who have considered all the world and wandered over it, seeking those first experiences and trying to feel as felt the earlier men in a happier time – yet these few rich men have not so felt and have not so found the things which they desire. I have known men who have thought to find them in the mountains, but would not climb them simply enough and refused to leave their luxuries behind, and so lost everything, and might as well have been walking in a dirty town at home for all the little good that the mountains did to them. And I know men who have thought to find this memory and desire in foreign countries, in Africa,

*Sailing – Philosophy for Everyone: Catching the Drift of Why We Sail*, First Edition.
Edited by Patrick Goold.
© 2012 John Wiley & Sons, Inc. Published 2012 by John Wiley & Sons, Inc.

hunting great beasts such as our fathers hunted; yet even these have not relit those old embers, which if they lie dead and dark in a man make his whole soul dusty and useless, but which if they be once rekindled can make him part of all the centuries.

Yet there is a simple and an easy way to find what the men who made us found, and to see the world as they saw it, and to take a bath, as it were, in the freshness of beginnings; and that is to go to work as cheaply and as hardly as you can, and only as much away from men as they were away from men, and not to read or to write or to think, but to eat and drink and use the body in many immediate ways, which are at the feet of every man. Every man who will walk for some days carelessly, sleeping rough when he must, or in poor inns, and making for some one place direct because he desires to see it, will know the thing I mean. And there is a better way still of which I shall now speak: I mean, to try the seas in a little boat not more than twenty-five feet long, preferably decked, of shallow draught, such as can enter into all creeks and havens, and so simply rigged that by oneself, or with a friend at most, one can wander all over the world.

Certainly every man that goes to sea in a little boat of this kind learns terror and salvation, happy living, air, danger, exultation, glory, and repose at the end; and they are not words to him, but, on the contrary, realities which will afterwards throughout his life give the mere words a full meaning. And for this experiment there lies at our feet, I say, the Channel.

It is the most marvelous sea in the world – the most suited for these little adventures; it is crammed with strange towns, differing one from the other; it has two opposite people upon either side, and hills and varying climates, and the hundred shapes and colors of the earth, here rocks, there sand, here cliffs, and there marshy shores. It is a little world. And what is more, it is a kind of inland sea.

People will not understand how narrow it is, crossing it hurriedly in great steamships; nor will they make it a home for pleasure unless they are rich and can have great boats; yet they should, for on its water lies the best stage for playing out the old drama by which the soul of a healthy man is kept alive. For instance, listen to this story:

The sea being calm, and the wind hot, uncertain, and light from the east, leaving oily gaps on the water, and continually dying down, I drifted one morning in the strong ebb to the South Goodwin Lightship, wondering what to do. There was a haze over the land and over the sea, and through the haze great ships a long way off showed, one or two of them, like oblong targets which one fires at with guns. They hardly moved in spite of all their canvas set, there was so little breeze. So I drifted in the slow ebb past the South Goodwin, and I thought: "What is all this drifting and doing nothing? Let us play the fool, and see if there are no adventures left."

So I put my little boat about until the wind took her from forward, such as it was, and she crawled out to sea.

It was a dull, uneasy morning, hot and silent, and the wind, I say, was hardly a wind, and most of the time the sails flapped uselessly.

But after eleven o'clock the wind first rose, and then shifted a little, and then blew light but steady; and then at last she heeled and the water spoke under her bows, and still she heeled and ran, until in the haze I could see no more land; but even so far out there were no seas, for the light full breeze was with the tide, the tide ebbing out as strong and silent as a man in anger, down the hidden parallel valleys of the narrow sea. And I held this little wind till about two o'clock, when I drank wine and ate bread and meat at the tiller, for I had them by me, and just afterwards, still through a thick haze of heat, I saw Grisnez, a huge ghost, right up against and above me; and I wondered, for I had crossed the Channel, now for the first time, and knew now what if felt like to see new land.

Though I knew nothing of the place, I had this much sense, that I said to myself, "The tide is right down Channel, racing through the hidden valleys under the narrow sea, so it will all go down together and all come up together, and the flood will come on this foreign side much at the same hour that it does on the home side." My boat lay to the east and the ebb tide held her down, and I lit a pipe and looked at the French hills and thought about them and the people in them, and England which I had left behind, and I was delighted with the loneliness of the sea; and still I waited for the flood.

But in a little while the chain made a rattling noise, and she lay quite slack and swung oddly; and then there were little boiling and eddying places in the water, and the water seemed to come up from underneath sometimes, and altogether it behaved very strangely, and this was the turn of the tide. Then the wind dropped also, and for a moment she lollopped about, till at last, after I had gone below and straightened things, I came on deck to see that she had turned completely round, and that the tide at last was making up my way, towards Calais, and her chain was taut and her nose pointed down Channel, and a little westerly breeze, a little draught of air, came up cool along the tide.

When this came I was very glad, for I saw that I could end my adventure before night. So I pulled up the anchor and fished it, and then turned

  HILAIRE BELLOC

with the tide under me, and the slight half-felt breeze just barely filling the mainsail (the sheet was slack, so powerless was the wind), and I ran up along that high coast, watching eagerly every new thing; but I kept some way out for fear of shoals, till after three good hours under the reclining sun of afternoon, which glorified the mist, I saw, far off, the roofs and spires of a town, and a low pier running well out to sea, and I knew that it must be Calais. And I ran for these piers, careless of how I went, for it was already half of the spring flood tide, and everything was surely well covered for so small a boat, and I ran up the fairway in between the piers, and saw Frenchmen walking about, and a great gun peeping up over its earthwork, and plenty of clean new masonry. And a man came along and showed me where I could lie; but I was so strange to the place that I would not take a berth, but lay that night moored to an English ship.

And when I had eaten and drunk and everything was stowed away and darkness had fallen, I went on deck, and for a long time sat silent, smoking a pipe and watching the enormous lighthouse of Calais, which is built right in the town, and which turns round and round above one all night long.

And I thought: "Here is a wonderful thing! I have crossed the Channel in this little boat, and I know now what the sea means that separates France from England. I have strained my eyes for shore through a haze. I have seen new lands, and I feel as men do who have dreamt dreams."

But in reality I had had very great luck indeed, and had had no right to cross, for my coming back was to be far more difficult and dreadful, and I was to suffer many things before again I could see tall England, close by me, out of the sea.

But how I came back, and of the storm, and of its majesty, and of how the boat and I survived, I will tell you another time, only imploring you to do the same; not to tell of it, I mean, but to sail it in a little boat.

## NOTE

1  "The Channel" from *Hills and Sea* by Hilaire Belloc. Reprinted by permission of Peters Fraser & Dunlop on behalf of the estate of Hilaire Belloc.

# NOTES ON CONTRIBUTORS

**GREGORY BASSHAM** is Professor and Chair of the Philosophy Department at King's College (Pennsylvania), where he specializes in philosophy of law and critical thinking. He co-edited *The Lord of the Rings and Philosophy* (2003) and *The Ultimate Harry Potter and Philosophy* (2010), and is co-author of *Critical Thinking: A Student's Introduction*. A veteran armchair sailor, Gregory has rounded the three Capes on many voyages of imagination.

**TOD BASSHAM** is a lawyer, writer, and sailor in Portland, Oregon. He races and cruises obsessively on the Columbia River, the Salish Sea, and wherever else he can cadge a berth. He is blessed with a tolerant wife and two forgiving children, and still laughs with childish delight when the wind fills the sails.

**HILAIRE BELLOC**, who lived from 1870 to 1953, was a prolific writer of poetry, essays, novels, histories, and political and social commentary. He was also an ardent yachtsman and his experiences at sea were a frequent subject of his essays.

**LUÍSA GAGLIARDINI GRAÇA** is an avid Portuguese sailor who likes to keep her country's great tradition of navigation alive. She holds a masters

*Sailing – Philosophy for Everyone: Catching the Drift of Why We Sail*, First Edition.
Edited by Patrick Goold.
© 2012 John Wiley & Sons, Inc. Published 2012 by John Wiley & Sons, Inc.

in sport sciences with emphasis on sport aesthetics from the Faculty of Sport, University of Porto (Portugal), where she is currently working on her PhD as she focuses on the intersection between aesthetics and ethics in sport. She has presented her work numerous times at conferences such as the International Association for the Philosophy of Sport and the European Association for the Philosophy of Sport. She is a licensed captain, and has sailed extensively in the Mediterranean, the Atlantic, and the North Sea, whether as crew in a tall ship race or a more manageable sloop or catamaran – so long as it floats, she'll sail it. Her next sailing adventure will be in the Aegean Sea. Ideally, she'd like to explore the whole world by sea … and she is working on that, only that it will have to wait until the winds or the whims of the sea deities are more favorable.

**PATRICK GOOLD** is Associate Professor of Philosophy at Virginia Wesleyan College. His current research focuses on defining rationality. He is co-editor with Steven Emmanuel of the Blackwell anthology *Modern Philosophy from Descartes to Nietzsche*. Patrick is passionate about sailing, and, in addition to maintaining a small daysailer and a cruising boat of his own, frequently crews on the boats of others. The bays and sounds of Virginia and North Carolina are his home waters but he has sailed the length of the East Coast of the United States from Hilton Head to Long Island Sound, made a Bermuda crossing, done club racing in Brittany, and cruised in the Lesser Antilles.

**NICHOLAS HAYES** is the author of *Saving Sailing, The Story of Choices, Families, Time Commitments, and How We Can Create a Better Future* (Crickhollow Books, 2009). *Saving Sailing* won an Independent Publisher 2010 Living Now Silver Medal, was a ForeWord 2009 Book of the Year Award finalist. Nick is a veteran of fifteen Mackinac Races and of uncounted other offshore sailing races in three decades of racing on Lake Michigan. He lives in Shorewood, Wisconsin, with his wife Angela and their daughters Kate and Elizabeth, all decorated sailors. The Hayes family campaign their B-32 sailboat *Syrena* out of the South Shore Yacht Club and sail together for fun as often as they can.

**STEVEN HORROBIN** has sailed oceangoing yachts since the age of fifteen, completing his first long sea voyages in the later 1980s. Prior to returning to the study of philosophy, he was a playwright, actor, theater manager, and designer. His PhD, at the University of Edinburgh, was on the subject of the nature of the value of life to persons conceived as processes, and he has published, edited, tutored, and lectured in the subjects of general philosophy, bioethics, meta-ethics, and ontology in books, academic journals, and universities internationally for much of the past decade. He is a commercially certified Yachtmaster and Cruising Instructor and a passionate diver and freediver.

RICHARD HUTCH completed his MA and PhD at the University of Chicago, his BD at Yale University, and his BA at Gettysburg College in the United States. Since 1978, he has been Reader in Religion and Psychological Studies in the School of History, Philosophy, Religion, and Classics at the University of Queensland in Australia. For the past fifteen years he has skippered his twenty-seven-foot yacht, *Impulse*, off the coast of Brisbane, not only trying his hand at racing on Moreton Bay but also cruising over short runs up and down the coasts of Queensland and New South Wales. He has written five academic books including one based on his sailing experiences, *Lone Sailors and Spiritual Insights: Cases of Sport and Peril at Sea* (2005). His love of sailing was triggered during his boyhood years in the United States, where he sailed small boats on Barnegat Bay in New Jersey, where he grew up.

JESÚS ILUNDÁIN-AGURRUZA is an Associate Professor of Philosophy and Allen and Pat Kelley Faculty Scholar at Linfield College in Oregon. He hails from landlocked Pamplona, Spain, where he learned to yearn for the sea. His specialties are the philosophy of sport, aesthetics, and metaphysics. The horizons of his teaching and research span the philosophy of literature, Asian philosophy, ethics, and the philosophy of mind. He has published in journals such as *Sports, Ethics, and Philosophy* and *Proteus*; he co-edited Wiley-Blackwell's *Cycling – Philosophy for Everyone*; and has chapters in anthologies on sports and risk, soccer, childhood and sports, the Olympics, hunting, and others (some in Spanish). Of lesser sailing experience than his writing crewmates, he matches their love for sailboats and the azure.

JOSÉ ÁNGEL JÁUREGUI-OLAIZ, from Pamplona (Spain), did his best to follow in the wake of Juan Sebastián Elcano, who was among the first crew to circumnavigate the Earth and was born about forty nautical miles northwest of Pamplona as the seagull flies. He is a former Second-Class Pilot in the Spanish Merchant Navy who has sailed and cruised the Atlantic Ocean, the Mediterranean, the Cantabric Sea, and North Sea in all kinds of weather both for pleasure and professionally. Aboard his now-gone sloop *Snowgoose* he spent a literally tempestuous yet happy honeymoon. Nowadays retired as a seaman, he takes care of the family business and voraciously reads sailing books (enjoying narratives of solo exploits the most). Any chance he gets finds him on the waves. His current dream is to save enough money for another sailboat where he and his crew – wife Chus, daughter Marina, and son Lorenzo – may humor him pretending to follow his orders.

**GARY JOBSON** is the president of US Sailing, the national governing body of sailing in the United States. He has authored seventeen sailing books and is Editor at Large of *Sailing World* and *Cruising World* magazines. His newest book is *Gary Jobson: An American Sailing Story*. He has been ESPN's sailing commentator since 1985. Gary has won many championships in one-design classes, the America's Cup with Ted Turner, the infamous Fastnet Race, and many of the world's ocean races. He currently races a Swan 42, *Mustang*, and an Etchells, *Whirlwind*. Also an active cruising sailor, Gary has led ambitious expeditions to the Arctic, Antarctica, and Cape Horn. In 1999 he was honored with the Nathanael G. Herreshoff Trophy, US Sailing's most prestigious award. This trophy is awarded annually to an individual who has made an outstanding contribution to the sport of sailing in the United States. A fuller account of Gary's many awards and accomplishments can be found on his website: www.jobsonsailing.com.

**SEBASTIAN KUHN** teaches physics at all levels (from large undergraduate survey courses to highly specialized graduate classes) at Old Dominion University (Norfolk, Virginia). He also probes the innermost life of nuclei, smashing atoms at the Thomas Jefferson National Accelerator Facility (Newport News, Virginia). He obtained his doctorate in physics in 1986 (University of Bonn, Germany) and had stints in Berkeley and Stanford before moving to the East Coast. In his spare time, he loves to cruise on the Chesapeake Bay with his wife Kathrin (and occasionally his daughter and son) on an aging Vega 27″ sloop. He'd be happy to discuss physics and sailing with anyone – contact information can be found at http://odu.edu/~skuhn.

**CRISTA LEBENS** is an Associate Professor of Philosophy teaching a wide range of courses, including feminist philosophy and philosophy of race, to students at the University of Wisconsin-Whitewater. Her area of specialty is social ontology. Crista is active in the Midwest Society for

Women in Philosophy, and attends the California Roundtable on Philosophy and Race as often as possible. She began sailing on an old wooden X-Scow (the *Firefly*) at age eight, and was told to stay down in the cockpit and watch out for the boom. She liked watching the water creep up the deck as the boat "high-sided" and soon learned to sail from her father, a business owner and former Marine pilot who, after retiring from the reserves, decided that sailing was an enjoyable alternative to flying. Crista finds herself out on the water less than she'd like these days, but still notes whether or not the wind is good for sailing. She continues to be fascinated by the notion that the sail on a boat works on the same principle as the wing of an airplane. Crista says, "This one's for you, Dad."

**STEVE MATTHEWS** is Senior Research Fellow at the Plunkett Centre (a center for medical ethics), at the Australian Catholic University. His research areas include personal identity, agency and autonomy, philosophy of psychiatry, and applied ethics. His work has appeared in a range of journals including *Philosophical Studies*, *The Monist*, and *American Philosophical Quarterly*. He has been sailing since 1999.

**JOHN D. NORTON** is Director of the Center for Philosophy of Science and past Chair of the Department of History and Philosophy of Science, University of Pittsburgh. His research is in the history and philosophy of physics, with special attention to Einstein's work in special and general relativity; and he also works in general topics in the philosophy of science, including inductive inference, causation, and thought experiments. He thinks philosophy while sailing the rivers around Pittsburgh's point and wonders why there are no others sailing there regularly.

**JOHN ROUSMANIERE** (pronounced "Room-an-ear," with a silent "s") was educated at Columbia University (bachelor's and master's degrees in history) and Union Theological Seminary (M Div). He taught history and writing, then edited *Yachting* magazine for several years, eventually becoming a freelance writer. He is the author of more than two dozen books on sailing, yachting history, and New York history. His sailing books include *The Annapolis Book of Seamanship*, *A Berth to Bermuda: One Hundred Years of the World's Classic Ocean Race*, *Fastnet Force 10: The Deadliest Storm in the History of Modern Sailing*, *The Golden Pastime: A New History of Yachting*, *In a Class by Herself: The Yawl Bolero*, and *Sailing at Fishers: A History of the Fishers Island Yacht*

*Club*. John has sailed on most of the world's oceans, logging some 35,000 miles on the water.

TAMAR M. RUDAVSKY is Professor of Philosophy at The Ohio State University. She specializes in medieval Jewish philosophy and has edited or co-edited three volumes: *Divine Omniscience and Omnipotence in Medieval Philosophy: Islamic, Jewish, and Christian Perspectives* (1984), *Gender and Judaism: The Transformation of Tradition* (1995), and, along with Steven Nadler, the *Cambridge History of Jewish Philosophy: From Antiquity through the Seventeenth Century* (2009). Her volume *Time Matters: Time, Creation and Cosmology in Medieval Jewish Philosophy* appeared in 2000. Her most recent book (2010) on Maimonides appeared in Wiley-Blackwell's "Great Minds" series. She is also the author of numerous articles and encyclopedia entries, and her major research continues to focus on issues connected to philosophical cosmology in medieval Jewish and scholastic thought. She learned to sail in the Charles River in Boston, and has continued sailing in Ohio.

NATHANIEL RUDAVSKY-BRODY graduated from Northwestern University with a degree in mathematics. He continued his studies in mathematics and medieval literature. He currently works as a translator in Brussels. He learned to sail on Lake Michigan, where even in good weather he preferred staying close to shore.

JESSE STEINBERG teaches philosophy at the University of Pittsburgh at Bradford. He has published articles on a variety of topics including ethics, metaphysics, and philosophy of mind. Jesse grew up in California and thoroughly enjoyed the Pacific Ocean. Now that he lives in Pennsylvania, time on the water is sadly reduced, though he has enjoyed sailing with co-author Michael Stuckart on Lake Ontario immensely.

JACK STILLWAGGON comes from a seafaring family. Three generations before him were tugboat men in New York harbor. His grandfather captained troopships during World War II in both the Pacific and European theaters. His great-grandfather was captain of a schooner that ran out of Liverpool for exotic ports of call in South America. Jack chose a business career instead of a life on the water but did serve as a "soldier of the sea" as an officer in the Marines. Since that time, he has owned both sailboats and powerboats and tries very hard to never lose sight of land. Jack has spent over thirty years in business in general management.

He currently advises private equity firms, facilitating smooth transitions of the CEOs of acquired companies into new working environments for greater growth and strong partnerships.

**MICHAEL STUCKART** teaches anthropology at the University of Pittsburgh at Bradford. As an anthropologist, he specializes in traditional arts, tourist arts, religion and culture, and Latin America. He grew up in Huntington, Long Island and has sailed for over fifty years. His major blue-water experience involved crossing the Gulf of Mexico, and he enjoys single-handed sailing on the Great Lakes.

**JAMES WHITEHILL** is Professor Emeritus of Religion and Philosophy at Stephens College, Columbia, Missouri, where he taught Asian religions, Zen Buddhism, and philosophical ethics for thirty-six years. He directed the College's Japan Studies Program for thirty years and was awarded a Fulbright senior lecturer fellowship to Japan in 1991–1992. He co-founded and directed the Columbia Zen Center, a *zazenkai*, and practiced in Soto and Rinzai Zen monasteries. His publications include a book on meditation practice, *Enter the Quiet*, and several articles and chapters on Buddhist and Zen ethics. He sailed since his high-school days, and has owned small boats over the decades, auspiciously named *Miko, Hotei, Blue Lotus*, and, since his retirement to Cape Cod, *Garuda*.